Instructor's Manual with Test Bank and Solutions to

THINKING
CRITICALLY

Techniques for Logical Reasoning

Georgia State University

Nicholas J. Caste
University of North Carolina-Charlotte

Minneapolis/St. Paul   New York   Los Angeles   San Francisco

WEST'S COMMITMENT TO THE ENVIRONMENT

In 1906, West Publishing Company began recycling materials left over from the production of books. This began a tradition of efficient and responsible use of resources. Today, 100% of our legal bound volumes are printed on acid-free, recycled paper consisting of 50% new paper pulp and 50% paper that has undergone a de-inking process. We also use vegetable-based inks to print all of our books. West recycles nearly 27,700,000 pounds of scrap paper annually—the equivalent of 229,300 trees. Since the 1960s, West has devised ways to capture and recycle waste inks, solvents, oils, and vapors created in the printing process. We also recycle plastics of all kinds, wood, glass, corrugated cardboard, and batteries, and have eliminated the use of polystyrene book packaging. We at West are proud of the longevity and the scope of our commitment to the environment.

West pocket parts and advance sheets are printed on recyclable paper and can be collected and recycled with newspapers. Staples do not have to be removed. Bound volumes can be recycled after removing the cover.

Production, Prepress, Printing and Binding by West Publishing Company.

 TEXT IS PRINTED ON 10% POST CONSUMER RECYCLED PAPER  Printed with **Printwise** Environmentally Advanced Water Washable Ink

CONTENTS

Introduction vii

PART ONE: THE ANALYSIS OF ARGUMENTS

Chapter 1 - A TECHNIQUE FOR THINKING CRITICALLY
Chapter Outline and Key Terms 1
Overview 2
Solutions to Exercise Questions 5
Test Bank with Answers 7

Chapter 2 - DISAGREEMENTS AND ARGUMENTS
Chapter Outline and Key Terms 13
Overview 14
Solutions to Exercise Questions 16
Test Bank with Answers 27

Chapter 3 - LOGICAL ASSUMPTIONS, IMPLICATIONS, AND ARGUMENT
DIAGRAMS
Chapter Outline and Key Terms 39
Overview 40
Solutions to Exercise Questions 41
Test Bank with Answers 54

Chapter 4 - CLARIFYING MEANING
Chapter Outline and Key Terms 63
Overview 64
Solutions to Exercise Questions 65
Test Bank with Answers 69

PART TWO: THE EVALUATION OF ARGUMENTS

Chapter 5 - FALLACIES
Chapter Outline and Key Terms 75
Overview 76
Solutions to Exercise Questions 78
Test Bank with Answers 85

Chapter 6 - THE CATEGORICAL SYLLOGISM
Chapter Outline and Key Terms 95
Overview 97

Solutions to Exercise Questions 98
Test Bank with Answers 139

Chapter 7 -   THE SYLLOGISM REFINED
               Chapter Outline and Key Terms 147
               Overview 148
               Solutions to Exercise Questions 150
               Test Bank with Answers 165

Chapter 8 -   SYMBOLIZING STATEMENTS
               Chapter Outline and Key Terms 171
               Overview 172
               Solutions to Exercise Questions 174
               Test Bank with Answers 178

Chapter 9 -   ARGUMENT FORMS
               Chapter Outline and Key Terms 185
               Overview 186
               Solutions to Exercise Questions 187
               Test Bank with Answers 195

Chapter 10 -   TRUTH TABLES, EQUIVALENCE AND VALIDITY
               Chapter Outline and Key Terms 201
               Overview 202
               Solutions to Exercise Questions 203
               Test Bank with Answers 220

Chapter 11 -   STATEMENT FORMS: CONTRARIES, CONTRADICTIONS, AND
               TAUTOLOGIES
               Chapter Outline and Key Terms 227
               Overview 228
               Solutions to Exercise Questions 229
               Test Bank with Answers 235

PART THREE: APPLICATIONS

Chapter 12 -   INDUCTIVE REASONING
               Chapter Outline and Key Terms 243
               Overview 244
               Solutions to Exercise Questions 246
               Test Bank with Answers 251

Chapter 13 - STANDARDIZED TESTS AND LOGICAL PUZZLES
              Chapter Outline and Key Terms 257
              Overview 257
              Solutions to Exercise Questions 259
              Test Bank with Answers 263

Chapter 14 - ARGUMENTATIVE WRITING
              Chapter Outline and Key Terms 273
              Overview 273
              Solutions to Exercise Questions 275
              Test Bank with Answers 276

Appendix A - TRANSPARENCY MASTERS A-1

INTRODUCTION

Because logic and critical thinking courses have become such an integral part of the undergraduate (and to a limited extent, the graduate) curriculum at most colleges and universities, many of you who find yourselves teaching this class may come to the realization that a substantial percentage of your undergraduate teaching load is occupied by this class. This Instructor's Manual is written to lighten that load a bit. We will try to offer as many tips as we can based upon numerous years of experienced failures as well as successes (our colleagues and our own). For instance, it is not a bad idea to keep a folder handy in which you continually deposit tidbits of reasoning from the sublime to the ridiculous. These may come from your excursions to the grocery store or the movies just as easily as those to the library or "internet." A folder full of examples may provide you (a) with timely, vivid, often humorous examples that will spice up your classes, (b) with the fodder for pertinent, up to the minute questions for your quizzes, tests, exams, and (c) perhaps even the well stocked larder you will need when you make your own course pack or write your own text!

The Instructor's Manual is organized to coincide with each of the chapters in the textbook. Each chapter will be summarized again with some tips for how to introduce and use the chapter. We will provide a chapter outline and list of key terms and, then, explain how the Critical Technique applies to that chapter. Next, we include the solutions to all of the exercises in the chapter. We have found this helpful because, in the case of other texts we have used, when all of the solutions are not centrally localized, it becomes difficult or cumbersome to use the solutions effectively. Moreover, you are encouraged to challenge answers which are provided here and in the text. It may sharpen your students' critical thinking skills for them to see you taking issue with or augmenting the explanations that have become static in print. Finally, we conclude each chapter with a test bank, structured quite similarly to the textbook itself. The initial questions, mostly multiple choice, fill in the blank, and short answer are designed to ensure comprehension of the material in the chapter. The second set of questions is intended to test how well the student can *apply* the concepts and technique to concrete problems. The final set of questions contains deeper level problems geared to making the student reason for herself or himself. Again, feel free to alter these in any way you find useful and, if you come up with some questions you find really intriguing, please share them with us and we will disseminate them to others, if you so desire.

A PLEA

In fact, because we believe that logic, rationality, critical thinking, and intelligence are very much social processes, we ask that you share your comments with us—both what works in the classroom for you and what doesn't work. If, for example, your students find some form of Euler Diagramming much easier to master and remember as well as find it more useful on standardized testing in lieu of the Venn Diagrams we included, let us know. If you have particularly wonderful or instructive student essays that are turned in to you, we will be glad to credit both you and the student, if we may include them in subsequent editions. This offer extends to blurbs and examples you find in the text or any other comments. We really would appreciate them all. In fact, one of the carrots Kiersky dangles before his classes is the following: "The student this term who turns in the best critical analysis of the text itself will get an A in the class regardless of test grades!" In virtually every case, he has not had to give up very much as the student with the best critique has been one with a 98-100 average anyway. But it does get students to read the text, assimilate it, *and* think critically about it. Contact Kiersky at the Department of Philosophy at Georgia State University or in care of West Publishing Company.

Chapter 1

A TECHNIQUE FOR THINKING CRITICALLY

CHAPTER OUTLINE

A Critical Technique
Summary
Exercises
Case Study

KEY TERMS

Argument - A set of related claims in which one is said to follow from or be based on the others. The two types of claims in an argument are premises and conclusions.

Argument Structure - How the premises of an argument are related to the conclusion.

Claim - A declarative assertion capable of being assessed as true or false.

Conclusion - The claim that is to be established or proven in the argument.

Critical Technique - An eight-step method of analyzing and evaluating reasoning presented in this book.

Critical Thinking - The ability to correctly validate or refute claims presented for our belief.

Fallacy - An error in the reasoning process. Do not confuse it with a false claim.

Hidden Assumption - An unstated premise in an argument, sometimes also called a logical presupposition.

Inductive Argument - reasoning in which the truth of the premises makes the truth of the conclusion more or less probable, but can never guarantee it. They are classified from strong to weak according to the degree of probability with which the conclusion is established.

Invalid Deductive Argument - An argument

presented as if its conclusion had to be true, but due to a flaw in the argument's structure, it is possible for all of the premises to be true, while the conclusion is nevertheless false.

Meaning - How a word, phrase, sentence, or gesture is understood, as well as how it is used in context.

Premise - A claim offered in support of the conclusion.

Valid Deductive Argument - An argument is deductively valid if and only if it is impossible for all of the premises to be true and the conclusion to be false at the same time.

OVERVIEW

The initial chapter plunges the reader quickly into the pool of logic and critical thinking. Several important points surround the first chapter. First, the reader is introduced to the "Critical Technique:" an eight step program around which the entire book is organized. In our experience, when the student does not have a sense of the whole endeavor in which she or he is asked to participate, there is little chance of more than a superficial mastery of the concepts involved with even less chance of understanding how and when they apply. We try to stress that the Critical Technique is not the only way of analyzing, evaluating, or constructing arguments or lines of reasoning, but that it happens to be the way we organized this particular introduction to the topic. Each part of the text that follows is devoted to a particular phase of the process of reasoning and each chapter within that part is concerned with developing certain skills that a critical thinker should understand at that particular stage of thinking. As the students progress they should be encouraged to amend the Technique and tailor it to their own unique interests and needs.

The Technique is one method for organizing our analysis and evaluation of lines of reasoning that are presented for our acceptance and belief. Basically, it involves being able to distinguish between lines of reasoning, called arguments, and other kinds of thinking. Both critical thinking and logic deal almost exclusively with arguments and their components (statements or claims).

STEP ONE of the Technique asks us what is the major claim or the point of the reasoning? What is the reasoning trying to get us to do or believe? This phase of the reasoning process is discussed in the first chapter and in the beginning of the second chapter of the text.

STEP TWO of the Technique points us in the direction of identifying the arguments and their component premises and conclusions. At this point of the reasoning process we are non-judgmentally analyzing the structure of the reasoning involved in order to give it the fairest assessment possible. This stage of the Technique is discussed in the second chapter of the text.

STEP THREE of the Technique bids us look for the parts of the arguments that are not stated. In other words, are there any logical assumptions (missing premises) or implications (unstated conclusions) which need to be made explicit in order to complete the structure of the argument as a whole? This facet of reasoning is elucidated at the end of Chapter Two and in Chapter Three. It will also reappear in the latter half of Chapter Seven.

STEP FOUR of the Technique requires us to take an objective look at the content or meaning of the words, phrases, and language involved. Are there points which require clarification, definitions that need assessing, vague or ambiguous uses of language, equivocal phraseology, grammatical misconstructions? These points are systematically covered in Chapter Four, which rounds out the analytical phase of the Technique.

STEP FIVE of the Technique opens the evaluative phase of the process by examining fallacies that occur in the course of reasoning. Fallacies, or errors in reasoning, are distinguished in a very simple taxonomy in Chapter Five of the text. Beginning students usually find this phase one of the most enjoyable parts of the entire process. It makes fairly good sense to many of them to begin by asking - is the evidence for this particular claim true and accurate? And, even if it is true, is it relevant? Even if it is both true and relevant, is it fair (or is it slanted and one-sided)? Even if it is true, relevant, and fair, is it adequate? Is it enough or sufficient to support the particular claim it is supposed to support?

STEP SIX of the Technique raises the very important question of the argument's structure. Is the argument inductive or deductive, and why should the answer to that question matter? If the argument is deductive in nature; that is, if the premises are supposed to guarantee the truth of the conclusion without any further evidence, then we can assess the <u>validity</u> of the form of the argument <u>before</u> we even look at the content (which includes the truth, relevance, fairness, and adequacy) of the premises. Because this concept is so central to logic and critical thinking, it is covered from several different angles in Chapters Six through Eleven. We also cover the importance of understanding the major forms of inductive reasoning in Chapter Twelve.

STEP SEVEN of the Technique bids us look for what further conclusions can be drawn from the arguments that are given. This phase has been partially touched upon in Chapters Three, Seven, Nine, and Ten. However, it is given a peculiarly practical application to the field of standardized testing in Chapter Thirteen. Similarly, although the applicability of the Technique to the sphere of argumentative writing is a part of the exercises in virtually every chapter throughout the text, it is the exclusive concern of Chapter Fourteen.

STEP EIGHT of the Technique concludes the process of evaluation by asking us whether we agree or disagree with the conclusion or point of the argument <u>now</u> that we have looked at the content and the form of the evidential support it has been given. Four outcomes are possible: (1) we agree with the conclusion and we agree with the argument. Is there anything else we might add in support of it? (2) We agree with the conclusion, but we find the argument lacking. In this case, what evidence would <u>we</u> offer as grounds for believing in the conclusion? (3) We disagree with the conclusion, and we find the argument lacking. Is there anything else we would need to bring out about the reasoning? (4) We disagree with the conclusion, although we find the arguments to be extremely good ones. Is there anything else in our analyses we have not yet mentioned? One final point should also be considered: how important is the tool of critical thinking (or the Technique) in dealing with the particular issue at hand?

In order to bring this bare-bones outline to life for the students, we often give examples during the first or second class period, sort of concretizing the outline for the student as we explain it. So, as we illustrate Step One, we might bring out how many more instances there are than we can imagine where reasoning is occurring: we decide to get up (because we have to go to work or school); we turn on the radio/television/CD (because we need some stimulation or information); we brush our teeth (because we don't want cavities or bad breath); and so on.

Step Two is easily illustrated by using the same examples. We now have a whole argument: "I have decided to bicycle to school today (conclusion), because I don't have any gas in my car and I don't have any money to get any more gas (premises or reasons)." Step Three is likewise illustrated by showing that parts of arguments are often missing (and for a very broad variety of reasons). For instance, the old commercial from Burger King is still vivid: "The bigger the burger, the better the burger; the burgers are bigger at Burger King," is really two statements that imply a missing conclusion—"Therefore, the burgers are better at Burger King." Even more often, a premise may be missing. "Ollie North was lying to Congress; therefore you can't trust him," is an inductive argument missing a premise that "you can't trust anyone who lies to Congress."

Step Four is illustrated by explaining how often we have to clarify the language and the grammar that occurs in reasoning. We may be duped by bait-and-switch advertising. Definitions play a central role in reasoning and require careful scrutiny. The dangerous duo of vagueness and ambiguity require close monitoring. Step Five, the identification of fallacies, can be illustrated by showing the students some real life examples you have witnessed or that have happened to you.

We explain the importance of Step Six by showing how most people who listen to someone else's reasoning usually end up either agreeing or disagreeing with their conclusion without actually listening to or understanding their entire arguments. By carefully paying attention, we often may be able to show the invalidity of a line of reasoning without even having to give our own opinion as to the truth or falsity of their conclusion.

When we get to Steps Seven and Eight, we sometimes explain seven by pointing out that, normally, people either believe the conclusion or point of the argument or they don't believe it. Rarely, if ever, do they stop to consider whether they find the argument to be a good one or not. But, an important part of critical thinking is finding out whether or not we have good reasons to accept a particular claim. And, with Step Eight we try to explain that there are situations where the use of reasoning (as opposed to other problem-solving or decision-making procedures) is extremely helpful, useful, important, essential, and just as importantly, that there may be situations where reasoning may not be of much avail or utility. In fact this latter point is an excellent opportunity to engage the class in some discussion. Try to get them to come up with some scenarios wherein critical thinking might not be all that helpful.

You may want to mention to the class that logic/critical thinking is a skills course, frequently quite different from any other philosophy course they may have had, not because there's no skill to philosophy, but rather because there are definite and measurable outcomes pertinent to this class. Indeed, now is a good time to mention objectives and goals of the text and of thinking critically. For us, these may include, but certainly are not limited to:

1. increasing our awareness of the variety of ways human beings think, reason, justify, explain, rationalize, persuade, etc. and to help develop critical abilities (a) for analytically understanding even the most technical and obtuse thinking, and (b) for being able to fairly assess and judge the worth of those lines of reasoning;

2. sharpening our organizational, written, and presentational skills;

3. helping us understand how standardized test questions are formulated so that we may improve our scores on a range of aptitude tests (from the GMAT, GRE, and LSAT, to the MCAT);

4. increasing our self-awareness through techniques such as being able to spot our hidden presuppositions and assumptions;

5. increasing our understanding of the interconnectedness of much of our educational exposure with that of our lived experiences;

6. helping us to change our attitudes about problems, conflicts, and disagreements so that they become challenges rather than nuisances;

7. helping us become better listeners as well as more effective speakers;

8. helping us improve the quality of life for ourselves as well as others.

SOLUTIONS TO EXERCISE QUESTIONS

Answers to Exercises on Pages 9 through 11

Level A

1. *   B
2. *   A

5

Chapter 1

3. * It can be A, B, or D
4. * D
5. * B, although it could be A, C, D, or even E
6. * Premises (or the premise set)
   Conclusion
7. * Hidden, Unstated, Tacit, or Implicit
8. * Logical Presupposition
9. * Deductive
10. * Inductive

Level B

1. * Conclusion: That the defendant was guilty (or innocent) of committing a particular crime.
   Evidence: That the defendant was somewhere else at the time, had an iron clad alibi, that someone else committed the crime....

2. Conclusion: That you should vote for that politician.
   Evidence: That politicians will represent your needs and wants better than any other candidate. (e.g., will lower your taxes, pay all your bills, take care of your retirement, etc.)

3. * Conclusion: That you should buy that particular brand of toothpaste.
   Evidence: Buying that particular brand will lower your rate of cavities and/or brighten your teeth, etc. better than any other brand of toothpaste.

4. Conclusion: My paper is one week late.
   Evidence: It was due in one week ago and I am just now turning it in, because (a) I have been in the hospital, (b) my dog ate it, (c) I had to go out of town for an emergency, (d) my boss wouldn't let me off work for a week, etc.

5. * Conclusion: Smoking cigarettes is hazardous to your health.
   Evidence: There is a high degree of correlation between smoking cigarettes and the incidence of lung cancer.

6. Conclusion: My car was illegally parked in the "No Parking" zone.
   Evidence: I had to bring an emergency package into the Dean's office immediately.

7. * Conclusion: People should not "Cry 'Wolf'."
   Evidence: Other people will no longer listen to a person who continually cries for help when it is not needed or is a joke.

8. Conclusion: That people should behave morally and not sin.
   Evidence: That sinners will pay a heavy price, whereas virtue will be rewarded.

9. * Conclusion: This concert was absolutely awesome!
   Evidence: It was the best rendition of this particular piece I have ever heard and I liked it anyway to begin with.

10. Conclusion: We are trying to help raise money for AIDS victims.
    Evidence: Because we believe that this is a worthwhile endeavor and that they

6

deserve our support and compassion.

Evidence Questions

11. *   Evidence: Your client has no motive or opportunity and an ironclad alibi.
12.   Evidence: Your friend will be much better off under the political leadership and policies of this particular politician.
13. *   Evidence: There are terrific tax benefits for making such a contribution and your friend believes in the ideas espoused by that particular charity.
14.   Evidence: The instructor has a written policy in her syllabus guaranteeing students the right to a make-up exam in case of bona fide illness.
15. *   Evidence: That cheating is wrong from an ethical point of view and that the consequences of being detected outweigh any possible benefits of doing so.
16.   Evidence: Pro positions may use rational, causal, or cosmological premises such as order in the universe, etc.; anti positions often use the unnecessary pain and suffering or existence of evil arguments or the inherent unfairness in the universe arguments.
17. *   Evidence: Rational arguments would rely on what conditions are necessary to sustain life as we know it, showing that Mars either meets or fails to meet these conditions. More empirical arguments would utilize premises showing what facts we have already uncovered and what data have been compiled from astronomic observations.
18.   Evidence: That classic music has withstood the test of time that rock music has yet to endure; or that rock music is relevant to the cultural needs of contemporary society while classical music has outlived any such utility. (Or that one simply "sounds" a lot better than the other!)

TEST BANK

Multiple Choice Questions

1. How do Logic and critical thinking differ?
   A. Logic is not judgmentally evaluative, while critical thinking is judgmentally negative.
   B. They differ according to their subject matter.
   C. Logic concerns the province of facts, while critical thinking pertains to opinions.
   D. Logic is concerned more with the structure or form of discursive reasoning while critical thinking includes logic but is the larger endeavor of analyzing and evaluating reasoning in order to determine which claims are worthy of belief and which are not.
   E. Logic is concerned with the origin of human beliefs, while critical thinking is concerned with their validation.

ANSWER: D

2. What is the point of critical thinking?
   A. To show that a conclusion is false.
   B. To be able to win any disagreement or debate.
   C. To be able to "snow" or win opponents over to your way of thinking.
   D. To test our beliefs and those of others.
   E. To avoid controversy.

   ANSWER: D

3. Suppose you come across an article in a reputable publication and your attention is captured by the title, "College Students Losing Interest in Core Courses Due to Electronic Brain Stimulation." You are hooked and read on to discover the authors are contending that undergraduate students by the hundreds are getting "high" from the EBS and consequently suffering from poor class attendance, lowered test grades, more interest in "fringe" elective courses, and general malaise about education and the curriculum overall. How do both logic and critical thinking pertain to this scenario?
   A. They don't, since the report merely gives information.
   B. They do pertain, because this report attempts to be factual.
   C. They do pertain, because this entire topic is highly controversial.
   D. They do not pertain, because this is a causal rather than a logical explanation.
   E. They do pertain, because the report tries to establish a claim (that EBS has certain adverse effects) based upon some evidence (the performance of hundreds of college students) and so one could apply the Critical Technique to it.
   F. They do not apply, because (1) this report is stupid and totally fabricated (there is no such thing as EBS) and (2) even if there were, it only pertains to a handful of students and not the vast and normal majority of college students.

   ANSWER: E

4. Identify the main point or claim of each of the following passages:
   A. You shouldn't go in to work today: the weather is terrible.
   B. Noot got more votes than his opponent, Ben; no wonder he won the election.
   C. Codependency is an oppressive concept; you should be wary of using it.
   D. Hot coffee will scald you; I saw it happen to my mom once.
   E. Emptiness cannot be. What is empty is nothing and nothingness can not be.

   ANSWER: A. You shouldn't go in to work today.
              B. No wonder Noot won the election.
              C. You should be wary of using it.
              D. Hot coffee will scald you.

     E. Emptiness cannot be.

5. Which of the following claims are statements?
   A. Why was he in the car in the first place?
   B. Cool beans!! Totally awesome!!
   C. Help is on its way.
   D. How long has it been since you saw her?
   E. Go to the next question, please.

   ANSWER: C

6. How does the analytical phase of critical thinking differ from the evaluative phase?
   A. The analytical phase is non-judgmental; it is the step that seeks a fair and impartial breakdown of the reasoning into its component parts. The evaluative phase is judgmental, attempting to determine if the argument is a good one or not and attempting to determine whether the conclusion is worth believing or not.
   B. The analytical phase is concerned with the source or origin of a particular belief, while the evaluative phase is concerned with the verification or validation of that belief.
   C. The evaluative phase builds upon the analytical phase so that the two are integrally woven into one continuous process of reasoning and problem-solving.
   D. The analytical phase is more quantitative, whereas the evaluative phase is more qualitative.
   E. Both A and C above.

   ANSWER: E

7. What is the purpose of having a technical vocabulary in a field of study that is meant to apply to almost every area and aspect of life?
   A. It definitely helps increase ones vocabulary and word power.
   B. It allows for precision of expression and also for people to have a simpler way of referring to more complex matters.
   C. It will definitely impress people who are unfamiliar with the terms so that one who is able to use such terminology correctly will appear to be much more intelligent than someone who cannot do so.
   D. The purpose is actually academic: courses gain their significance and their rationalization within the educational community to the extent that they have a technical language that must be taught and mastered.
   E. All of the above.

   ANSWER: B

8. Which of the following questions would not be important for the critical thinker?
   A. What claims are being made?

    B. Are there any logical assumptions or implications?
    C. From where did those claims arise?
    D. What fallacies are involved?
    E. What is the argument's structure and is it valid?

ANSWER: C

Short Answer Questions

In the following questions, state the <u>conclusion</u> (if any) that would most probably be advanced in the situation. Then state what evidence might be offered in support of this claim.

9. An advertisement for a soft drink company.

    ANSWER:
        Conclusion: You should buy Gola Cola.
        Evidence: Gola Cola will increase your lifespan threefold.

10. A sports editorial.

    ANSWER:
        Conclusion: Major league baseball will never be the same.
        Evidence: Too many lifelong fans have been permanently soured by the strike.

11. A letter to the editor of a newspaper about euthanasia.

    ANSWER:
        Conclusion: Dr. Jack Kevorkian is a saint and should be knighted.
        Evidence: He has helped more persons cope with suffering than Clara Barton.

12. An essay on multiculturalism.

    ANSWER:
        Conclusion: We should all be very proud of our multicultural heritages.
        Evidence: Experiences that contribute to our individuality and uniqueness likewise redound to society's benefit.

13. A TV celebrity and ex-drug addict talking to a high school audience.

    ANSWER:
        Conclusion: You should learn to say, "No," and stand up for yourself early in life.
        Evidence: I would be a much richer person if I had done so. And, I have seen others

who have fared far worse than I did.

14. A political lobbyist for a major medical insurance company speaking to an influential senator.

    ANSWER:
      Conclusion: You should vote for House Bill Umpty Ump (which will protect my company's position in the market).
      Evidence: A pro vote will mean a six figure contribution to your retirement account.

15. A corporate board member speaking at a board meeting on the prospect of bringing out a new product.

    ANSWER:
      Conclusion: You should come out with this product as soon as possible.
      Evidence: Marketing analysis shows we will make a fortune from it.

16. An accountant advising a taxpayer client.

    ANSWER:
      Conclusion: You should begin keeping all of your mailing receipts, as well as your copying expenses.
      Evidence: These are legitimate business expenses and can save you tax money.

17. A biologist trying to determine what sort of lifeform a particular organism is.

    ANSWER:
      Conclusion: It cannot be an influenza.
      Evidence: We can see it under normal magnification through a microscope.

Short Essay Questions

18.   State what you take to be the purpose and function of the Critical Technique.

19.   Explain the difference between the origin of a belief and the verification or validation of that belief.

20.   Write a brief argumentative essay for or against one of the following topics:
    A. A college education helps a person become a more responsible voter and citizen.
    B. A semester system of education is better than the quarter system.
    C. Students should not have to take any kind of core curriculum courses.
    D. Censorship of reading materials at the high school and college level is actually harmful (or beneficial) to democracy.

Chapter 2

Disagreements and Arguments

CHAPTER OUTLINE

2.1 Disagreements
      Exercises
2.2 Arguments
      Exercises
2.3 Inductive and Deductive Arguments
      Summary
      Exercises
      Case Study: NPR's Weekend Edition

KEY TERMS

Argument - A set of related claims. Two types of claims in an argument are premises and conclusions. Arguments are often used to settle disagreements.

Conclusion - The claim or statement to be established or proved in an argument.

Disagreement - A difference of opinion, attitude, or belief between two or more persons, or within one and the same person.

Evaluative Disagreement - Difference in the assessment of the moral, aesthetic, or practical worth of an event, object, or course of action.

Explanation - Usually a special kind of argument in which the conclusion is more familiar or better known than the support for it.

Extraneous Statement - A claim that is neither a premise nor a conclusion.

Factual Disagreement - A dispute about an empirical matter, settleable by observation or experiment.

Inductive Argument - Reasoning wherein the truth of the premise makes the truth of the conclusion more or less probable, but does not guarantee it.

Interpretive Disagreement - Conflict between different readings or understandings of the same set of facts.

Premise - A statement or claim designed to support a conclusion.

Strong Inductive Argument - Reasoning in which the truth of the premises establishes a relatively high degree of probability that the conclusion is true too.

Verbal Disagreement - Misunderstanding resulting from different uses of the meaning of a word or phrase.

Weak Inductive Argument - Reasoning in which the truth of the premises establishes a relatively low degree of probability that the conclusion is also true.

OVERVIEW

Chapter Two comes quickly to the main point of logic and critical thinking: the study of discursive, point by point reasoning also called arguments. Disagreements are distinguished from arguments for several reasons. The textbook keeps close to the street or ordinary sense of disagreement as a dispute, a difference of belief, attitude, or opinion, or a conflict, or a puzzle or problem, and so forth. The word "argument" becomes the first technical term developed in the book. Without a precise understanding of the concept and a way to distinguish it from other forms of human cognition, the study of reasoning would be rendered much more difficult. Finally, the chapter concludes with a discussion of the differences between deductive and inductive lines of reasoning as well as an explanation for why we draw the distinction as we do. Chapter Two thus corresponds to step two of the critical technique.

2.1   Disagreements

Differences of opinion, disputes, conflicts may be distinguished according to different ways of approaching and resolving them rationally or critically. Indeed, the purpose for delineating between factual, interpretive, verbal, and evaluative disagreements or disputes is to show that different kinds of arguments are required to resolve different types of disputes and problems. Be sure to emphasize that these distinctions are not hard and fast, that there is a great deal of overlap between them, that in the case of most real life disagreements there is more than one kind at play, and that these four types are not completely exhaustive of all the possibilities. Still, they may be workable and helpful, particularly if they are recognized as one of the principal incentives for thinking about how to settle them.

Factual Disagreements are disputes that may be settled by appeals to empirical, observational, or some kind of operational or experimental basis, in principle, if not in practice. As such, the kinds of arguments which will resolve them often hinge upon one or more crucial empirical statements that may be verified as either true or false.

Interpretive Disagreements are disputes that very well may appeal to the same set of "facts," but have different ways of reading, seeing, or understanding those data. As such, an appeal to facts will not necessarily resolve the problem. Usually, interpretive disagreements require as part of the premises a theoretical framework that explains why one way of seeing the data is better than the other (and it also generally explains why the other explanation *appears* plausible).

Verbal Disagreements are pseudo-disputes in which the parties end up talking past one another usually because a critical word or phrase is being understood in two different ways. As such, this type of disagreement is not so much resolved as *dissolved* once the parties recognize what is happening. Quite often, another kind of disagreement will arise once the verbal morass is cleared up.

Evaluative Disagreements are one of the most widespread of all and they involve a difference in attitude toward or judgment about something. Very often the parties involved may agree on the facts of the situation and perhaps even the interpretation of how the facts are to be construed. The difference concerns the worth or importance or rightness or wrongness of some aspect of the situation. As such, the arguments used to resolve this kind of disagreement will require as part of the premises a moral principle or some type of evaluative statement in order to reach the desired conclusion.

2.2   Arguments

An argument in logic is a line of reasoning composed of two types of statements, or declarative assertions, capable of being assessed as either true or false. Premise statements provide the grounds or the evidence for the conclusion statements (claims which are the point of the argument). Indicator words help us determine which statements are premises and which are conclusions. Where no indicator words exist, the "so-because" test may be helpful. So is the source or author of the argument, and so is the context itself.

Once we have begun to identify the argument or arguments, it will be important to make sure we have not confused any complex statements, such as hypothetical or conditional statements, with the arguments themselves. They very well may be components of an argument. It is also important to eliminate extraneous or irrelevant statements from consideration. And, it is also helpful to distinguish particular kinds of arguments called "explanations" in which the conclusion is at least as well established as the premises offered in support of it. By the time we have completed sections 2.1 and 2.2 and practiced a number of examples, we will have addressed steps one and two of the critical technique.

2.3   Inductive and Deductive Arguments

15

Chapter 2

Inductive reasoning may be distinguished from deductive reasoning insofar as the latter is couched in language that makes it seem that the premises by themselves establish the conclusion beyond the shadow of a doubt. Indeed, if this is true, the conclusion of deductive arguments is contained in the premises already so that there is in fact no new information in the conclusion which was not already in the premises. Another way of phrasing this same feature is to note that in deductive reasoning which is valid, it would be a contradiction to say that the premises are true but the conclusion is false. In inductive reasoning, no such contradiction arises. The conclusion goes beyond what is contained in the premises, and the premises may support the conclusion to a very, very strong degree, but they do not guarantee it. It is always possible for all of the premises to be true in an inductive argument but for the conclusion to turn out to be false anyway. An argument is deductively valid if and only if it is impossible for all of the premises to be true while the conclusion is false.

SOLUTIONS TO EXERCISE QUESTIONS

Answers to Exercises on Pages 21 through 24

Level A

1. * A Disagreement is a difference of opinion, attitude or belief while an Argument (for the purposes of Logic or Critical Thinking) is a line of reasoning composed of a premise set and a conclusion.
2. * An Interpretive Disagreement is straightforward in the sense that it is a dispute centering around the meaning or significance of some thing or event. A Verbal Disagreement is *not* straightforward because it involves the kind of misunderstanding in which people are talking past one another usually because they are using a crucial word or phrase in two different senses and they do not recognize that this is happening.
3. * Evaluative. (Probably Moral, Social or Political)
4. * False. (Quite often several different kinds of disagreement are embedded in one and the same dispute.)
5. * False again. (It is possible to have a disagreement that is purely Factual, or purely Verbal, or purely Evaluative, or purely Interpretive.)
6. * False yet again. (The reason for drawing the distinction in the first place was to show that different kinds of disagreements generally require different kinds of arguments to resolve them.)
7. * Evaluative. (Note the operative word, "better.")
8. * Factual
9. * Probably Interpretive
10. * Probably Interpretive
11. * Mostly Evaluative with some Interpretive overtones (if they are disagreeing about the significance of certain aspects of the problem) and possibly some Factual overtones (if

they are disagreeing about predictable consequences of sending such aid).

12. * Evaluative
13. * Evaluative - Practical (since this concerns an action to be taken), but there are Factual dimensions concerning the actual effects of increased or reduced cholesterol levels.
14. * Evaluative with some Interpretive overtones as to what constitutes "private." (This could also be seen as Factual, if we are talking about what are the *legal* limits.)
15. * Evaluative
16. * Evaluative
17. * Evaluative - Practical (this can be seen as Factual)
18. * Evaluative - Aesthetic
19. * Factual
20. * Interpretive

Level B

1. * The question of who actually wrote the novel, *The Outsider* is a Factual Disagreement in this case. It was written by Richard Wright. Note that there is no disagreement as to Frantz Fanon's writing abilities; if there were it would probably be an Evaluative Disagreement. Also, when spoken, if the last word, "right," is taken to be "Wright," it may generate a Verbal Disagreement (although it is not at this point.)

2. In this case, Daniel and Cynthia are talking past one another; she is talking about a moral right, while he is talking about a legal right. The Disagreement is Verbal.

3. * The Disagreement about the "Best way" is an Evaluative one, even if it is a Practical one. It may evolve into an Interpretive Disagreement if by "Best" Roger means "quickest" and Judy means "most scenic." Since she actually indicates this, the dispute is probably Evaluative. If the disagreement were which of the two routes is actually the fastest, then the dispute would be Factual.

4. The Disagreement is primarily Evaluative (it concerns what course of action *should be* taken). We need to see how this disagreement develops. If the two CPA's are in agreement about the principles and objectives involved then the dispute will probably be resolved when Arthur finishes his demonstration. If there is a disagreement over either principle or objective (say, one wants to cast the Annual Report in the most favorable light while the other wants to help lower corporate tax liability or reduce the price of the corporate stock so that the company can buy up more shares) then it would be Evaluative. It could be a factual Disagreement if the two agree on all the salient points and there is simply a computational discrepancy.

5. * This one is tricky. At face value, it is a Verbal Disagreement: George is talking about the actual consequences that ensued from Desert Storm; while Jimmy is talking about the motives that led to the decisions to become involved with Desert Storm. To that extent, they are talking past one another. (Typical of politicians!) But there is clearly an Evaluative component as well, for George obviously approves of the policy and its results while Jimmy disapproves.

6.   This one has several overlapping components. First, there is an Evaluative Disagreement as to whether this statue should be ranked among the "best." Second, there is an Interpretive Disagreement as to whether this piece of sculpture should be considered a "work of art" or "one of fine technical merit (but not art)." The Disagreement with respect to whether Fred X is an "Italian artist" or not is either Factual (if they disagree as to where in fact he was actually born) or Interpretive (if one believes that an "Italian" artist must come from Italy, while the other believes that an "Italian" artist may include people who live and were trained in Italy or come from Italian ancestry). But, it is not a Verbal Disagreement because the two are not (yet anyway) talking past one another.

7. *   This is a Factual Disagreement! Can this particular river be canoed by anyone or is it navigable only by experienced open-boaters? If the Disagreement hinged around the subject of just what constitutes "an experienced open-boat canoeist," then the dispute would be Interpretive. If we are disagreeing about how much experience is actually needed to canoe the Upper Gauley, then the dispute might be Evaluative—Practical.

8.   The question is whether this is a *good* time for Michele to buy a new home or not. On the one hand, that is an Evaluative Disagreement, even if a Practical one. To a lesser degree, neither side disagrees about the facts in this case, although each side adduces a different set of considerations as to why this is or is not "the perfect time ..... to buy a new house." This aspect of the difference of opinion is Interpretive.

9. *   Ellen's statement is a factual one, even if it is couched in evaluative language (like "horrible"). Barbara has taken Ellen's words to mean something more and different and so is really talking past Ellen, making this a Verbal Disagreement. If both persons were also disagreeing about whether the government *should* allocate resources for AIDs research, then the dispute would be Evaluative.

10.   This dispute is a judgment call concerning which course of action is better to take in a dangerous situation. Jim thinks it is better to try to avoid the storm and the lightening, while Cathy thinks that it is better to minimize the time spent in the dangerous situation. The Disagreement is Evaluative.

Answers to Exercises on Pages 30 through 32

Level A

1. *   Premises (the evidence) and Conclusion (the point of the reasoning)

2. *   A *statement* in logic is a declarative utterance which is capable of being assessed as true or false. All Statements are sentences. But, not all *sentences* are statements, for some sentences are commands, directives, exclamations, questions, and other forms of language usage than declarations. Moreover, some sentences contain more than one statement within them.

3. *   *Arguments* are lines of reasoning in which premises are used to support a conclusion which is not as well known or accepted as the premises, whereas *explanations* are lines of reasoning in which the conclusion is already known or better accepted than the premises

which are being used to account for that conclusion. As such explanations can be seen as one kind of argument.

4. * Therefore, Thus, Hence, Consequently, So, ...

5. * Because, Since, For, As, For the reason that .....

6. * True. This is because all reasoning is contextual and it will depend upon the particular argument in question as to whether a given statement is a premise or a conclusion in that argument.

7. * False. (If you have trouble with this, look back at some of the examples, particularly on pages 25 and 28.)

8. * False. While it is true that all statements are sentences, the concept of sentences is broader than that of statements.

9. * True. This is one of the uses of the So-Because Test. It is also helpful in determining which of two statements is a premise and which is a conclusion when there are no indicator words present.

10. * True

Level B

1. * P-1: Dickie and Debbie are trying to control their cholesterol intake.

   C: Dickie and Debbie prefer meals that are low in saturated fats.
   Premise Indicator: Because

2. P-1: Dickie and Debbie prefer meals that are low in saturated fats.

   C: Dickie and Debbie will probably reduce their risk of coronary heart disease.
   Premise Indicator: Because

3. * P-1: We spent all of our money at the ball game last night.
   P-2: We only have six dollars between us.

   C: We should just get a rental movie tonight.
   Premise Indicators: Since, After all

4. P-1: Spike Lee's movies deal with subject matter that few other directors would consider putting on film.
   P-2: They focus on sensitive issues without being superficial.

   C: Spike Lee's movies are daring and provocative.
   Premise Indicator: Because. (Also the word, "AND," lets you know that the last statement is on the same logical level as the statement preceding it—that is, in this case they are both premises.)

19

5. *   P-1:   Clinton was able to win back Democratic voters who had gone for Bush and Reagan in previous elections.

   _____

   C: Clinton won the election.
       Premise Indicator: The main reason that
       This example is clearly an Explanation. (We know that Clinton won the election. The question is whether this is the main reason or premise that explains WHY he won.)

6.   P-1:   Mary and Maggie don't like any extra ingredients other than mushrooms on their pizza.

   _____

   C: We should probably order the plain one.
       Premise Indicator: Since
       Extraneous Statement: "Morgan likes anchovies on her pizza."

7. * Strictly speaking this is not an argument at all. It is cast in the form of a hypothetical or conditional statement, and in this particular case it is also followed by a question mark (which often indicates that it is a non-statement, such as a question). However, it may be read as a rhetorical question and turned into a set of two statements that in the present case could be considered an argument:
   P-1:   The Earth's average temperature has risen sharply since the beginning of the industrial age.

   _____

   C: Global warming is taking place.

Note that the reasoning in this example _may_ be read in just the opposite mode: in other words, it makes sense to say that "Because global warming has been taking place, therefore the Earth's average temperature has risen sharply since the beginning of the industrial age." The example in question is phrased in such a way that the former reading is much more apropos than the latter in this case because of the phraseology in this context.

8.   We are problem-solving here and attempting to draw a conclusion, so, yes, there is an argument. But there are no indicator words in the passage. So, we will have to apply our "So-Because" Test:
   P-1:   The power is on in the rest of the house and none of the circuit breakers have been tripped.
   P-2:   The clock and timer are both still working and so is the oven.

   _____

   C: It is highly unlikely that the problem is external to our electric range itself.
       Note that the word "So" in P-2 means "also" or "too" in this context and not "therefore." It is not a Premise Indicator or a Conclusion Indicator here, but a

conjoining word to indicate that the clock *and* the time *and* the oven are all working.

9. *   Again, we are reasoning out the answer to a problem and drawing a conclusion. And again, we are not given indicator words. The "So-Because" Test will work fine here, too.

P-1:   We are sailing toward the pole star.

P-2:   The last two stars in the Big Dipper point to it (the pole star).

P-3:   The wind, which is out of the east tonight, is directly off our starboard (right) beam (side).

P-4:   The compass is pointing at 360 degrees (helps a bit).

_____

C: We have to be sailing a northerly course.
        Extraneous words or expressions: "Just look;" "And;" "Of course"

10.   This time we have a complex statement, a hypothetical or conditional statement, as one of the premises.

P-1:   If timing were not the crucial factor that it is, then it would not matter when you completed your assignment.

P-2:   It does matter when you complete this task.

_____

C: Timing is a crucial factor.
        Indicator words: "If, then" indicate a conditional statement.
                          "Since" indicates a premise.
                          "However" functions like a conjoiner to show that these two statements are on the same level.
                          "Must" indicates a conclusion to be drawn in this instance and may be rendered as "is" (or you can keep the "must" at this point) when writing the conclusion.

11. *   This one is a little trickier and can be read in more than one way.

P-1:   He (Bill Clinton) can keep at least a half-dozen Southern states in play.

_____

C: (He can) keep President Bush from the traditional Republican lock on the Confederacy's 147 electoral votes.

P-2:   (He can) keep President Bush from the traditional Republican lock on the Confederacy's 147 electoral votes.

_____

C: For now, Bill Clinton needs a healthy third force in this campaign.

P-3:   For now, Bill Clinton needs a healthy third force in this campaign.

_____

    C: He (Bill Clinton) needs Ross Perot.

          Indicator words: "Thus" indicates a conclusion to follow.

                     "So that" here paradoxically introduces a reason why and hence is a premise indicator.

12.   P-1:   Our political mythology imbues us with the idiocy of "We're No. 1!"

        P-2:   U.S. Politicians are still trying to erase Vietnam from their memories.

    C: We aren't very good at handling defeats in war—and no good at all at learning ... from them.

          Indicator words: "So" here indicates a conclusion.

One may want to argue that the first sentence, which we have included as P-2, is actually extraneous to this particular argument. However, it seems more likely that it functions as an example, perhaps one of the prime ones at that, in recent history to bear out P-1. As such P-1 and P-2 together do a better job of supporting the Conclusion than does either one of the Premises by itself.

13. * P-1:   Two world wars have proved that the United States ignores events in Europe at its own peril.

    C: All of the arguments [urging the U.S. to reduce its military forces in Europe] are flawed.

If this were the whole of the argument, it would be a very hasty generalization. The point of what was included in this little excerpt was to show how, quite often, we back up our conclusions with words indicating our main reasons, as Nixon has done here by the use of the word "First." Each subsequent point would then follow numerically (e.g., "Second," "Third" .....)

14.   P-1:   Their [people's] moods govern how much money they spend.

        P-2:   Consumer spending accounts for about two-thirds of all economic activity.

    C: How people feel, deep down, is critical (Dr. Zullow says).

          Indicator words: "Because" indicates a premise or reason.

                     "And" in this case indicates the point that follows is on the same logical level as the point which preceded it (which was a premise).

15. * P-1:   Six million people were exterminated (he says).

        P-2:   There are still people in the world who are savages.

    C: Home Depot Chairman Bernard Marcus has pledged $1 million to the U.S. Holocaust Memorial Museum in Washington.

This example is an *Explanation.*   Indicator words: "Why?" indicates a premise to follow.

"Because" also indicates a premise. "And"
again conjoins two premises in this instance.

Answers to Exercises on Pages 35 and 36:

Level A

1. *   In at least one of three ways: (1) Are the premises asserted as if they definitely and irrevocably guaranteed the truth of the conclusion without any further information at all? (2) Is the conclusion, as stated, already contained in the premises themselves, or does the conclusion go beyond anything contained in the premises? (3) Would it be a contradiction to say that these premises are true, but the conclusion is or may be false?

2. *   In inductive or non-deductive arguments, the premises may support the conclusion to a greater or lesser degree, but they never can absolutely guarantee its truth. There may be some other reason why it ultimately turns out to be false.

3. *   By saying that the conclusion of a deductive argument is contained within the premises what is meant is that there is no new information which appears in the conclusion which is not already in the premises. Indeed, that information may be spread out over many different premises and the combination in one place for the first time may seem a novelty, but all of the pieces of the puzzle were in fact given at the outset.

4. *   False

5. *   Probably True. (But, if one adds the unstated premise that goes with arguments of this type—such as "The future will exactly resemble the past." —then it may be a deductive argument.

6. *   False

Level B

1. *   P-1:   Every day that the traffic is reported to be congested I always take the subway to town.

    P-2:   The traffic report is for another day of gridlock.

    _____

    C: I will take the subway to town today.
          Premise Indicator: "Since"

If you take P-1 as a statement about the past (in other words, "every day up until today"), then the argument is Inductive since the conclusion goes beyond the premises to talk about today. However, P-1 is more likely a statement about "every day," past, present, and future, and, hence, the argument is a Deductive piece of reasoning that looks something like

    P-1:   If A (traffic is congested), then B (I take the subway)

    P-2:   A (traffic is congested)

    _____

    C: B (I take the subway)

23

2.   P-1:   Every day this year that the traffic has been reported to be congested Carole has taken the subway into town.
       P-2:   The traffic is supposed to be congested again today.

       _____

       C: She (Carole) will probably take the subway again today.
                Conclusion Indicator: "So"

This example is even more borderline than the first one. On the one hand, it can be regarded as an Inductive argument insofar as P-1 concerns every individual day this year up through yesterday and the conclusion is about what will happen today. On the other hand, it is probably better seen as a Deductive argument because the conclusion is not that Carole will definitely take the subway again today (that would be an Inductive argument), but rather that, because she has behaved in a certain way under certain conditions, she will probably behave that same way under those conditions today. Even if it turns out that she doesn't take the subway today, the *odds* were that she would do so based on past behavior. Still, one could counter that the reason why she took the subway when the traffic was congested was because it was also raining on each of those previous days and although the traffic reported to be congested today, since it is not raining, she chooses to drive or carpool or maybe not even go to town today!

3. *   P-1:   Anniece has taken her dry cleaning to three of the twelve Acme Dry Cleaning stores and has been dissatisfied with their work each time.

       _____

       C: Acme Dry Cleaners must not do very high-quality work.
                Conclusion Indicator: "She has concluded that"

This one is an Inductive argument. She may have been unfortunate in the few times she took her clothing to those cleaners. It is also possible that the other nine out of twelve stores do outstanding quality work and never leave customers unsatisfied while the three she did visit normally do excellent work too.

4.   P-1:   The bigger the taco is, the better the taco is.
       P-2:   Nacho Momma's has the biggest tacos around.

       _____

       C: Nacho Momma's has the best tacos around.
                Conclusion: "So, you can be sure ....."

This one is definitely a Deductive argument. Whether or not Nacho Momma's has the best tacos around, *if* they have the biggest ones around, and *if* the biggest ones around are the best ones around, *then* it has to be true that Nacho Momma's has the best ones around.

5. *   P-1:   I was on flight 108 from Salem to San Diego at the time.
       P-2:   Nobody can be two places at once.

       _____

       C: I could not have been driving the car at that time.

Indicator Word: "Because" indicates a premise.
                   "And" indicates another premise in this case.
Extraneous Expression: "Your Honor"

This argument is intended to be Deductive. If it is true that I have an iron-clad alibi where I was at the time and if it is equally true that no one can be two places at the same time, then it must be true that I could not have been at a second place simultaneously. (Okay, suppose it was one of those huge transports and the car was on the plane!!)

6.   P-1:   The Broncos have won every game in which speedster Trak Starr has played.
       P-2:   Trak Starr is playing in tomorrow's game.
       _____

       C: The Broncos are bound to win tomorrow.
               Indicator Word: "So" indicates the conclusion.

Because P-1 is about the past (every game that Trak Starr has played for the Broncos up until now), even though P-2 is about tomorrow's game, it is quite possible that P-1 and P-2 are both true while the conclusion turns out to be false. This argument is Inductive.

7. *   P-1:   Senator Snort said he would not enter the upcoming gubernatorial race unless the Democrats made him angry.
        P-2:   So far no one has aroused his ire.
        _____

        C: Senator Snort doesn't plan on entering the race.
                Indicator Words: The first "So" is not used to indicate a conclusion, but a point in time (hence it is temporal, not logical).
                                  The second "So" indicates a conclusion.

There are at least two ways of looking at this example. First, the form of the argument is basically one in which someone is claiming:

        If   X does not happen, then Y will not happen.
(And)   X is not happening.
        _____

(So)   Y will not happen.

This is a Deductive Argument.

The second way of looking at the example is to notice that there is a difference between *saying* that you will not enter the race and *not planning* to enter the race. Because of this, perhaps subtle, distinction, the conclusion may go beyond what is claimed in the premises and, hence, make this more of an Inductive or Non-Deductive Argument. We would favor looking at the example in the former way but would not quibble with the second reading. After all, politicians have been know to *say* one thing when they were *planning to do* something quite different.

8.   P-1:   Rising interest rates have always been followed by falling ones.
       P-2:   (Conversely,) Falling interest rates have always been succeeded by rising ones.

C: Market conditions have always tended to be cyclical in some appreciable manner.

There are no indicator words to help us decipher this passage. The "So-Because" Test helps us see that for this first part of the argument, we have an Explanation of *why* market conditions have always tended to be cyclical. This Argument/Explanation is Inductive in nature because the premises are talking about rising and falling interest rates while the conclusion speaks of market conditions. The conclusion is not contained in the premises, unless we make explicit the assumption that rising and falling interest rates are market conditions or at least are partially or wholly constitutive of market conditions.

Then, the conclusion of the first part of the argument, (C), becomes a premise for the ultimate claim of the passage:

P-1:   Market conditions have always tended to be cyclical in some appreciable manner.

C: The rates will go back up eventually.

Again, this argument is Inductive for any number of reasons. For instance, the premise is about the past; the conclusion is about the future. The premise is about market conditions; the conclusion is about "the rates."

Finally, there is a third part of the argument which utilizes the conclusion of the second part as its premise:

P-1:   The rates will go back up eventually.

C: There is no need to worry.

This final part of the Argument is also Inductive. The premise concerns "the rates" while the conclusion concerns the "need to worry."

9. *   P-1:   They don't card anyone.
        P-2:   They've got the best juke box around.
        P-3:   They've got the cheapest beer prices.

        C: Mack's is the best bar around.

This rather terse Argument is definitely Inductive. The "fact" that a bar does not "card" anyone or has the best juke box around or the cheapest beer prices does not necessarily mean that it is the best bar around, unless one is underage or likes being with underage drinkers or likes the particular music in the juke box or prefers drinking cheaper beers or a host of other concerns.

10.   This argument occurs in two parts:
        P-1:   Coal seams have been discovered in Antarctica.

        C: The climate there was once warmer than it is now.

Indicator Words: "This means that ....." shows that a conclusion is about to follow.

This part of the Argument is Inductive. The fact that coal seams have been found does not necessarily mean that the climate was once warmer unless it is also true that coal seams are only found in climates which are appreciably warmer than that of Antarctica at the present time.

The second part of the Argument takes off from the conclusion of the first part:

P-1:   The climate there was once warmer than it is now.

_____

C: Either the geographical location of the continent has shifted or the whole earth was once warmer than it is now.

Indicator Word: "Thus" precedes the conclusion.

Also, the "Either-Or" here indicates a complex statement which is the conclusion of the Argument. If you said that there are TWO conclusions to the Argument, taking the simple statements (1) the continent shifted geographical location, and (2) the whole earth was once warmer than now, this is a permissible reading PROVIDED THAT you indicated the relationship between them was that one of the two statements has to be true (perhaps even both of them) but NOT NECESSARILY either one by themselves.

Whether this is an Inductive or Deductive Argument is a more difficult question. Our leaning is to say that it is an Inductive Argument which is missing a link between the premise (the climate in Antarctica was once warmer than now) and the conclusion (either Antarctica was in a different geographical location then or the whole earth was once warmer). If these were the *only* two possibilities, then the argument would indeed be Deductive. But, barring this assumption, there seem to be other Logical Possibilities (however farfetched) such as (a) maybe the geographical location was the same but the rotational axis of the earth changed from an east-west to a north-south one? or (b) there were at one time tremendously active volcanoes in Antarctica which caused or aided the formation of coal seams, or (c) a giant meteor made of coal crashed into the region and left such a deposit, and so forth. Therefore, it is possible that the premise is quite true, but the conclusion could turn out to be false anyway.

TEST BANK

Multiple Choice Questions

1. In logic, an argument
    A. must have at least one premise.
    B. must have more than one premise.
    C. must have a conclusion.
    D. both A and C above

E. both B and C above

ANSWER: D

2. In logic, arguments are
    A. the opposite of explanations.
    B. controversial--at least to some extent.
    C. relational--having two parts: a premise set and a conclusion.
    D. all of the above.
    E. none of the above

    ANSWER: C

3. In logic, sentences that come in the form, "If A, then B," or "Whenever A is true, then B is true," are called
    A. complex arguments.
    B. simple arguments.
    C. conditional statements.
    D. Misuse of Hypothesis Fallacies.
    E. counterfactuals.

    ANSWER: C

4. Which of the following words would *probably* not be a conclusion indicator?
    A. Thus
    B. However
    C. Hence
    D. Therefore
    E. Consequently

    ANSWER: B

5. Which of the following words would *probably* not be a premise indicator?
    A. Sense
    B. Because
    C. For
    D. As is shown by
    E. Due to

    ANSWER: A

6. Two people disagreeing about whether the television program they were watching is a re-run

or not are *probably* engaged in which kind of disagreement?
A. Factual
B. Interpretive
C. Verbal
D. Practical
E. Aesthetic

ANSWER: A

7. Two people disagreeing about what they should do in a particularly problematic situation are *probably* having which kind of disagreement?
A. Factual
B. Interpretive
C. Verbal
D. Evaluative
E. Stupid

ANSWER: D

8. Which of the following statements is true of inductive and/or deductive reasoning?
A. Inductive arguments always proceed from specific statements to a generalization.
B. Inductive arguments are based on opinions while deductive arguments are based on facts.
C. The premises of inductive arguments may support, but they never guarantee the truth of their conclusions.
D. Inductive arguments are ones in which it should be a contradiction to say that the premises are true but the conclusion is false because the conclusion is already contained in the premises.
E. Inductive arguments proceed from premise set to the conclusion, while deductive arguments begin at the conclusion and proceed to the premises.

ANSWER: C

9. Which of the following is/are true of the differences between an interpretive disagreement and a verbal one?
    I   An interpretive disagreement is straightforward and concerns the meaning or significance of something while a verbal one involves a misunderstanding that results in the parties talking past one another.
    II   An interpretive disagreement is a dispute about the meaning or significance of a thing or event while a verbal disagreement concerns the meaning of a verb.
    III An interpretive disagreement is basically a straightforward dispute about the interpretation of something while a verbal disagreement is a straightforward dispute about some linguistic construction.

    A. I only

    B. II only

    C. III only

    D. I and II only

    E. I and III only

ANSWER: A

10. What is the difference between an argument and an explanation in logic?

    A. Arguments concern opinions while explanations are about facts.

    B. Explanations are usually one kind of argument, the difference being that in explanations the conclusion is at least as well known as the premises.

    C. Explanations function more like excuses, while arguments are more like disagreements.

    D. An argument is hypothetical; an explanation is unconditional.

    E. Both A and D above.

ANSWER: B

11. Two nations having a dispute about where the border between them should be drawn are *probably* engaged in which type of disagreement?

    A. Factual

    B. Interpretive

    C. Verbal

    D. Evaluative

    E. Unresolvable

ANSWER: D

12. Arguments

    A. are always composed of statements.

    B. are always hypothetical or conditional in nature.

    C. are generally controversial.

    D. always have indicator words.

    E. always occur between two or more persons or groups.

ANSWER: A

13. In logic, a claim or statement is

    A. the same thing as a sentence: any claim or statement is expressible as a sentence and any sentence is a claim or statement.

    B. a simple declarative utterance capable of standing as a sentence; all statements are sentences but not all sentences are statements.

C. a simple or complex declarative utterance capable of expression as a sentence; all statements are sentences but not all sentences are statements.

D. expressible as a sentence, just as all sentences are expressible as claims or statements.

E. Both A and D above.

ANSWER: C

14. "Bill Clinton won the 1992 election because people were tired of 'government as usual' and wanted to see some kind of significant change." This sentence is best interpreted as

A. a hypothetical or conditional statement.

B. an argument.

C. an explanation.

D. a statement, but not an argument.

E. It could be either B or C above.

ANSWER: E

15. "Do me a favor and bring my notebook with you." This sentence is best interpreted as

A. an argument but not an explanation.

B. a simple statement but not an argument.

C. an argument but not a statement.

D. a complex statement but not an explanation.

E. a non-argumentative use of language.

ANSWER: E

16. Which of the following could be a claim or statement for the purposes of logic?

A. Wow! Fantastic!

B. Could you tell me what time it is?

C. Just skip this question altogether.

D. Just once I would like to win the lottery.

E. When will you start keeping up with your assignments?

ANSWER: D

17. In logic, the minimum number of premises an argument can have is

A. zero.

B. one.

C. two.

D. three.

E. It doesn't matter as long as it has a conclusion.

ANSWER: B

Questions 18 through 20 pertain to the following scenario:
Suppose someone were to reason that "Everytime I take Marta to school I am always 10 to 15 minutes late for class. Therefore, I am going to have to start driving to school or catching a ride with a friend."

18. This passage is best characterized as
    A. a statement.
    B. an argument.
    C. an explanation.
    D. a hypothesis or conditional.
    E. a lame excuse.

    ANSWER: B

19. There is an "indicator" word in this passage:
    A. Everytime
    B. Always
    C. Therefore
    D. Or
    E. With

    ANSWER: C

20. If there is reasoning in this passage, it is best characterized as
    A. Deductive.
    B. Inductive.
    C. Reductive.
    D. Non-argumentative.
    E. Explanatory.

    ANSWER: B

Questions 21 through 25 pertain to the five passages below, lettered from A to E:
A. Your water boiled over onto the stove because you left the heat on too high for too long.
B. Your water will boil over onto the stove if you leave the heat on too high for too long.
C. Your water will boil over onto the stove because you are leaving the heat on too high for too long.
D. You left your water on the stove for too long. The temperature was way too high. Then, it boiled over onto the stove.
E. Whenever you leave water on the stove for too long with the temperature too high, it will boil

over onto the stove. You left your water on the stove for too long with the temperature too high. It is bound to be boiling over onto the stove right now.

21. Which one of the passages above best characterizes an inductive argument that is not an explanation?

    ANSWER: C

22. Which one of the passages above best exemplifies a hypothetical or conditional statement which is not an argument or an explanation?

    ANSWER: B

23. Which one of the passages above best exemplifies a deductive argument?

    ANSWER: E

24. Which one of the passages above best exemplifies an explanation which is also an argument?

    ANSWER: A

25. Which one of the passages above best exemplifies a description which is not an argument, nor an explanation, nor a hypothetical or conditional statement?

    ANSWER: D

Short Answer Questions

In the following passages, identify arguments by (i) circling the conclusion, (ii) underlining the premises, (iii) putting a box around any indicator words, (iv) "X"ing out any extraneous or irrelevant information, (v) indicating the presence of an explanation by the letters "EXP." If the passage is not an argument, write, "NOT AN ARGUMENT."

26. Juan and Jomo went to the park where they spent over an hour. Then, they walked for a mile or so. Finally, they went to the movies.

    ANSWER:
        (Not an argument, but a description.)

27. Paulette and Maya went to the movies also, since they were intent on seeing Juan and Jomo there.

ANSWER:

(Paulette and Maya went to the movies also,) | since | <u>they were intent on seeing Juan and</u>

<u>Jomo there.</u>

    (Definitely an argument, possibly an explanation, particularly if the person making this argument actually saw them at the movies.)

28. If the players thought that the owners would give in to their demands, they were about to find out they had miscalculated badly.

    ANSWER:

    (Not an argument, but a complex statement which is phrased as a conditional statement.)

29. To Whom It May Concern:
I recommend Ms. Moffitt most highly for the graduate teaching assistantship you have open in nasal archeology. She is incredibly bright. Other professors have commented to me about her intelligence. She is extremely well-motivated and has superb teaching skills. Moreover, she has outstanding laboratory techniques. I have observed them firsthand.

    ANSWER:
~~To Whom It May Concern:~~

(I recommend Ms. Moffitt most highly for the graduate teaching assistantship you have open in nasal archeology.)

<u>She is incredibly bright.</u> <u>Other professors have commented to me about her intelligence.</u> <u>She is extremely well-motivated and has superb teaching skills.</u> <u>Moreover, she has outstanding laboratory techniques.</u> <u>I have observed them firsthand.</u>
    (An argument supporting Ms. Moffitt's candidacy for a GTA based upon four main premises--two of which are further supported.)

30. To The Editor:
I say parimutuel betting should be legalized in this state. The tax revenues it will generate will help fund better educational facilities. And, we all know this is a high priority of the governor. But even if it weren't, it is still a good idea to improve our educational system, for it is one of the weakest in the nation. Not only that, but betting will give a lot of people a chance to improve their financial condition in life. And to those who scream about morality, betting on the dogs and ponies is no more sinful than playing bingo at the local church on Wednesdays which a lot of people are already doing.

ANSWER:

~~To The Editor:~~

(~~I s~~X~~y~~ parimutuel betting should be legalized in this state.) <u>The tax revenues it will generate will help fund better educational facilities. And, we all know this is a high priority of the governor.</u>

~~But even if it weren't,~~ (it is still a good idea to improve our educational system,) [for] <u>it is one of the weakest in the nation.</u> ~~Not only that,~~ ~~but~~ <u>betting will give a lot of people a chance to improve their financial condition in life.</u> A~~X~~d <u>to those who scream about morality, betting on the dogs and ponies is no more sinful than playing bingo at the local church on Wednesdays which a lot of people are already doing.</u>

(An argument in favor of legalizing parimutuel betting based upon three main premises)

In the following passages, identify arguments (i) by circling the conclusion, (ii) by underlining the premises, (iii) by putting a box around any indicator words, (iv) by lining through or striking out any extraneous or irrelevant information or language, and (v) by indicating whether the reasoning is inductive or deductive. Be sure to explain why you think so.

31. Any time the fishing conditions are just right, I always drop what I'm doing and go; and the fishing conditions are just right now. So, I'm headed out of here right now and going fishing.

    ANSWER:
    <u>Any time the fishing conditions are just right, I always drop what I'm doing and go; and the fishing conditions are just right now.</u>

    [So,] (I'm headed out of here right now and going fishing.)

    (A deductive argument if the first premise is read as a blanket claim covering past, present, and future. A student may want to read it as a claim only about the past; i.e., up until now, wherever the fishing conditions were right, I'd always go fishing. In that case, the argument could be seen as inductive insofar as the conclusion would concern the present, and the premises concern only the past, and hence the conclusion would go beyond the premise.)

32. Global politics have always been tied to economics in some appreciable manner. Therefore, the political unrest in Algeria must be due to unseen economic factors at play.

    ANSWER:
    <u>Global politics have always been tied to economics in some appreciable manner.</u>

35

Therefore,

the political unrest in Algeria must be due to unseen economic factors at play.

(This is a borderline example which seems to be slightly more inductive than deductive for at least two reasons. First, the premise is clearly about the past, while the conclusion is about what is happening now. The conclusion goes beyond anything contained in the premises. Second, the alleged "fact" of a link between global politics and economics does not necessarily mean that the link is either causal, as implied in the conclusion, or uni-directional.)

33. If business were the socially responsible institution it claims to be, then environmental pollution would not have become steadily worse over the past three decades. But, in point of fact, environmental pollution has worsened since the second World War. Obviously, business is not the socially responsible institution it claims to be. Either business is the socially responsible institution it claims to be or it must be regulated by government. You can see then, that business must be regulated by government.

ANSWER:

If business were the socially responsible institution it claims to be, then environmental pollution would not have become steadily worse over the past three decades. BXt, iX poXnt Xf fXct, environmental pollution has worsened since the second World War.

Obviously,

business is not the socially responsible institution it claims to be.

Either business is the

socially responsible institution it claims to be or it must be regulated by government.

You can see then, | thXt

business must be regulated by government.

(There are actually two deductive arguments at play in this example, the conclusion of the first argument then becoming a premise in the second argument.)

34. We are not going to have an outside speaker tomorrow, because we had one today and we have never had an outside speaker two days in a row.

ANSWER:

We are not going to have an outside speaker tomorrow, | because | we had one today and we have never had an outside speaker two days in a row.

(Again, this example is inductive because the second premise only concerns what has happened in the past. If it had been a policy, say for example in a syllabus that there will never be an outside speaker two days in a row, then perhaps this would be a deductive argument.)

35. Dad is not at work and he is not at any of his usual hangouts. Therefore, he must be at home.

ANSWER:

<u>Dad is not at work and he is not at any of his usual hangouts.</u> | Therefore, |

(he must be at home.)

(Definitely an inductive argument. Dad might have been delayed in traffic, caught in a malfunctioning elevator, involved in an accident, or any number of other possibilities, such that the premises may all be true, but the conclusion could very likely turn out to be false.)

Short Essay Questions

36. Explain the difference between a factual disagreement and an interpretive one.

37. What is the purpose of the "so-because" test and how does it work?

38. What makes a conditional statement different from an argument?

39. Explain the difference between an interpretive disagreement and a verbal disagreement.

40. Explain the differences between inductive and deductive reasoning. Why would it be important to draw such a distinction?

More Difficult Essay Questions

41. Construct an argument of your own on the topic of smoker's rights.

42. It has often been claimed that deductive reasoning is the fundamental form of human reasoning and that inductive reasoning is a subsidiary and derivative cousin of its pure form. Construct an argument at least one and a half pages in length but not more than two pages in favor of such a position. Then, construct an argument of similar length that inductive reasoning is in fact the primary form of argumentation and that deductive reasoning is merely a derivative and ancillary form of inductive thinking. Finally, in an essay of not more than two pages, state what you really think to be the case concerning these two kinds of reasoning.

Chapter 3

Logical Assumptions, Implications, and Argument Diagrams

CHAPTER OUTLINE

Spotting Hidden Assumptions and Implications
Exercises
Diagramming Arguments
Summary
Exercises
Case Study

KEY TERMS

Compound Argument - Reasoning in which two or more premises combine to imply a conclusion they would not necessarily imply independently.

Convergent Argument - Reasoning where two or more independent claims or premises imply the same conclusion.

Divergent Argument - Reasoning in which the same statement generates two or more independent conclusions.

Explicit Assumption - A claim actually stated and functioning as a premise in an argument, but which is not itself supported by another premise (i.e., an unsupported claim).

Implication - A claim that follows from another claim such that, if the original claim is true, then the implication must also be true. (Also called an *unstated conclusion.*)

Implicit Assumption - An unstated claim functioning as the premise of an argument. (Also called an *unstated premise* or logical presupposition.)

Linear Argument - Reasoning in which the premises and conclusions can be arranged such that each claim implies the next.

Principle of Fairness - The working idea that one should be as unbiased as possible in assigning unstated premises and conclusions to arguments.

Unstated Conclusion - A conclusion not explicitly stated by which follows as from the given content and structure of the argument. (Also called a *logical implication.*)

Unstated Premise - A missing link in an inductive argument connecting the content of the premises with the content of the conclusion so as to turn the argument into a deductive one. (Also known as implicit or hidden assumptions or logical presuppositions.)

Unsupported Claim - A statement functioning as a stated premise in an argument, but which does not itself have another statement to support it.

OVERVIEW

Two main functions of Chapter Three are to fill in and deepen the understanding of arguments by learning how (1) to spot what is missing as well as what is actually stated, and (2) to give definiteness to the structure of entire arguments through preliminary diagramming techniques. There are two sub-parts to the first function: one is learning to detect unstated premises which may be called "logical assumptions," "presuppositions," or "hidden assumptions"; the other is learning to figure out unstated conclusions, sometimes called "logical implications."

Each of these functions corresponds to step three of the critical technique, in which we are asked to complete the structural analysis of an argument. It is important at this juncture to stress what we call the principle of fairness, a general rule of thumb requiring us to be as unbiased and even-handed in assigning unstated premises and conclusions to the arguments of others as we would have them do for ours. Put negatively, we are admonished not to impute assumptions and implications simply for the purpose of making it easier to refute the conclusions of others or to misrepresent their arguments.

When we speak of *logical* assumptions and *logical* implications we do not mean a psychological analysis of the reasoner, her motives, or the hidden agenda she brings to the situation. Rather, we are talking about something fairly straightforward: what is it that is included in the conclusion that is not included in the premises? And, secondly, what information is there in the premises which does not occur in the conclusion but which is relevant to it? When we connect the answer to these two questions, we can ascertain the maximum information necessary for the truth of the premises to guarantee the truth of the conclusion. For example, if someone were to argue that Becky is an excellent editor, therefore she would never have missed such a glaring mistake, the reasoning in question is inductive. The premise is about the quality of Becky's editorial capabilities. The conclusion is about something she would or would not have done. The missing premise that functions as the logical assumption of this argument is that excellent editors would never have missed such a glaring mistake. There are many, many ways this could have been phrased: No excellent editor would ever have missed such a glaring mistake; or, if one is an excellent editor, then one would never miss such a glaring mistake; etc. Spotting missing implications is slightly harder, because we have no such easy barometer to let us know when one is missing. Special techniques for determining logical implications will have to await discussions in Chapters Six through Eleven and Thirteen.

In the latter half of Chapter Three, we turn to the larger picture of completing the structure of entire lines of reasoning. One type of argument we consider is the *linear* argument in which each premise implies a conclusion which becomes the premise for the succeeding conclusion and so forth. Then, we take a look at *convergent* arguments in which different premises offer independent support for the same conclusion. *Divergent* argument forms occur when the same claim or piece of evidence offers support for two different conclusions which are independent from each other. *Compound* argument forms are those in which the premises depend upon each other to mutually imply the conclusion. Moreover, it is helpful to be able to assign relatively more weight to premises which are more important, crucial, relevant to the conclusion and less weight to those which are only tangential to the conclusion or of lesser importance to it. It is at this point in the discussion of arguments and their analysis that we find it helpful to spend a fair amount of in-class time going over longer arguments with the students. Although this might seem a little tedious, you may lighten it up with a little humor and a lot of input from the students who are going to have to be your chief yardstick for how well this material has been assimilated.

SOLUTIONS TO EXERCISE QUESTIONS

Answers to Exercises on Pages 47 through 50

Level A

1. *   In logic and in critical thinking, an ASSUMPTION is an unstated premise. Sometimes we use the word "PRESUPPOSITION" to express the same idea of a part of the evidence which is missing but which, when combined with the rest of the stated reasons, would turn the argument into a Deductive one.

2. *   An IMPLICIT ASSUMPTION is the missing premise which would make the argument an ironclad Deductive one. Once that premise has been formulated, explicitly stated, and becomes a part of the newly restated argument, it is an EXPLICIT ASSUMPTION.

3. *   A HIDDEN ASSUMPTION is the same thing as an IMPLICIT ASSUMPTION or PRESUPPOSITION. An UNSTATED CONCLUSION is a conclusion which is not actually stated but which is implied by the stated parts of the argument. As such it may also be called the IMPLICATION of an argument insofar as it logically follows from the evidence which is given.

4. *   An IMPLICATION may be an UNSTATED CONCLUSION or it may actually be stated but in either case it is the CONCLUSION of a line of reasoning, while a HIDDEN ASSUMPTION is always a PREMISE in that part of the reasoning.

5. *   The PRINCIPLE OF FAIRNESS is the working idea that we remain as unbiased as possible in making explicit the assumptions and implications of any line of reasoning.

6. *   True, initially. Of course, once they are recognized and formulated, then they become EXPLICIT ASSUMPTIONS and actually stated parts of the argument.

7. *   True. The EXPLICIT ASSUMPTION is the IMPLICIT ASSUMPTION once it is actually stated.

8. *   True. UNSTATED PREMISES may be recognized by noting that there are parts of the conclusion which are not stated in the premises and then connecting the parts of the premises not in the conclusion with the parts of the conclusion not in the premises, whereas there is no easy rule of thumb for spotting unstated conclusions.

9. *   False. Most Deductive arguments have premises which are sufficient to guarantee the truth of their conclusions. To be sure, in every argument there are premises which must themselves be unsupported (otherwise we have an infinite regress) and, hence, we have an unsupported claim in every argument. But, an unsupported claim is not necessarily an unstated premise.

10. * True. This is an important part of the Principle of Fairness—to treat any argument with the same respect as if we were making the claim ourselves.

Level B

1. *   P-1:   You were asked to serve on the jury.

     _____

     C: You are ("Must be") a registered voter.
     Inductive argument missing the assumption which could be stated in an indefinite number of ways:

     A. Only registered voters are asked to serve on juries.
          If you were asked to serve on a jury, then you must be a registered voter.
          All persons asked to serve on juries must be registered voters.
          People cannot be asked to serve on juries unless they are registered voters.
     (Note that we are now leaving out the indicator words and any extraneous material.)

2.   P-1:   You would have seen the Empire State Building.
       A-1:   All people who have been to Manhattan have seen the Empire State Building.
       A-2:   (From P-1 - You are telling me) You did not see the Empire State Building.

     _____

       C: You have never been to Manhattan.

Again, the assumption (A-1) may be stated in any number of logically equivalent ways; e.g., "If you haven't seen the Empire State Building, then you haven't been to Manhattan." But, notice from this example that the assumption or unstated premise does NOT NECESSARILY HAVE

TO BE TRUE. What we are looking for in each case is the missing link which IF IT WERE TRUE would help to guarantee the truth of our conclusion.

3. *   P-1:   Every time you wreck the car you get a stupid look on your face.

      C: You wrecked the car.

Note that even if we add the assumption that "You have that stupid look on your face right now," it would not guarantee the conclusion because there could still be other times you get that stupid look on your face. So, there are really *two* assumptions needed in this instance:

     A-1:   Only when you wreck the car do you get that stupid look on your face.
     A-2:   You have that stupid look on your face right now.

4.   P-1:   The hit-and-run victim's lungs are too clean.
     A-1:   People from around here do not have lungs that clean.

      C: The hit-and-run victim is not from around here.

5. *   P-1:   You have been walking to school for the past week.
     A-1:   If your parents would let you drive the car any more, then you would not be walking to school

      C: Your parents won't let you drive the car any more.

6.   P-1:   You have a big test tomorrow.
     A-1:   Whenever you have a big test the next day, then you really should take it easy the night before.

      C: You really should take it easy tonight.

7. *   P-1:   Anyone who makes more than $400 in interest income has to report it on their tax return.
     P-2:   You made about three times that much (more than $400 in interest).

  (Imp. C):   You have to report your interest income on your tax return.

8.   P-1:   A karaoke bar is a great place for a person to make a spectacle of herself.
     A-1:   Cathy would really enjoy going any place she could make a spectacle of herself.

      C: Cathy would really enjoy going to a karaoke bar.

9. *   P-1:   John was the only person in the car.
     A-1:   Any time you are the only person in the car you must be behind the wheel!

C: John must have been behind the wheel.

10.   Here you just have two statements:
         S-1:   Bob just graduated with honors.
         S-2:   You have a better GPA than Bob does.

One cannot conclude that therefore you graduated with honors too or that you graduated with "better" honors than Bob did, because this may be your first semester in school, you may be at a different university than Bob, or any other number of possibilities.

Level C

1. *   Answer (B). (C) is not a bad answer, but in the passage by the use of the term "best" the author assumes that there are at least three forms of adjustment and we have to link three or more with "many."

2.   The correct answer is (D). Even if (A), (B), and (C) are true, they do not guarantee the conclusion because in each of these cases it is possible for someone other than a soccer player to wear a soccer jersey. Answer (E) is totally irrelevant to this particular argument.

3. *   The correct answer here is (B). We are looking for what conclusion HAS TO FOLLOW from the fact that 45% of all Americans are displeased with the shape of their nose. It does not have to mean that (I) many Americans wish they could have their noses fixed. They may be more afraid of the surgery or unable to afford the cost or a host of other concerns. It does mean that (II) many (at least 45%) of the Americans are dissatisfied with their facial characteristics because we are going to assume that, in virtually all of these cases, the noses are part of the facial characteristics. Note that it does not necessarily mean that (III) most (i.e., over 50%) of American adults are displeased with one of their physical attributes. To be sure, you would think that if 45% didn't like their noses, that surely another 6% would be dissatisfied about something else, BUT NOT NECESSARILY from the data given. Both (I) and (III) go beyond what is contained in the originally given statement. Only (II) does not.

4.   As in the previous example we are looking for the missing conclusion or implication(s) of a line of reasoning. There are several ways to approach such a problem. Here is one: taking the word "ONLY" which appears in every one of the given statements as equivalent in meaning to "THEN" in a conditional statement we can rephrase the given argument as below—

         If LD (legally drive), then VL (you have a valid license)
         If VL (valid license), then PDT (passed the driving test)

         ――

         If LD (legally drive), then PDT (passed the driving test)

Now let us look to see what is NECESSARILY ENTAILED by this piece of reasoning (regardless of whether it is true or not). (I) If a person does not have a valid license (not VL), then he cannot legally drive (not LD). Actually, this is logically the same statement as the first premise in the argument, so yes (I) has to be true too if P-1 is true. (II) If a person does not have a valid license, then she has not passed the driving test is NOT NECESSARILY entailed by P-2. She may not have a valid license even though she passed the driving test because, for example, it may have been revoked due to her amassing too many points from tickets or for some other reason. So, (II) is not necessarily true. Finally, (III) anyone who has not passed the driving test cannot legally drive is logically the same statement as the conclusion of the given argument (only those who pass the driving test can legally drive). So, the correct answer is (C) both I and III must be true, but not necessarily II.

5. * Again we are looking for the logical implications which follow from a given statement or set of statements. In this case, if there are no fewer than three but no more than five people in this class who understand the nature of this problem, then there MUST BE either three or four or five people who understand it. (We are assuming that a half a person does not count; in other words that the whole person either understands it or does not.) Statement I—that four people in the class understand the problem—may be true, but it doesn't HAVE TO BE, since there could be three or five people in the class who understand it. So, even if the answer had been phrased "At least four people in class ....." it would not necessarily have been true. Statement II is that there are more than two people in this class who understand the problem and since three, four, and five are all "more than two," this answer MUST BE true. Statement III is that there are more than three people in the class who understand the problem. Well, if there are four or five people who do, then this answer is correct. But, if there are only three people who understand it, then the answer is incorrect for three is not "more than three." So, the correct answer is (B) Statement II only.

6. Now we are back to looking for the missing premise or premises which would help to guarantee the truth of the conclusion which in this instance is that "the greatest chance for the existence of extra-terrestrial life is on a planet beyond our solar system." The premise for this claim is that the Milky Way Galaxy alone contains a hundred billion other suns, possibly accompanied by planets similar enough to Earth to make them capable of supporting life. What is missing here is an assumption that in order for life to occur on another planet, that planet would have to have conditions similar to those found on Earth (otherwise, why not begin by looking within our own solar system). Answer (A) is actually too strong, for we are only talking about extra-terrestrial life, not necessarily what they would HAVE TO LOOK LIKE. Answer (B) looks better than answer (A) except that it is also too strong insofar as it makes the claim that such life CANNOT exist on other planets within our solar system. Answer (C) is also too strong a claim since it is saying that appropriate physical conditions are not only a necessary condition, but a

sufficient condition for life to exist. In other words, if this were true, every time we found a planet with conditions similar to Earth, it too would have to contain life forms. Answer (D) is not an assumption of the argument because it is actually stated in a weaker form right in the premise itself. Answer (E) and only Answer (E) makes explicit what is missing from the line of reasoning and so is the correct answer.

7. *   Note that in this example, the premises concern the preferences of English tea drinkers and the price of Earl Blue Tea relative to Lippy's Tea. The conclusion is that Americans should purchase Earl Blue too and that they will save (money?). As such, one obvious missing link between premises and conclusion is that American preferences are (or should be) the same as those of their English counterparts. Answer (B) then is the best answer. Answer (A), that a cheaper brand of tea must be better, is not warranted by this argument. That is too strong. However, if the assumption were that a cheaper brand of tea is not significantly worse than a more expensive brand, it might have been a better answer. Answer (C), that Lippy's is a poor quality tea is clearly unwarranted also. Indeed, it may even be a superb brand of tea and that would not damage this argument a bit. Answer (D), that teas are all alike in quality, so people should buy the cheapest brand of tea, is an interesting argument, but it is not relevant to THIS particular line of reasoning. Neither premises nor conclusion address the QUALITY of either brand of tea. Answer (E) is that Earl Blue is the best and cheapest brand of tea available. This is not even suggested in the premises or the conclusion. In fact the only part of this statement related to the argument is that Earl Blue is cheaper than Lippy's and THAT is actually stated, not implied or assumed. So, (B) is the only correct answer here.

8.   Again we are given an argument with one premise (regarding the correlation between cardiovascular fitness and exercise shown by scientific testing) and one conclusion (that it is essential for people to run or swim for at least a half-hour three times a week). We are asked to pick out the missing premise that would guarantee the truth of this conclusion. Answer (A) is that people must achieve cardiovascular fitness to be considered in good health. This is too strong insofar as the premise only mentions a "significant correlation" NOT a one-to-one reality. Moreover, even if it were true, that would not guarantee that the ONLY WAY to achieve cardiovascular fitness would be to run or swim for at least 30 minutes three times a week. In fact, looking for this criterion, which is what it would take to make this argument valid, we can rule out Answer (C) and Answer (D), too, because (C) doesn't limit the forms of exercise to running and swimming or specify the exact amount of time and while (D) does limit the forms to running and swimming, it does not specify the time limit or the frequency. Only Answers (B) and (E) contain all the necessary information to link the premise with the conclusion. The problem with Answer (B) is that the argument never attempts to GUARANTEE THAT, if people do run or swim for 30 minutes three times a week, they will DEFINITELY achieve cardiovascular fitness. What the conclusion is saying is that IF THEY DON'T run or swim 30 minutes three times a week, then they won't achieve C-V fitness. And, this is what Answer (E) and only Answer

(E) states.

Answers to Exercises on Pages 55 and 56

Level A

1. *   A CONVERGENT ARGUMENT is one in which two or more premises each independently support the same conclusion.
2. *   A DIVERGENT ARGUMENT is a line of reasoning in which one premise or piece of evidence supports two or more independent conclusions.
3. *   A COMPOUND ARGUMENT is one in which two or more premises rely upon each other to support a conclusion when none of the premises would adequately do so by themselves. A DIVERGENT ARGUMENT takes off to support two or more independent conclusions from the same premise or premise set.
4. *   A simple CONVERGENT ARGUMENT might be expressed in the following words and diagrammed as below:

    P-1:   You are yawning.
    P-2:   You cannot keep your eyes open.
    _____
    C: You must be sleepy.

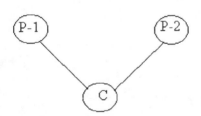

5. *   A simple DIVERGENT
    ARGUMENT might be expressed in words as follows and diagrammed as shown below:

    P-1:   I overslept.
    _____
    C-1:   I am going to be late.
    C-2:   I will not have time to clean up.

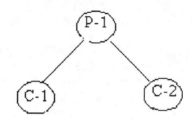

6. *   FALSE. Agreement or disagreement of the disputants has nothing to do with the form of the argument.

7. *   FALSE. Many arguments are linear or compound.

8. *   TRUE. In that way, each conclusion becomes a successive premise for the next conclusion (which then becomes a premise, until the last one).

9. *   PROBABLY FALSE. Probably just as many arguments are convergent or compound as are linear.

10. * TRUE. And we now have a way of representing this by making that line of implication darker than the other lines.

Level B

1. *   Statements: Diagram:
        1 = Ben is a Member of Congress.
        2 = Ben can send all of his official
                mail for free.
    A-1 = Members of Congress can send
                official mail for free.

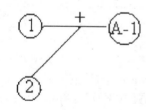

2.   Statements: Diagram:

    1 = Ben is a Member of Congress.

   A-1 = Members of Congress can send
            official mail for free.

    2 = Ben can send all of his official
            mail for free.

   A-2 = If you can send mail for free, then
            you don't have to pay postage.

    3 = Ben doesn't have to pay postage.

   A-3 = If you don't have to pay postage,
            then you don't have to worry
            about licking stamps.

    4 = Ben doesn't have to worry about
            licking stamps.

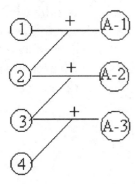

Note that we did not have to make Statement 3 a separate statement in this argument because in this context, although the words are different from the wording in Statement 2, the two statements IN THIS CONTEXT are identical in meaning. In other words, it could be done just as correctly as shown below:

    1 = Ben is a Member of Congress.

    2 = Ben can send all his official mail for free (Ben does not
            have to pay postage for his official mail.)

    3 = Ben does not have to worry about licking stamps.

3. *   Statements: Diagram:

    1 = Betty didn't invite Veronica to
            her party.

    2 = Betty and Veronica had just had a
            fight.

    3 = Betty and Veronica's husbands
            often get into heated arguments
            when they are together.

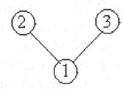

4.   Statements: Diagram:
       1 = Clinton ought to be able to help
              out the economy.
       2 = Clinton wants to bring down the
              cost of health care.
       3 = Clinton intends to try to reduce
              the budget deficit.

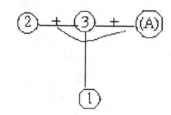

This is an inductive argument in which both of the premises are supposed to reinforce each other in support of the conclusion. The missing assumption, granted it is a weak one, is (A) Wanting to bring down the cost of health care and intending to try to reduce the budget deficit ought to be able to help out the economy.

5. *   Statements: Diagram:
       1 = I was late for the examination.
       2 = Professor Reed gave me an 'F'.
       3 = My grade point average is going
              to go way down.
       4 = If my GPA goes way down, I'll
              lose my scholarship and my
              parents will take away my car.

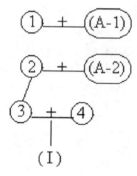

In this case, Statements (1), (2), and (3) form a linear argument with each link being inductive. The link from (1) to (2) relies on the assumption (A-1) Being late for an examination is sufficient for Professor Reed to give someone an 'F'. (In other words, it was the lateness and not the performance on the exam that merited the grade.) The link from (2) to (3) relies on the assumption (A-2) Getting an 'F' grade will make my GPA go way down. The conclusion of this linear argument, Statement (3), when combined with Statement (4) deductively, leads to the final conclusion which is implied but not actually stated, (I) = I will lose my scholarship and my parents will take away my car. Granted there is probably a line of reasoning in that statement itself—it makes a lot more sense to say that Because I will lose my scholarship, therefore my parents will take away my car than to say, Because my parents will take away my car, therefore I will lose my scholarship. But, because it is phrased the way it is, we will take it at face value for the moment. Notice also the Statement (4), for example, is what we call a Complex Statement. It actually is composed of three statements: (i) My GPA is going to go way down, (ii) I'll lose my scholarship, and (iii) My parents will take away my car. Within this complex statement are both a hypothetical or conditional statement {If (i), then [(ii) and (iii)]} and a conjunction {which is the [(ii) and (iii)] part}. We will see how to deal more effectively with Complex Statements as we refine the Technique further.

6.   Statements:

        1 = Cigarettes cause health problems.
        2 = Cigarettes can cost a lot of money.
        3 = You should give up smoking.

Diagram:

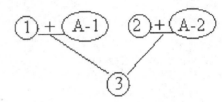

Several points are worthy of note in this example. First, the phrase "because of the health problems" in the third sentence indicates a premise which is not in itself a complete statement. Actually, it merely reiterates and underscores the first statement and so is redundant logically and need not be given a separate number since it says precisely the same thing as Statement (1). The fourth sentence is likewise redundant, reiterating Statement (2). So, there are really only three logically distinct statements in this example. Second, the passage is phrased in such a way that the first statement is meant to be a more important reason than the second. We have indicated this in the diagram by making the line from (1) to (3) darker than the line from (2) to (3). Third, the reasoning is put forth as if the two premises were meant to stand independently from one another and so we have shown the argument as Convergent. That is, even if you had all the money in the world, cigarettes would still cause health problems and this would constitute a reason for stopping. Fourth, the reasoning in both cases is inductive and so there are assumptions associated with each converging fork. (A-1) would be the assumption that if something causes health problems, then you should stop doing it. (A-2) would be the assumption that if something is an expensive habit, then you should break it (or stop doing it).

7. *   Statements:

        1 = The U.S. ought to try to make peace with Iraq.
        2 = Iraq is one of the most powerful nations in the region.
        3 = The U.S. (i.e., "we") should try to be on peaceful terms with all influential nations.
        4 = The U.S. (i.e., "we") have lost enough lives already trying to solve our differences through the use of force.

Diagram:

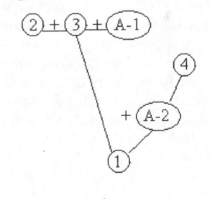

There appear to be two main parts to this line of reasoning. The first contains two premises, Statements (2) and (3) which together form a compound argument that is almost deductive. We need add only none small link between the two premises themselves, (A-1), "Any nation which is one of the most powerful in its region is an influential nation." If (2), (3), and (A-1) were all true, then the conclusion, (1), would have to be true too. The second part of the reasoning is inductive and is missing the unstated premise (A-2), "Whenever a country loses enough lives trying to solve its differences by force, then it ought to seek peace." It is a more difficult question to determine whether the first part of the reasoning is alleged to be of more importance than the second. We have represented both as being of equal importance, although a good case could be made for making the line between (2), (3), (A-1), and (1) darker than that between (4), (A-2), and (1).

8. Statements:
    1 = The U.S. ought never to make peace with Iraq.
    2 = Iraq tortured American prisoners (in the Gulf War).
    3 = Hussein is power-hungry.
    4 = Hussein will try to take over all the oil in the region.
    5 = If Hussein takes over all the oil in the region, then the U.S. will be at his mercy economically.

Diagram:

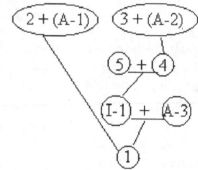

This piece of reasoning is comprised of two main arguments leading to the same conclusion: (1), The U.S. ought never to make peace with Iraq. The first convergent fork uses only Statement (2) as a premise and is inductive. The assumed premise (A-1) is that "If a country tortures your prisoners, then you ought never to make peace with them." The second convergent fork is slightly more complicated. Even though the indicator words may be misleading, this part of the reasoning begins with Statement (3) "Hussein is power-hungry." BECAUSE of (3), not "AND" but "THEREFORE" (4), he will try to take over all the oil in the region. There is an assumption to this one premise—one conclusion inductive argument: (A-2), "Power-hungry people will try to take over all the oil in the region. The next piece of the puzzle is a compound argument. Statements (4) and (5) go together to form premises that might better be expressed: (4) and If (4) is true, then (5) is true. Together they imply an unstated conclusion (I-1), The U.S. will be at his mercy economically. This Implication together with the assumed premise that (A-3) If an action puts us at someone else's mercy economically, then we ought never make peace with them.

9. * Statements:

Diagram:

1 = If Senator Gramm runs as the Republican nominee for President in '96, that will mean the conservative wing of the party has taken control.

2 = If the conservative wing of the party takes control, then abortion will be a big issue.

3 = If the conservative wing of the party takes control, then gun-control will be a big issue.

4 = If abortion becomes the big issue, the Republicans will lose.

5 = If gun-control becomes the big issue, then the Republicans have a chance.

6 = If either (4) or (5), then it doesn't look very good for the Republicans in '96.

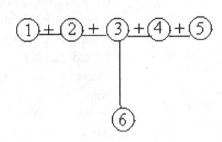

This example actually shows why we need a more sophisticated method for displaying the structure of complex arguments and complex statements as well. Given the method we have so far, Argument (9) is a compound argument with Statements (1) through (5) together providing deductive support for the conclusion which is Statement (6). The problem is that we do not yet have a way to show that this is an Invalid or Bad way of reasoning. There really are no links left out. The reasoning simply looks like a kind of chain of hypothetical or conditional statements:

(1) If A, then B
(2) If B, then C
(3) If B, then D
(4) If C, then E
(5) If D, then F

_____

(So) (6) If (E or F), then not F

10.   Statements: Diagram:

    1 = If the economy is bad in 1996 and
           Clinton's popularity starts
           slipping, the Republicans will
           recapture the White House.

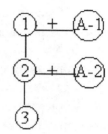

    2 = Five of the last seven Presidential
           elections were won by
           Republicans.

    3 = If that doesn't tell you which
           party is the most popular, nothing
           will.

Again we need a more in-depth method for showing the structure of complex statements and arguments. As we now have it, this argument is a linear one with Statement (1) being given as a premise for Statement (2). Together with the assumption (A-1) that the Republicans won the elections of 1988, 1984, 1980, 1972, this argument becomes deductive. Statement (2) in turn is offered as evidence for Statement (3). That piece of reasoning is also inductive until one adds the assumption (A-2) that any political party which wins 5 out of 7 Presidential elections is the most popular party.

TEST BANK

Multiple Choice Questions

1. "Sam and Diane did not study at all for this test. Basically, they goofed off all week. Therefore, they will not do well on this test." The author of this passage is logically assuming
    A. Sam and Diane are not very bright.
    B. Sam and Diane are basically goof offs.
    C. people who goof off do not study.
    D. people who don't study for this test won't do well on it.
    E. Sam and Diane might think about dropping the course.

    ANSWER: D

2. Suppose the following quotation represents the sketch of an argument. What is missing? "O.J. Simpson has the best legal defense money can buy. Therefore, he is bound to get out of this mess without going to jail."
    A. A premise is missing, but assumed.
    B. A conclusion is missing, but implied.
    C. Nothing is missing; there are simply two statements.
    D. There is an insinuation that Simpson is really guilty.

E. There is the assumption that Shapiro, Bailey, et al. are the best legal defense money can buy.

ANSWER: A

3. For the purposes of logic or critical thinking, an *assumption* is
   A. an unstated conclusion.
   B. something implied by what is implicitly stated.
   C. an unstated premise.
   D. an unsubstantiated claim which is part of an argument.
   E. an unprovable part of an argument.

ANSWER: C

4. For the purposes of logic or critical thinking, an *implication* is
   A. an unstated premise.
   B. an unstated conclusion.
   C. a part of an argument that a person is thinking but does not want to say.
   D. a way of pointing an accusing finger at someone or something without incurring any liability.
   E. all of the above.

ANSWER: B

5. A logical assumption or presupposition
   A. expresses a link between the contents of the premises and that part of the conclusion that is not contained in the premises.
   B. requires us to psychologically analyze the motives or desires of the person who is making the argument.
   C. must ultimately be true or the conclusion of the argument will have to be false.
   D. is that part of the premises of an argument which is stated but which is not itself supported by any evidence.
   E. is something found only in deductive arguments.

ANSWER: A

6. A major reason why a person would want to figure out what the logical presuppositions or assumptions of an argument are would be
   A. to find out what would be the minimal information necessary for the truth of the premises to guarantee the truth of the conclusion.
   B. to determine what information would link the contents of the premises with the contents of the conclusion.

   C. to help direct further inquiry either by way of clarifying what disagreements are occurring or by way of identifying what additional information is needed.

   D. to facilitate the analysis of an argument by completing the picture of the structure of that argument.

   E. any one of the four answers above.

ANSWER: E

7. Consider the following argument:

"You have made her very angry. Consequently, she is not going to go out with you tomorrow night, and also she is not going to help you study for the chemistry examination."

Which of the following best expresses the structure of the reasoning in this passage?

   A. Divergent Argument

   B. Convergent Argument

   C. Linear Argument

   D. Compound Argument

   E. Argument with Differently Weighted Premises

ANSWER: A

8. "Salita must be a master chef; she is wearing a master chef apron." The conclusion of this argument is validly drawn only if it is true that

   A. master chefs often wear this kind of apron.

   B. every master chef wears this kind of apron when cooking.

   C. master chefs never wear any other kind of garment but a master chef apron.

   D. actually, master chefs are required by law to wear master chef aprons.

   E. only master chefs wear master chef aprons.

ANSWER: E

9. "If Elaine is on the steering committee, then she is on the central committee." This statement can be logically deduced from which of the following statements?

   A. All members of the central committee are on the steering committee.

   B. Elaine is on either the central committee or the steering committee.

   C. Everyone who is on the steering committee is on the central committee too.

   D. Only those members of the steering committee are on the central committee too.

   E. Elaine has got to be on the steering committee, and she might be on the central committee too.

ANSWER: C

10. Assume that the following quotation represents the sketch of an argument. What is missing? "People who understand this question will have no trouble answering it, and you obviously understand this question."
    A. A premise is missing but assumed.
    B. A conclusion is missing but implied.
    C. Nothing is missing; you just have two statements.
    D. There is an insinuation that you don't really understand the question.
    E. The question itself is missing.

    ANSWER: B

11. What is the minimal logical assumption necessary to guarantee the conclusion of the following argument? "Sam shouldn't go skydiving. She has severe lower back problems."
    A. People with severe lower back problems shouldn't go skydiving.
    B. Most people with severe lower back problems shouldn't go skydiving.
    C. Women with severe lower back problems shouldn't go skydiving.
    D. Most women with severe lower back problems shouldn't go skydiving.
    E. Most people shouldn't go skydiving.

    ANSWER: C

12. "Because you have a lot of money in the bank, you have a lot of economic power. Because you have a lot of economic power, you can live a happier life style."
    Which one of the following most closely resembles the reasoning in the passage above?
    A. If you exercise a lot, then you can work more efficiently. If you can work more efficiently, then you will earn more money. Therefore, if you exercise a lot, then you will earn more money.
    B. You can actually live a fuller lifestyle if you gain more power and control over your life. And, you can gain more power and control over your life if you learn to save money. Therefore, if you save money, you can actually live a fuller lifestyle.
    C. You are ultimately going to be a healthier person because you work out daily. You work out daily because you foresaw the benefits of regular exercise.
    D. Since your diet is an extremely healthy one, you will maintain better cardiovascular health. Since you exercise on a very consistent basis, you will maintain better cardiovascular health.
    E. If you have a lot of money in the bank, you will inevitably have more friends hanging out with you. If you have a lot of money in the bank, you will be able to do more things that you want to do.

    ANSWER: C

13. "European and Asian schoolchildren devote some portion of each day's studies to training in mathematics, whereas North American schools have been reluctant to offer this much background in math. On tests, European and Asian schoolchildren score much better on mathematics sections than their North American counterparts. Therefore, we must conclude that North American schoolchildren can improve their mathematics skills up to the levels of their Asian and European counterparts only if they devote some portion of each day's studies to training in mathematics."

Which of the following is a logical assumption basic to this passage?

A. Any child can improve their mathematics skills by increased practice and exposure.

B. All schoolchildren will attain the same level of competence in math by the same degree of practice and exposure.

C. Basic training in mathematics on a daily basis in schools is the only significant way to improve ones mathematical test scores and skills.

D. If a schoolchild is not interested in mathematics and skills, then no amount of exposure and training will help improve their test scores.

E. Superior mathematical skills produce superior intellectual skills, which redounds not only to the student's, but to society's benefit as well.

ANSWER: C

Short Answer Questions

For each of the passages below, state what is missing—a premise or a conclusion. Then state exactly what that missing premise or conclusion is.

14. That watch cannot possibly be a genuine Rolex because the second hand moves in discrete ticks and not continuously.

ANSWER:
Inductive argument missing the assumption that
   "No Rolex watches have second hands that move in discrete ticks and not continuously."
   (or)
   "All Rolex watches have second hands that move continuously and not in discrete ticks."
   (or many other ways; e.g.)
   "If a watch has a second hand that moves in discrete ticks and not continuously, then it cannot be a Rolex."

15. It is probably raining outside right now because the streets are soaking wet.

ANSWER:
Inductive argument missing a premise as a logical assumption:
   "Usually when it is raining outside, then the streets get soaking wet."

16. Anyone who enjoys jazz at all would love Gato Barbieri's *Caliente*. Although Suleman and Jonah don't particularly care for jazz, Jameel really enjoys it a lot.

    ANSWER:
    This is the sketch of an argument with the implied but unstated conclusion: "Therefore, Jameel would love Gato Barbieri's *Caliente*."

17. Truly outstanding architecture either takes a back seat to the environment and is visually unobtrusive or is so functionally organized as to recreate that environment into a better place than it was before. The Vanderbilt mansion definitely does not take a back seat to the environment. In fact, it stands out quite prominently, but it is truly outstanding architecture.

    ANSWER:
    This too is the sketch of an argument with the implied but unstated conclusion: "Therefore, the Vanderbilt mansion is so functionally organized as to recreate its environment into a better place than it was before."

18. There's no way that flying insect is a bee; it stung you twice.

    ANSWER:
    Inductive argument missing the assumption:
      "Bees cannot sting you twice." or "Bees cannot sting more than once." or "If a flying insect stings you twice, then it cannot be a bee." (etc.)

19. Capital punishment should be abolished. It has many more bad effects than good ones.

    ANSWER:
    Inductive argument missing the assumption:
      "If something has many more bad effects than good ones, then it should be abolished."

20. People who really work hard at what they are doing will always succeed in the end. And, you not only appear to be working hard, but are actually doing so.

    ANSWER:
    Sketch of an argument with the unstated but implied conclusion:
      "You will succeed at what you are doing in the end."

Chapter 3

Short Essay Questions

Each of the passages numbered 21 through 28 contains a line of reasoning. Critically analyze that reasoning by at minimum answering the following questions about it:

    (1) What is the main point of the reasoning?

    (2) What premises and conclusions occur in the reasoning?

    (3) Are there any indicator words?

    (4) Are there any explanations?

    (5) Is the reasoning inductive or deductive as actually stated?

    (6) Are there any missing assumptions or implications?

    (7) What unsupported premises or claims are there?

    (8) What is the overall structure of the reasoning? (Diagram it.)

21. "Because I am cognizant of the interrelatedness of all communities and states, I cannot sit idly by in Atlanta and not be concerned about what happens in Birmingham. Injustice anywhere is a threat to justice everywhere. We are caught in a network of mutuality, inescapably tied in a garment of destiny. Whatever affects one directly affects all indirectly. Never again can we afford to live with the narrow, provincial 'outside agitator' idea. Anyone who lives in the United States can never be considered an outsider anywhere within its bounds."
    — paraphrase from Dr. Martin L. King, Jr., "Letter From the Birmingham Jail"

22. "I believe that the determination of accounting principles cannot be confined to either the private or the public sector. Accounting principles are polyglot. They represent the conglomeration of sociology, history, economics, communications, philosophy, law, mathematics, taxation, and accounting converging on itself. It therefore seems reasonable that no single narrow group should set the Generally Accepted Accounting Principles (GAAP).

    For the same reason, the accounting profession should abandon its quest for a single rule for each type of accounting transaction. There is just too much diversity to contend with. Instead, I would unshackle accountants from the bonds of uniformity and leave it to the marketplace of ideas to judge the quality of principles in practice."
    — from A. Briloff, "How Accountants Can Recover Their Balance"

23. "The most general and serious problem is that there are no grounds to assume that everything primates do is necessary, natural, or desirable in humans, for the simple reason that humans are not non-humans. For instance, it is found that male chimpanzees placed alone with infants will not 'mother' them. Jumping from hard data to ideological speculation, researchers conclude from this information that *human* females are necessary for the safe growth of human infants. It would be as reasonable to conclude, following this logic, that it is useless to teach human infants to speak, since it has been tried with chimpanzees and it does not work."
    — from Naomi Weisstein, "Psychology Constructs the Female"

24. "I say pari-mutuel betting should be legalized in this state. The tax revenues it will generate will help fund better educational facilities, and we all know this is a high priority of the Governor. But even if it weren't, it is still a good idea to improve our educational system, for it is one of the weakest in the nation. What is more, betting will give a lot of people a chance to improve their financial condition in life because it gives them a chance to win large sums of money. And anyhow, betting on the dogs and ponies is no more sinful than playing bingo at your local church on Wednesday nights, which a lot of people are already doing."
    — Letter to the Editor, *Atlanta Journal and Constitution*

25. "...Fascism and racialism can go together, but socialism and racialism are incompatible. The reason is easy to see. Fascism is the highest and most ruthless exploitation of man by man; it is made possible by deliberate efforts to divide mankind and set one group of men against another group...

    But the man or woman who hates 'Jews', 'Asians', or 'Europeans', or even 'West Europeans and Americans' is not a socialist. He is trying to divide mankind into groups and is judging men according to the skin colour and shape they were given by God. Or he is dividing men according to national boundaries. In either case, he is denying the equality and brotherhood of man."
    — from Julius Nyerere, *Ujamaa: Essays on Socialism*

26. "Pecuniary logic is a proof that is not a proof but is intended to be for commercial purposes......There is nothing basically novel in pecuniary logic, for most people use it more or less all the time in their everyday life. What business has done is to adopt one of the commoner elements of folk thought and to use it for selling products to people who think this way all the time. This kind of thinking—that accepts proof that is not proof—is an essential intellectual factor in our economy, for, if people were careful thinkers, it would be difficult to sell anything. From this, it follows that in order for our economy to continue in its present form, people must learn to be fuzzy-minded and impulsive, for, if they were clear-headed and deliberate, they would rarely put their hands in their pockets; or if they did, they would leave them there. If we were all gifted logicians, the economy would not survive; and herein lies a terrifying paradox, for *in order to exist economically as we are, we must try by might and main to remain stupid.*
    — Jules Henry, "Cultural Factors in Advertising"

27. "Sir: Your essay includes the following statement: 'Since tests proved that it took at least 2.3 seconds to operate the bolt on Oswald's rifle, Oswald obviously could not have fired three times—hitting Kennedy twice and Connally once—in 5.6 seconds or less.' This argument which has appeared in many publications since the assassination is faulty, and I'm surprised that I haven't seen it refuted before this. Assuming that the bolt of Oswald's rifle can in fact be operated in 2.3 seconds, Oswald could definitely fire three shots in 5.6 seconds or less, for a stop watch would be started when the first shot was fired; the second shot would be fired

when the watch read 2.3 seconds; and the third shot would be fired when the watch read 4.6 seconds. You have apparently overlooked the fact that, in the time it takes to fire three shots, it is only necessary to operate the bolt twice."

— F.T. Wehr, Letter to *Time*, 30 Sept. 1966.

28. "Accepting the decisions in these [earlier] cases...we think it evident that none of the rights announced in those cases bears any resemblance to the claimed constitutional right of homosexuals to engage in acts of sodomy that is asserted in this case. No connection between family, marriage, or procreation on the one hand and homosexual activity on the other has been demonstrated, either by the Court of Appeals or by respondent. Moreover, any claim that these cases nevertheless stand for the proposition than any kind of private sexual conduct between consenting adults is constitutionally insulated from state proscription is insupportable. Indeed, the Court's opinion in *Carey* twice asserted that the privacy right...did not reach so far."

— Bowers vs. Hardwick, 106 Supreme Court 2841 (1986)

More Difficult Essay Questions

29. Explain the difference between a logical assumption or presupposition and a logical implication. What is the function of each from the standpoint of critical thinking or logic?

30. Critical thinkers and logicians seem to be divided on the question of whether inductive arguments always have at least one or more missing premises which are the logical assumptions of that argument. Those who believe that many inductive lines of reasoning do not have missing premises point to scientific predictions based on known laws and facts, or to moral lines of reasoning, particularly those concerning an action to be taken as a result of decision-making and deliberation. Those who believe that it is still *logically* possible to turn any inductive argument into a deductive one point out (a) that the assumption, "If P, then C," would guarantee any inductive argument and (b) that while such assumptions are not necessarily a part of every inductive line of reasoning, they can be added in order to complete the picture of the structure of that reasoning and to show what it would take to make the argument watertight. This has the added advantage of showing where the disagreements may be and what is needed to have full faith in the conclusion. Which side seems to have the better argument and why?

Chapter 4

Clarifying Meaning

CHAPTER OUTLINE

4.1 Ambiguity and Vagueness
Exercises
4.2 Definitions
Summary
Exercises
Case Study

KEY TERMS

Ambiguity - Confusion resulting from the fact that a word or phrase has more than one definite meaning and it is unclear which one is meant in the context.

Connotation - The set of conditions for a term's use.

Definition - What a word means and the conditions governing its usage.

Denotation - The set of objects, events, or conditions to which a term is taken to refer.

Equivocation - The usage of a crucial word or phrase in at least two different senses in the same argument or disagreement.

Grammatical Ambiguity - Confusion resulting from faulty sentence construction open to two or more definite interpretations, and the context does not help clarify which is meant.

Meaning - What a word or phrase signifies, represents, or how it is used in a specific context.

Quantitative Vagueness - Occurs when an expression is used that refers to an indefinite amount or quantity.

Referential Ambiguity - Results from using a

word that can refer to two or more things or places and it is not apparent which is intended.

Referential Vagueness - Lack of clarity resulting from the use of a term in a way not specific enough to indicate the conditions under which it would apply.

Reportive Definition - The actual usage in ordinary language of what a word or phrase means, now or in the past.

Stipulative Definition - Specifies the precise meaning of how a term is going to be used in a particular context.

Term Mention - A referral to the actual word or phrase itself as opposed to using that particular word or phrase.

Term Use - The actual employment of a word or phrase in normal speech, discourse, writing when we are not actually talking about the word itself.

Vagueness by Stress - The fact that the same set of words may be understood differently depending on how the words are stressed or accentuated.

OVERVIEW

Step Four of the Technique is concerned with linguistic meaning. By linguistic meaning, we are talking about that which a word, phrase, or sentence signifies, represents, or portends, and it generally includes the set of conditions governing the use of that word. Clarifying the meaning of words, phrases, and sentences allows us to have a better understanding of the speaker's intended meanings, and it also allows us to make our own ideas clearer to other people. It would be hard to overestimate the importance for clarity of meaning in relation to critical thinking and logical reasoning. The old adage, "Garbage in; garbage out," is particularly apropos. No matter how valid the structure and form of a line of reasoning may be, if the content of that argument is garbled, ambiguous, vague, indefinite, or any of a host of related problems, the outcome is extremely suspect.

In Chapter Four, we focus in on just a few of the problems that may arise when linguistic meaning is not clarified in the context of reasoning. Understanding of the meaning of a term or phrase may help us construct clearer and less diffuse arguments. It may even aid in the spotting of hidden assumptions and unstated conclusions. The meaning of a term can often cause confusion because it is ambiguous, which means that the terms has two or more possible, very definite meanings and the intended meaning is not apparent or obvious. *Equivocation* is one special kind of ambiguity occurring when the term in question is used such that it is conducive to reasoning errors. It does this by relying on one meaning in one use, and a different meaning in another use, so that a link that is supposed to be made is not in fact present. One way of illustrating this quickly for the class is to use the example below and ask them what is wrong with it:

> A weighs more than B
> B weighs more than C
> So,   A must weigh more than C

The form of this argument is perfectly valid. Therefore, we should be able to substitute any values we like for A, B, and C. They could be Al, Bob, and Chuck. Suppose, however, we insert the word "Nothing" for B; the word "Lead" for C; and the word "Feathers" (or "I" or "You") for A. Ask the class what is wrong with this line of reasoning. (Finally, one of them may point out that the word "Nothing" is being used in two different senses or meanings; i.e., equivocally.)

Referential ambiguity is another form of linguistic confusion resulting when the connotation of a term is apparent, but the denotation is not. *Vagueness* results when the application of a term is not apparent or is unclear or indistinct. *Quantitative vagueness* results from the use of unclear or open-ended terms indicating amounts such as *lots* or *a few, many* or *some*, etc., when a more precise quantifier is needed. *Referential vagueness* occurs when it is not clear to what specific objects, events, or places, a term is meant to apply. *Vagueness by stress* results from the intonation or accent given to a particular part of a statement or gesture, thereby altering its meaning. The *Use-Mention* distinction may be a useful one to bring up, insofar as an understanding of it may be helpful in reducing confusion that results when we are critically talking *about* a word or phrase as opposed to using that word or phrase.

One of the most important points in the clarification of meaning is to be able to give good definitions when needed and to be able to assess the definitions that others put before us. *Reportive definitions* indicate the way terms are actually used, whereas *stipulative definitions* tell us how a particular term is going to be used in a specific context (not that it *actually* means this). Each of the two types is evaluated differently. Some of the major points to look for in evaluating reportive definitions are their accuracy and precision, their adequacy and relevance, their clarity, and their fairness. Within these broad categories we distinguished at least seven criteria for evaluating reportive definitions, some of which overlap:

1. Avoid using irrelevant features.
2. Avoid characterizations that are too broad or too narrow.
3. Avoid circular definitions (that repeat the term being defined).
4. Avoid obscure characterizations (that are harder to understand than the word being defined).
5. Avoid language that is vague, ambiguous, metaphorical, or figurative.
6. Avoid descriptively negative characterizations.
7. Avoid persuasive or judgmentally loaded characterizations.

SOLUTIONS TO EXERCISE QUESTIONS

Answers to Exercises on Pages 66 and 67

Level A

Chapter 4

1. *   *Ambiguity* refers to the lack of clarity caused by language usage which is susceptible of multiple meanings and it is not clear from the context which of two or more definite meanings is intended.

2. *   *Equivocation* refers to the use of a crucial word or phrase in two or more distinctly different senses in one and the same context.

3. *   Pronouns which are indefinite: such as "this", "that", "whose", "which", and so forth. Place indicators: such as "here", "there", "the other side". *Referential ambiguity* can occur whenever words or phrases are used to refer to two or more possible things, states, or affairs, and it is not clear from the context which one is intended.

4. *   Actually, a list of common expressions conveying *referential vagueness* would be endless: any time a term or phrase is used in such a way that it is unclear whether a set of conditions applies or not could be a case of referential vagueness. For example, "Wear a BLUE tie," might be an example. "Don't spend TOO MUCH money tonight," could be another.

5. *   Quantitative vagueness occurs when an indefinite numerical expression is used when a more precise one is appropriate. Words like "some", "any", "a few", "a whole bunch", "lots", "scads", "a veritable plethora", "almost none", and so forth are prime candidates for quantitative vagueness indicators. (This does *not* mean that they *always* indicate vagueness.)

6. *   True

7. *   False (It is used, not mentioned.)

8. *   True

9. *   True

10. *   False (Intentionality does not matter.)

Level B

1. *   You say "yes," while I say, "I'll think about it."

2.   Every time you say 'now' it is always then.

3. *   Magic Johnson got his name from his mother.

4.   James wrote the name 'Jim' on his notebook.

5. *   I know what I mean, but you don't know what 'you' means.

6.   Anyone who can write well can write 'well'. (Although it could also be written: Anyone who can write 'well' can write well. Or any combination thereof.)

7. *   Either way: (a) Nick had written his name in the margin on the first page. or (b) Nick had written 'his name' in the margin on the first page. (It depends on whether he wrote, "Nick," or "his name.")

8.   'Stupid' is a stupid word to spell.

9. *   Several ways seem possible:
        (a) The sign said 'The Greatest Show on Earth is playing at the big top.'
        (b) "The sign," said The Greatest Show on Earth, "is playing at the big top."
        (c) The sign 'said The Greatest Show on Earth' is playing at the big top.

(d) The sign said 'The Greatest Show on Earth' is playing at the big top.

10.   'Life' is the name of a magazine.

11. *   "Last Summer" may be vague: right now it could indicate, say, 1994. Said last year; 1993. If that is referentially vague, the phrase "a bunch of" is quantitatively vague. It could mean anything from two to one hundred and seventy-six.

12.   The adjective "large" is both quantitatively and referentially vague.

13. *   By italicizing the word "men," we have created the possibility of Vagueness by Stress.

14.   Ellen's response to Al's question is equivocal. The word "right" could mean "correct" or it could mean that he should turn ninety degrees clockwise.

15. *   No problem here, because the quotation marks serve to show that the word "love" is being mentioned, not used. And, yes, as a word, it has four letters. If anything untoward is being implied about the nature of love, then perhaps there is a problem with connotation.

16.   This is grammatically ambiguous: It is not clear whether Maggie went on to slap Mary after insulting her, or Mary slapped Maggie after Maggie insulted her.

17. *   Again, Vagueness by Stress: This time, we made it look like Cathy normally drinks too much but tonight, for a change, she did not. However, it could be the case that she does not drink at all.

18.   The term "a few" is quantitatively vague and it also serves to obscure the problem of failing the exam in the first place.

19. *   Either the second "hate" uttered by the Reformer should be in quotation marks to show that she is talking about the word itself, or the skeptic has misunderstood the Reformer's intentions due to referential ambiguity (or equivocation, which comes to the same thing here).

20.   The term "best" in this instance may be indicative of referential vagueness. Are we talking about the most expensive wines or the wines from the "best" regions in a particular part of the world or what?

Answers to Exercises on Pages 73 and 74

Level A

1. *   A Reportive Definition is an explanation of how a word or phrase is, or has been, used in ordinary language or in accepted technical jargon.

2. *   A Stipulative Definition is an explanation of how a particular word or phrase is going to be used when that usage (a) differs from the normal meaning of the term, (b) is a completely new and made-up word, or (c) is done hypothetically or conditionally to pursue a line of reasoning.

3. *   Connotation includes all of the conditions pertaining to the use of a word or phrase, particularly the emotional flavorings which tinge the meaning. Denotation is the actual set of objects, events, conditions to which the word or phrase refers.

4. *   Definitions may be formulated:

    (a) By Ostension - actually pointing to or touching an example of the term.

Chapter 4

> (b) By Citing Examples - mentioning particular cases to which the word or phrase applies.
> (c) By Complete Inventory - that is, citing all of the possible instances covered by the use of the term.
> (d) By Synonym - that is, giving another, hopefully more familiar, term that has the same meaning in the situation.
> (e) By Connotation - by setting forth the correct conditions for the proper usage of a word or phrase. This may also incorporate any or all of the other four methods.

5. * "Adequacy of a Definition" refers to scope of the meaning being ascribed to a word or phrase; a good definition should not cover more or less than a term's denotation.

6. * False. More often than not dictionaries report how terms are actually used in everyday ordinary language, whatever that language may be.

7. * False. More than likely it would be a Connotative one.

8. * True

9. * True

10. * False. It is a definition that repeats the term being defined, or gives as the definition a word or phrase that for all practical purposes is identical to it and unhelpful in understanding that term.

Level B

1. * As a Reportive Definition, this one is lacking on at least two counts: first, it fails to state the essential attributes of the word being defined (or put negatively, it states irrelevant features), and, second, it is too broad—true, a human being is a featherless biped, but so is a bear or, for that matter, a plucked chicken.

2. This one is too broad. The definition could also apply to a circle, a square, a pyramid, and an indefinite number of other shapes.

3. * Clearly a Circular Definition, repeating the term being defined.

4. If this were offered as a Reportive Definition, it is purely metaphorical or figurative and not a literal definition.

5. * As a "Complete Inventory" definition, this one is okay. In reality, it might be more helpful to add that we are talking about students who have completed successfully one or more years of their high school or college education.

6. As a Stipulative Definition, this characterization simply informs the listener or reader of the speaker's idea of a "good car." If it were a Reportive Definition, then it (a) would be a Definition by Citing Examples, and (b) might be Vague insofar as no criteria were specified as to what makes a car a "good" one.

7. * An Ostensive Definition.

8. If we added the proviso that this figure occurs in one and the same plane, then we would have a very good Reportive Definition by Connotation that seems to meet all of our criteria.

9. * This is a persuasive definition designed to poison someone's attitude against "liberals."

68

10. When formulated in the U.S. Constitution, this definition was at first Stipulative, specifying the conditions under which a person was to be legally recognized as a citizen of the U.S. Now, that definition is a Reportive one.

11. * Both too narrow and too broad. Too narrow because instructors often teach people other than children. Too broad because other people who are not instructors often guide or teach children (e.g., parents).

12. A persuasive definition (originally attributed to Mark Twain, later to Archie Bunker) designed to poison ones attitude against religious faith.

13. * A totally negative description of what "good" means, by telling us what it does not mean.

14. * Perhaps too broad insofar as there could be other cities with an elevation of 5,280 feet or higher; irrelevant feature, the Broncos—it used to be Denver long before the NFL football franchise was there. You might also say that "mile high city" is metaphorical.

15. * Metaphorical or figurative language (of course it will be irrelevant too, whenever it is metaphorical).

16. Way too narrow. Portraits do not have to be done in oil, nor in painting (there are photographic portraits), nor on canvas, and perhaps it could be argued that they do not have to depict a person.

17. * Straight out of the dictionary and it is both *circular*, repeating the term being defined, and it is a *totally negative description*, telling us what anti-social is not, but not what it is.

18. Again, right out of the dictionary, and it is *obscure*, just as hard to understand as the word being defined.

19. * This is a *stipulative definition*, not assessable in terms of truth or falsity but found in a contract or piece of legislation telling us how a term is going to be understood henceforth.

20. A *circular* definition.

21. * Too broad. Money, cash, silver certificates are also negotiable instruments.

22. *Totally negative description*, when we could do so positively in terms of telling the truth.

23. * A *stipulative definition*, this time by citing an example.

24. A *complete inventory* definition.

25. * A *loaded* definition designed to poison attitudes against the SAT.

TEST BANK

Multiple Choice Questions

1. Which of the following is an example of *ambiguity* (as opposed to vagueness or simple word play)?
   A. The slithy toves did gyre and gimble in the wabe.
   B. My vision for the future is a thousand points of light in a kinder, gentler America.
   C. Chestertown cigarettes have that uptown flavor.
   D. Patrons must remove clothes when dryers turn off.
   E. It's nice to be important, but it's more important to be nice.

ANSWER: D

2. "I am going to use the word 'wrongo' to refer to any argument that has a mistake in the reasoning process in it, plus a false conclusion." What kind of definition is this?
   A. Stipulative Definition
   B. Ostensive Definition
   C. Reportive Definition
   D. Persuasive Definition
   E. Analytical Definition

   ANSWER: A

3. Which of the following is an example of *quantitative vagueness*?
   A. Put it right over there for me, please.
   B. And while you are at it, bring me back some paper for this machine.
   C. And, I need you to call 555-1212 right now for me please.
   D. After you've finished that, you can take a lunch break.
   E. However, I will need you to be back here by 2:00 pm.

   ANSWER: B

4. The remark, "Try to turn in a decent copy of your essay by tomorrow morning," is mainly guilty of
   A. referential ambiguity.
   B. quantitative vagueness.
   C. vagueness by stress.
   D. referential vagueness.
   E. equivocation.

   ANSWER: D

Questions 5 through 14 concern the definitions given below. For each definition, evaluate what, if anything, is wrong using the following criteria:

   A. Avoid being too broad or too narrow (specify which)
   B. Avoid circular definitions
   C. Avoid using metaphorical, figurative, ambiguous, or vague language (specify which one of the four is violated)
   D. Avoid using obscure language
   E. Avoid totally negative descriptive characterizations
   F. Avoid persuasive or judgmentally loaded characterizations
   G. Avoid using irrelevant features

Assume the definitions given are reportive in nature and not stipulative. Numbers 8 and 10 have more than one correct answer. Also, make sure that there is not a more specific error than the one you have identified. For example almost every metaphorical or figurative definition, just as many persuasive definitions, will also rely on irrelevant features.

5. Alimony: the price one pays for screwing up a marriage

   ANSWER: F - judgmentally loaded characterization

6. All: a universal quantifier whose allusion is to the unmitigated totality of what is being referenced, albeit not necessarily with existential import

   ANSWER: D - obscure definition

7. Ant: a bug frequently attracted to picnics

   ANSWER: G - irrelevant feature (being attracted to picnics)

8. Antisocial: not social

   ANSWER: B, E - circular, repeating term and totally negative descriptive characterization

9. Art: the human endeavor to transform the indeterminate constituents of nature into a determinate synthesis having aesthetic qualities

   ANSWER: D - obscure definition

10. Asymmetrical: not symmetrical

    ANSWER: B, E - circular, repeating term and totally negative descriptive characterization

11. Atlanta: a Southern City; home of the Hawks

    ANSWER: A, G - too broad, and irrelevant feature (the Hawks)

12. Bread: the staff of life

    ANSWER: C - metaphorical or figurative language

13. Regent's Test: a discriminatory tool for keeping certain minority groups from obtaining college degrees

Chapter 4

ANSWER: F - judgmentally loaded characterization

14. <u>Talent:</u> the ability to do something

ANSWER: A - too broad

Short Answer Questions

Questions 15 through 20 pertain to the following headlines, advertisements, and other passages. State whether the passage is ambiguous, vague, equivocal, or any other content problems it may have, making sure that you also explain why it has the error or errors you claim it has. For example, if the passage is ambiguous, state the different ways in which it can be interpreted or understood.

15. Mid-Eastern Head to Seek Arms

ANSWER: Grammatically ambiguous: Is there a real head looking for a pair of biological arms or is this a chief of state searching for weapons?

16. City Crisis: Care of Needy Mushrooms

ANSWER: Grammatically ambiguous: Why would we need to provide assistance for some fungi? What is wrong with them? Or, are we speaking of the number of socially indigent persons rising?

17. Save 25% if you switch to MCI now.

ANSWER: Quantitative vagueness: Save 25% over what? The amount they would have overbilled you if you let them?

18. People who live in this country are free and you live in this country, don't you? So, you must be free right now. Therefore, you can go out with me now.

ANSWER: Equivocation: Two different meanings of free—(a) having liberties and rights, and (b) not doing anything at the moment.

19. Super Sale!!!   Incredible Savings!!!   Next Few Days Only!!!   Hurry!!!

ANSWER: Referentially and quantitatively vague: Savings on what? How much actual savings? How many days left?

20. Railroad Crossing Without Any Cars, How Can You Spell It Without Any R's?

ANSWER;   Use-Mention distinction: solved by putting the word "it" in quotation marks.

Matching Questions

Each of the definitions given on the left side commits one of the errors lettered on the right side. Match the definition on the left with the mistake on the right.

21. _____ Ancestor: a progenitor

A. Totally negative descriptive df.

22. _____ Animal: a live, two or four legged creature

B. Metaphorical df.

C. Obscure definition

23. _____ Antelope: not a deer, nor an elk, nor a bison

D. Too narrow and possibly irrelevant feature

24. _____ Antipasto: that delicious part of the meal that sets the stage for what is to follow

E. Persuasive, judgmentally loaded characterization

25. _____ Apple: The healthy staple that keeps the old doctor away

ANSWERS: C, D, A, E, B

Essay Questions

26. Explain the difference between vagueness and ambiguity. Give an example of each.

27. List at least five different ways of defining a term analytically or reportively (as opposed to stipulatively). What are some of the strengths and weaknesses of each of the different methods of definition?

28. Explain the difference between the *denotation* of a term and the *connotation* of a term. Why is this distinction important? Where do the emotional flavorings associated with words fit into this distinction?

29. What are some of the differences between reportive and stipulative definitions? What are some of the different ways reportive and stipulative definitions are used, and what are some of the different purposes behind using them?

Chapter 4

30. Why does language/meaning matter to logic and critical thinking?

Chapter 5

Fallacies

CHAPTER OUTLINE

5.1 Fallacies of Irrelevant Premises
Exercises
5.2 Fallacies of Inadequate Premises
Exercises
5.3 Fallacies of Unfair Premises
Summary
Exercises
Case Study: Love is a Fallacy

KEY TERMS

Fallacy - A mistake in the alleged connection between the premises and conclusion of an argument or within one of the premises.

Fallacy of Inadequate Premises - A mistake in which the premise may be relevant to the conclusion but actually provides insufficient grounds for that conclusion or not as much as it claims to provide.

Fallacy of Irrelevant Premises - One in which the evidence seems to support the conclusion but is in fact not relevant or germane to that conclusion.

Fallacy of Unfair Premises - Mistakes in the reasoning process involving a distortion of part of that reasoning or unfairly misconstruing or stressing parts of an opponent's claim or argument.

Chapter 5

OVERVIEW

As we move into Chapter Five on fallacies, we move from the analytical phase of the process of reasoning to the evaluative one. This is probably an excellent starting place for the introductory student, because it is easily identifiable, it seems fun to most of them, and it is something to which many can relate. Unfortunately, there are often some less than benign side effects that we, as instructors, would do well to remember. Perhaps one of the worst of these side effects is that students like to show off their new-found skills at picking apart *any* line of reasoning in much the same way that a five year old armed with a new "Super-soaker" likes to get anything in sight soaking wet. Or, as one of our colleagues put it bluntly one time, we are often guilty of producing the kind of person no one wants to be around at a cocktail party or social gathering of any sort.

In order to lessen the possibility of this happening, we generally have our students read the Case Study, "Love is a Fallacy," first, before reading and digesting the chapter. This, almost three quarters of a century old classic story by Max Shulman is as timely today as when it was written. And, it humorously shows the student what might happen from taking our newly minted skills too seriously. This is not to say that the study of fallacies is frivolous, but merely to put it in context for the student.

In fact, after they have read the case study, then it is a good idea to lead them into the study of fallacies by pointing out that fallacies, errors in the reasoning process, are contextual, not absolute or unconditional. In many instances, calling someone else a liar may be a fallacious way of drawing attention away from a line of reasoning, whereas in other cases, it is quite legitimate. How are they going to make the distinction? We need also to point out that fallacies work, are psychologically persuasive, in many instances because they parallel perfectly good and viable lines of reasoning. There is nothing inherently wrong with citing authorities. It is done effectively and correctly quite frequently. This is exactly why a Misuse of Authority Fallacy can work. Moreover, fallacies need not be intentional. We have even been known to pull them on ourselves unwittingly when we wanted to believe a conclusion badly enough. Fallacies are literally indefinite in number. There may never be a complete and exhaustive list of such reasoning errors because we are creative beings and will probably always keep coming up with new, improved mistakes.

At any rate, we have adopted a fairly simple taxonomy of fallacies in the text and it runs along the following lines: when looking at the content of the premises or evidence submitted in support of a conclusion, we may begin by asking ourselves if the evidence is relevant. Hence, section one deals with fallacies of irrelevant premises. However, even if the premises turn out to be true and relevant, the next question is are they fair? Or, are they biased, slanted, and one-sided, such that they are not typically representative of the conclusion they are supposed to support? This is taken up in section 5.3 under the rubric of Fallacies of Unfair Premises. Finally, even if the premises are true, relevant, and fair, what else could go wrong? One major answer is that there simply may not be enough evidence adequate to support the conclusion they are alleged to establish. Section 5.2 deals with Fallacies of Inadequate Premises.

5.1   Fallacies of Irrelevant Premises
          Psychologically Irrelevant Premises
                1. Personal Attack
                        Abusive
                        Circumstantial
                        The Genetic Fallacy
                        Praise- or Blame-by-Association
                        Poisoning the Well
                        You Too (Tu Quoque)
                2. Red Herring
                3. Appeal to Fear
                4. Appeal to Pity
                5. Misuse of Humor
                6. Appeal to Tradition
                        Appeal to Novelty
                7. Popular Appeals
                8. Bandwagon Fallacy
                9. Emotional Appeals
                10. Misuse of Authority

          Grammatically Irrelevant Premises
                11. Equivocation
                12. Amphiboly
                13. Composition
                14. Division

5.2   Fallacies of Inadequate Premises
                15. Hasty Generalization
                16. Accident
                17. Argument from Ignorance
                18. Begging the Question
                19. Assuming the Cause
                20. Assuming Existence
                21. Fakey Precision
                22. Faulty Analogy

5.3   Fallacies of Unfair Premises
                23. Misrepresentative Generalization
                24. Leading Question
                25. Limited Options
                26. Straw Man
                27. Fallacious Extension

28. Slippery Slope
29. Misuse of Hypothesis
30. Stress or Accent

SOLUTIONS TO EXERCISE QUESTIONS

<u>Answers to Exercises on Pages 87 through 89</u>

Level A

1. * The Red Herring. (Because they draw attention away from the point of the reasoning and focus it on something irrelevant to the issue.)
2. * The Bandwagon Fallacy may be considered one special kind of Popular Appeal in which support is sought for a conclusion on the basis of the fact that a lot of other people feel the same way.
3. * In the Fallacies of Psychologically Irrelevant Premises, support for the conclusion is logically missing, but in place of evidence there is some thing which is emotionally or otherwise psychologically persuasive. In the Fallacies of Grammatically Irrelevant Premises, support for the conclusion is again missing logically, but the premises or evidence seem at first glance to be germane until one notices that there is some error in the language or the structure of the language being used.
4. * False. This is not always a mistake. Rather, it is a mistake to question any change in procedure *simply* on the basis of reasoning to the effect that "But we have always done it that way!"
5. * False. The Fallacies of Composition and Division are not really Emotional Appeals at all, but Fallacies of Grammatically Irrelevant Premises.
6. * True. (Hopefully!)
7. * False
8. * False. Although it is a matter of terminology and the irrelevant attacking of a person's character rather than their reasoning is sometimes called "Poisoning the Well," we have reserved that term for only a special portion of those instances—namely, cases where language is used to make it embarrassing to disagree with the speaker.
9. * True. Although there are exceptions (such as journalistic protection of the identity of their news sources) which keep this from being an iron-clad rule.
10. * False. This is usually the heart of the You Too Fallacy (although, psychologically, it is very persuasive).

Level B

1. * Popular Appeals Fallacy. (The appeal to everyone to have a voice in government, "open doors", "forgotten citizens", "special favors" and "special interests" all contribute to this

one.)

2.   Appeal to Fear

3. *   Personal Attack - Circumstantial. The correctness of Dr. King's views is in no way diminished or enhanced because of where they originated...even if from a Bubble Gum wrapper.

4.   You Too Fallacy

5. *   Bandwagon Fallacy

6.   Poisoning the Well (with the phrase "any person with half a brain")

7. *   Emotional Appeals (with the use of the words "degrading", "disgusting", and "eyesores")

8.   Appeal to Tradition

9. *   Misuse of Authority

10.   Red Herring . (Perhaps sprinkled with a generous dose of Appeal to Pity)

11. * Composition. (What if all these recruits are point guards?)

12.   Equivocation. (Perhaps the officer has misunderstood the meaning of the phrase "take advantage of"?)

13. * Appeal to Pity

14.   You Too Fallacy

15. * Appeal to Novelty (the reverse of the Appeal to Tradition Fallacy)

16.   Division

17. * Amphiboly. (The sign is grammatically misleading: is it a hospital only for Christian children or is it a Christian hospital for any child?)

18.   Genetic Fallacy; Blame by Association

19. * Poisoning the Well (with the phrase, "even marginally informed voters know that")

20.   Appeal to Fear

21. * Misuse of Authority

22.   Equivocation. (Two different meanings of "hanging by the rafters")

23. * Emotional Appeals. (No evidence is given here, only negatively connotative words such as "naive", "mechanistic", and "robot-like" referring to one position; while positively connotative words such as "more informed" and "sophisticated" refer to the latter position.)

24.   Possibly Composition, although this looks like it might also be a Hasty or Misrepresentative Generalization or both.

25. * Bandwagon Fallacy

26.   Popular Appeals (This time by "snobbery")

27. * Could be either the You Too Fallacy if referring back to the accusing politician, or Red Herring if dragging us away from the charges at hand.

<u>Answers to Exercises on Pages 93 through 95</u>

Level A

1. *   The Fallacy of Hasty Generalization is the mistaken reasoning which jumps to a conclusion

about a whole population based upon insufficient evidence about some of its members. The Fallacy of Composition, by contrast, is mistaken reasoning which usually has sufficient evidence about the parts of a whole, but makes the leap in reasoning to assume that the whole will retain all the qualities that the parts have.

2. *   The Fallacy of Begging the Question may take one of several forms: (1) Assuming the Conclusion, (b) Circular Reasoning, (c) Definitional Dodgeball, (d) Misuse of Weasel Words. All of these forms of Begging the Question have the common trait of assuming the truth of what they in fact are trying to prove.

3. *   When one commits the Fallacy of Accident, one is assuming that because something is true as a general rule, therefore, it must be true in any particular instance.

4. *   False. Sometimes this is all the evidence we have, and, if we are careful not to claim any more strength for the conclusion than our evidence (or lack thereof) warrants, then the reasoning may not be fallacious. Remember, fallacies are contextual.

5. *   False. This could still be a fallacy if there was little warrant for the suspected cause in the first place *even if* it subsequently turns out to be the cause.

6. *   False. An incredible amount of human reasoning is done by analogy without our even being aware of it. Some of it is very well taken; some of it is not. Perhaps all of it is inductive, but just because the premises do not absolutely guarantee the conclusion beyond a shadow of a doubt does not necessarily mean that it is fallacious. Scientists use arguments from analogy when trying to determine how drugs which work on certain animals will work on humans. Lawyers and judges use arguments from analogy when they argue that certain cases are like earlier precedent cases and hence should be treated similarly.

7. *   False again. (Unless the illusion has been created that there is a corresponding entity for that term.)

8. *   False again. (Unless it needlessly detracts from a clear understanding of the issues in question.)

9. *   False. (What is being described is more like the Fallacy of Equivocation although even that one is not accurately captured here. The Fallacy of Accident is the misapplication of a generalization to a particular case whose "accidental" features make it outside the scope of that generalization.)

10. *   False. This could be one of the most frequently occurring forms of reasoning found in the human species.

Level B

1. *   Begging the Question by Assuming the Conclusion (the simplest form of Circular Reasoning). All we have done is repeat the premise in the conclusion with words that mean exactly the same thing: capital punishment = the death penalty; repeatedly convicted drug dealers = people who are found guilty of selling drugs again and again; and should be = justifiable.

2.   Hasty Generalization. This Volvo will be bad (conclusion) on the basis of my one

(Inadequate Premise) bad experience with a Volvo. The fact that reasoning mentions parts should not necessarily make you jump to the conclusion that this is a Composition or Division Fallacy. And, the part about the horn is not necessarily Misuse of Humor (unless you forgot the point of the exercise).

3. * Assuming the Cause. Even if the economy had started improving right after Clinton was elected, he would not necessarily be the cause of its having turned around.

4. Faulty Analogy. People are not exactly like tea kettles. There are too many relevant dissimilarities for this to be a decent piece of reasoning.

5.* This one can be seen in at least two distinct but related ways: (a) The Fallacy of Accident. It is true that freedom of reference is a fairly accepted practice *as a general rule*. The problem here is that we have misapplied that general rule to a specific case (students taking tests) whose special circumstances made that rule inappropriate. (b) When we get into the specifics of this argument about Doctors consulting books and X-Rays and Lawyers consulting their sources, there is a Faulty Analogy between the finished product of those studies and those who are in the process of learning their profession.

6. The Argument From Ignorance. Just because there is no material in a student's file cannot be a good reason for thinking that the student must be a good one (any more than it would be a reason for thinking the student must be a bad one).

7. * Of the fallacies we have discussed, this is probably closest to Assuming Existence, insofar as the passage seems to be implying that there is a distinct personality corresponding to "a Pisces" and that each person has a "fate."

8. Begging the Question (By Circular Reasoning). X is true (the Holy Book) because Y is true (it is the word of God). And Y is true (it is the word of God) because Z is true (the great prophets say so). And Z is true (the great prophets say so) because X is true (the Holy Book is true).

9. * Assuming The Cause. ACME Industries tripled in size *after* Mr. I became CEO. After this, therefore because of this.

10. Fakey Precision. In this case thirteen one thousandths of a second will not make any significant difference in the argument at hand, except to draw attention away from the more significant evidence to be found and conclusions to be drawn.

11. * Hasty Generalization

12. Accident

13. * Argument From Ignorance

14. Begging The Question (By Circular Reasoning)

15. * Assuming The Cause

16. Could be Fakey Precision. (Both sets of statistics might be correct!)

17. * Accident

18. Assuming Existence

19. * Argument From Ignorance

20. Hasty Generalization

21. * Begging The Question (By Definitional Dodgeball or Hedging)

22. Assuming The Cause (this time by getting the cause and effect mixed up)

Chapter 5

23. *   Faulty Analogy

<u>Answers to Exercises on Pages 99 through 102</u>

Level A

1. *   False. Quite often they are unintentional; we even use them on ourselves unwittingly.
2. *   True. Even though there is an "always" in the characterization, we would do well to consider this one true, because it is conceivable that under some set of circumstances the same line of thinking might be quite legitimate.
3. *   True. This holds true for both the psychologically and the grammatically irrelevant fallacies.
4. *   False. This sounds more like an Appeal to Fear. The Personal Attack Fallacy relies upon discrediting the person who is doing the reasoning rather than criticizing the reasoning itself.
5. *   False. One may reason quite legitimately through the medium of cartoons.
6. *   False. Although we did not put it in that category, a moment's thought would reveal that an Argument by Analogy may turn out to be faulty on any one of the three major grounds we have discussed: (a) there could be an inadequate number of similarities between the two situations being compared for the reasoning to be decent; (b) there could be irrelevant features being compared between the two situations; or (c) we could have singled out one or two atypical features and made the comparison on that basis (and hence have a Fallacy of Unfair Premises).
7. *   True. This is done in legal reasoning all of the time. Closer to home perhaps, parents who have set consistent guidelines with their children may do the same thing quite reasonably.
8. *   False. This is exactly an instance of the SLIPPERY SLOPE Fallacy.
9. *   False. It *may* involve this. But, it also involves unintentional misrepresentation. And, it may also involve misrepresenting different parts of the argument rather than the whole argument itself.
10. *   True. (More than likely.)

Level B

1. *   Misuse of Hypothesis Contrary To Fact. The antecedent of the conditional premise is "Billy Martin is still alive and managing the Yankees," and this happens to be false. Therefore, the consequent—"The Yankees would be in first place"—is actually indisputable because there is no way of being sure that this is correct or incorrect. We could cover ourselves and continue that the Yankees *might be* in first place for several additional reasons....
2.   Slippery Slope. We have gone from lowering interest rates by one quarter of a percent to twenty times that month by falling down that slippery slope.
3. *   Fallacious Extension. The argument began by drawing a conclusion about not raising the

cost of a college education. But, it then jumped illegitimately to other ramifications which were not even a part of nor yet a consequence of the original reasoning—namely, from education to food, housing, and health care.

4. Probably a Misrepresentative Generalization. The conclusion is how *most people in town* feel. It is based on letters to the editor in the local newspaper. Would a person be more likely to write such a letter if they were opposed to the club or in favor of it? (Hint: People rarely protest things they like.) Second, local neighborhoods are more likely to oppose the club than the rest of the town, since it affects them more directly. They are not necessarily representative of the entire town or even most of it. And, finally, perhaps there were only five letters to the editor or paper on this topic—we have no way of knowing. So, it may be a Hasty Generalization as well.

5. * Leading Question. We have already presumed in the asking of the question that higher education is a waste of time.

6. Limited Options. More than likely there are a host of other reactions possible and we have only picked out two extremes and then presented them in such a way as to make one of the (backing down) look very unattractive.

7. * Fallacy Of Stress. We have taken a statement by former President Truman and quoted him out of context to mean that you should spend as much money as possible to win (when his intention was to admonish people that they should *not* spend too much money).

8. This one can be looked upon at least two ways. The simplest is to see it as a case of Hasty Generalization. If we are generalizing on the basis of one case (Simone's) to conclude that Western nations may in fact be keeping pace with Eastern ones in mathematics training, then we certainly have not used a sufficient number of cases. But a second, more in-depth, way of looking at this reasoning is to see it as a case of the Straw Person Fallacy. One person has concluded that the West is not keeping pace with the East when it comes to training in Math. The second person disagrees, saying, "Not every Eastern person is better." This is clearly a warping of and strengthening of the first person's conclusion, which makes it a lot easier to blow away—the mark of the Straw Person Fallacy. All we have to do at that point is come up with one counterinstance. But, notice the original conclusion: one counterexample would not damage it a bit.

9. * Fallacy of Limited Options. Surely, there is something in between a good car and a cheap one, or maybe one that is both.

10. Misrepresentative Generalization. One hundred thousand college students (chosen at random) should be a sufficient number to generalize about the opinions of *college students*, but not necessarily of *Americans*. They may be an atypical subgroup of Americans.

11. * Leading Question. We have not given the defendant the chance to say that she did not run the red light.

12. Misuse of Hypothesis Contrary To Fact. This might be lessened by concluding that the Bulls *might* have had a shot at the title if Jordan had still been playing, as long as we back it up with some reasoning.

13. * Slippery Slope

14.   Fallacy Of Limited Options

15. *   Fallacy Of Stress

16.   Fallacious Extension. From a conclusion about the homeless, our reasoner has gone to food prices, AFDC, and gasoline prices.

17. *   Misrepresentative Generalization. Law students are *not* lawyers yet and may be a bit more idealistic and open.

18.   Straw Person Fallacy. Our arguer has misrepresented Dr. Sagan's conclusion in order to make it easier to refute.

19. *   Limited Options (False Dilemma)

20.   Misuse Of Hypothesis Contrary To Fact

21. *   Fallacious Extension (can be seen as a case of Slippery Slope)

22.   Straw Person (misrepresenting the first person's claim) and possibly a Leading Question (although it is probably meant as a rhetorical question)

23. *   Fallacy of Stress. (The student has misread the requirement of maintaining a *minimum* 2.0 average as if it must be *exactly* 2.0.)

24.   Division. Just because the company is young and aggressive does not mean that each and every employee is young and aggressive. (Also, there may be an Equivocation Fallacy here too, if being aggressive in business is different from being an aggressive driver.)

25. *   Limited Options

26.   Assuming The Cause

27. *   Several different forms of Personal Attack, from Circumstantial to Genetic

28.   First, Personal Attack—Blame by Association and Personal Attack, Abusive (by calling them "idiots"). Second, Slippery Slope, by claiming that first-trimester abortions is a necessary consequence of legal abortions for rape and incest. Also Fallacious Extension. (This could also be seen as Misuse of Hypothesis Contrary To Fact.)

29. *   First, perhaps a Misuse of Authority (just because your father and a priest tell you it is immoral does not make it immoral), and, second, Begging The Question by reiterating the conclusion in the premise. Also, the statement that "everybody knows that..." makes it either a Bandwagon Fallacy, or a case of Poisoning The Well.

30.   First, Bandwagon Fallacy, assuming that they are "good for you" on the basis of sales; and, second, Argument From Ignorance: perhaps no one has taken a look at the nutritional content of their burgers yet, or the study is still in progress.

31. *   This one begins with a huge Appeal to Pity and then shifts gears into an Appeal to Fear.

32.   Misuse Of Authority. Rush Limbaugh's conclusions need to be supported just like anyone else. Also, it ends with an Argument From Ignorance.

33. *   Appeal To Tradition. (Perhaps a trace of Poisoning The Well thrown in.)

34.   This may be a legitimate line of reasoning if, in fact, the precedent had been established as claimed.

35. *   Assuming The Cause. Concluding that the reason why we were robbed was due to the decrease in the penalty for burglary is to assume that since X came after Y, that Y must be the cause of X, with no more evidence to go on.

36.   Popular Appeals!

37. *   The You Too Fallacy. Even though this is cute and Nominee Clinton may even be right on the money here, has he responded to then-President Bush's charges, or merely thrown them right back in his face?
38.   Leading Question, by the way this one is phrased. Also, Emotional Appeals and Poisoning The Well, by referring to Arkansas as a "small, failed state."

TEST BANK

Multiple Choice Questions

1. All of the variations of the PERSONAL ATTACK Fallacy can be considered as subsets of which of the following fallacies?
   A. RED HERRING
   B. BANDWAGON Fallacy
   C. EMOTIONAL APPEALS
   D. APPEAL TO FEAR
   E. MISUSE OF HUMOR

   ANSWER: A

2. A BANDWAGON Fallacy is one particular type of
   A. APPEAL TO FEAR
   B. PERSONAL ATTACK Fallacy
   C. POPULAR APPEAL
   D. MISUSE OF AUTHORITY
   E. Grammatically Irrelevant Premise

   ANSWER: C

3. Whenever one encounters what in Chapter Four was described as a "Persuasive or Loaded Definition," in the context of an argument this would almost always be which one of the following fallacies?
   A. PERSONAL ATTACK
   B. POPULAR APPEALS
   C. RED HERRING
   D. EMOTIONAL APPEALS
   E. MISUSE OF AUTHORITY

   ANSWER: D

4. What is the difference between the Fallacies of HASTY GENERALIZATION and

COMPOSITION?

A. HASTY GENERALIZATION involves jumping to a conclusion without using enough cases, while COMPOSITION may use enough cases but assumes that what is true of these parts is also true of the organic whole they go together to form.

B. HASTY GENERALIZATION is a leap in reasoning that is done too quickly, while COMPOSITION is much more composed.

C. HASTY GENERALIZATION is a jump from some parts of something to all the parts of it, while COMPOSITION jumps from some parts of something to the whole entire thing.

D. HASTY GENERALIZATION is an inductive fallacy whereas COMPOSITION is a deductive fallacy.

E. Both A and C above.

ANSWER: E

5. What is the thread that all the different cases of BEGGING THE QUESTION have in common; that is, what makes them all cases of BEGGING THE QUESTION?

A. They all involve the use of definitions.

B. They all somehow assume the truth of what they are trying to prove.

C. They all involve some kind of question.

D. They all involve some kind of special pleading.

E. Both B and C above.

ANSWER: B

6. When a generalization which is held to be fairly reliable is used in an argument to support a special instance which is an exception to the general rule, the fallacy which is committed is

A. ASSUMING THE CAUSE

B. BEGGING THE QUESTION

C. ACCIDENT

D. HASTY GENERALIZATION

E. THE ARGUMENT FROM IGNORANCE

ANSWER: C

7. Misquoting or quoting out of context could most likely be the basis for which of the following fallacies:

A. Fallacy of STRESS OR ACCENT

B. Fallacy of AMPHIBOLY

C. Fallacy of EQUIVOCATION

D. MISUSE OF AUTHORITY

E. LEADING QUESTION

ANSWER: A

8. Which one of the following types of Fallacies works by distorting or misrepresenting either parts of another position or argument, or the assumptions or ramifications of that position?
   A. STRAW PERSON Fallacy
   B. FALLACIOUS EXTENSION
   C. MISUSE OF HYPOTHESIS
   D. SLIPPERY SLOPE
   E. All of the above

ANSWER: E

9. A person who reasoned, "All the men I meet are either gay or married or real dweebs. I guess there are no eligible single males around this part of the world," might be reproached for which of the following fallacies:
   A. PERSONAL ATTACK—YOU TOO FALLACY
   B. ARGUMENT FROM IGNORANCE
   C. BANDWAGON FALLACY
   D. HASTY GENERALIZATION
   E. APPEAL TO STUPIDITY

ANSWER: D

10. Suppose you read in "Pop Psychology Hints" that "When you're mad, don't hold it in! If a tea kettle couldn't blow off steam, it would explode! If you don't let the anger out when you're really mad, you'll blow up too." Which of the following best refutes this little gem of reasoning?
   A. Explosions are actually okay as long as they don't get into someone else's personal space.
   B. Experiments are needed to confirm that boiling tea kettles really will explode if the steam is not allowed to escape.
   C. This argument is actually inductive in nature and therefore only probably true.
   D. People are not tea kettles and "boiling mad" is only a metaphor. There are too many relevant dissimilarities here making this a Faulty Analogy.
   E. Actually the reasoning error in this case is a Hasty Generalization because it is not true that boiling tea kettles will explode every time they are overheated.

ANSWER: D

Exercises 11 through 20 concern each of the passages given below. Pick the appropriate answer from the multiple choices.

11. "My mother waited on her husband, hand and foot. So did her mother before her and her

87

grandmother before that. That is why I wait on Bluto hand and foot today."
    A. Appeal to Tradition
    B. Appeal to Pity
    C. Straw Man Argument
    D. Limited Options (False Dilemma)
    E. You Too Fallacy (Pointing to Another Wrong)

ANSWER: A

12. "All men are mortal. Socrates is a man. Therefore, Socrates is dead."
    A. Personal Attack
    B. Straw Man Argument
    C. Popular Appeals
    D. Emotional Appeals (Persuasive Language)
    E. None of the above

ANSWER: E

13. "You know that the media is and has long been biased from a liberal point of view. Despite
    allegations to the contrary from the Democrats, no one has ever been able to prove otherwise
    and now Newt Gingrich has told us the truth about the media."
    A. Argument from Ignorance and Misuse of Authority
    B. Personal Attack—Blame by Association and You Too Fallacy
    C. Emotional Appeals and Blame by Association
    D. Amphiboly and Appeal to Pity
    E. Composition and Misuse of Hypothesis

ANSWER: A

14. "Ford makes the best car in the United States today, since more people drive it than any other
    make."
    A. Personal Attack—Praise By Association
    B. Equivocation
    C. Bandwagon Fallacy
    D. Begging the Question
    E. Misuse of Authority

ANSWER: C

15. "The black community does not see the O.J. Simpson case as a racial issue. Neither Oprah nor
    Montel Williams feel this way."
    A. Straw Person Argument

B. Emotional Appeals
C. Misrepresentative Generalization
D. Argument From Ignorance
E. Accident

ANSWER: C

16. "No one in his or her right mind would even think of trying to go up against the stronghold of the new religious right wing that is taking over Congress."
A. Bandwagon Fallacy
B. Appeal to Fear
C. Hasty Generalization
D. Poisoning the Well
E. Popular Appeals

ANSWER: D

17. "Sammy is sixteen years old and pregnant. She has come to the conclusion that if Allan doesn't marry her, she will have to kill herself."
A. Appeal to Fear
B. Appeal to Pity
C. Misuse of Hypothesis
D. Slippery Slope
E. Limited Options—False Dilemma

ANSWER: E

18. "The Mariners are having a mediocre season. Therefore, Mariner outfielder Ken Griffey, Jr. must be having a mediocre season as well."
A. Appeal to Pity
B. Assuming the Cause
C. Division
D. Begging the Question
E. Fallacious Extension

ANSWER: C

19. "Business has increased dramatically since the new administration's tax cuts. See, I told you that policy would have wonderful consequences."
A. Assuming the Cause
B. Begging the Question
C. Argument From Ignorance

    D. Fallacious Extension
    E. Straw Person Fallacy

ANSWER: A

20. "I don't want to fail this exam; I'll just have to find some way to cheat."
    A. Poisoning the Well
    B. Appeal to Pity
    C. Argument From Ignorance
    D. Equivocation
    E. Limited Options—False Dilemma

ANSWER: E

Matching Questions

Questions 21 through 30 are matching questions about fallacies. Assume that the following passages occur in the context of arguments and that each one contains at least one major error. Match the passage number with the letter corresponding to the fallacy that names its most glaring error.

21. _____ Even though I am a brand new faculty member here at State Tech University, I have met several professors in my department and others as well. I'd have to say that we have the finest teachers anywhere.

    A. Equivocation

    B. Personal Attack—by Poisoning the Well

22. _____ The most successful junior executives today wear expensive tailored Italian suits, drive terribly expensive foreign cars and have cellular phones. So, one of the best ways you can become a successful junior exec is to go out and buy expensive foreign clothes and cars and a cellular phone.

    C. Misuse of Authority

    D. Straw Man Fallacy

23. _____ No one with a shred of intelligence would trust a woman who is on a mission, and, believe me, Hillary is on a mission with this health care reform business. Don't trust her.

    E. Misrepresentative and Hasty Generalization

24. _____ Your battery must be brand new: you just bought that car and it is brand new.

25. _____ O.J. Simpson must be innocent; otherwise someone would have been able to prove that he was guilty by now.

F. Division

26. _____ When do you think professors will start asking relevant questions on their examinations anyway?

G. Accident

27. _____ I have been teaching this logic course over twenty years now. So, you can be sure my interpretation of this argument is correct. Besides, you certainly do not want to fail this class.

H. Assuming the Cause

I. Appeal to Fear

28. _____ Nobody would make a better President than Clinton, and you are nobody: therefore, you would make a better President than Clinton.

J. Argument From Ignorance

29. _____ Noted astronomer and scientist, Carl Sagan, has remarked that human beings now have the capability to send people to the moon and to Mars. However, I think he has overstated his case: there is no way we can send any number of people anywhere in space whenever we want, and certainly not right now.

K. Leading Question

30. _____ Dan Quayle, as Vice President, must have been speaking rationally in his address to the people of El Salvador because he is a man, and, as Aristotle proved years ago, man is a rational animal. (This one has two mistakes, at least!)

ANSWERS: E, H, B, F, J, K, I, A, D, G and C (might give credit for A or F also)

Short Answer Questions

For each of the following passages, explain what fallacy or fallacies have been committed as well as how and why there are mistakes in the reasoning process.

31. "The *Times-Tribune-Picayune* has been accusing me of some questionable activities for a couple of weeks now. Just remember: they are guilty of some questionable activities themselves, so how can you trust them?"

ANSWER: Best answer is Red Herring; could also argue for You Too Fallacy.

32. "The basic cause of inflation is an unbalanced federal budget..."If the rate of inflation becomes too excessive, the result of this inflation is that the economy will stop...because the dollar will be losing value so fast people will stop exchanging goods of real value for dollars...Now this isn't conjecture; this has happened before, many times...If you don't control inflation...you will destroy the economy, and in a few weeks there will be no food to buy, little water, no electricity and services, and there will be such panic and disaster that some hard-pants general is going to move in and say, "I'm in charge here," and the Army or some military take-over will spell the death knell of democracy."

ANSWER: Starts off like an Assuming the Cause Fallacy but degenerates into a special kind of Fallacious Extension known as the Slippery Slope.

33. "It's so obvious why we didn't win the lottery last night: you must have been putting out some awful vibrations!"

ANSWER: Assuming the Cause. (Some may argue for Assuming Existence by the use of "bad vibrations.")

34. "The War in Vietnam occurred because U. S. corporations were afraid of losing millions of dollars of assets grounded there not to mention the millions of dollars of revenue. They were afraid of losing the assets and revenues because they would have had an awful lot of disgruntled stockholders. They would have had a lot of disgruntled stockholders because the U.S. public itself was becoming disgruntled and disenchanted because the War in Vietnam was occurring."

ANSWER: Begging the Question by circular reasoning. A is true because B is true; B is true because C is true; C is true because D is true; and D is true because A is true.

35. "I knew the SWAT Team was getting crazier and crazier; look what they've done now. Read the headlines, 'SWAT TEAM HELPS DOG BITE VICTIM.'"

ANSWER: Amphiboly: a misreading (?) of the headline to mean that the SWAT Team helped the dog bite the victim, rather than the SWAT Team helped the victim who had been bitten by a dog.

36. "If the President had responded differently to the touchy issue of gays in the military at the beginning of his Presidency, then we would not have seen such a reactionary backlash in last November's elections."

ANSWER: Misuse of Hypothesis contrary to fact. (Some will argue that it is also a kind of Assuming the Cause.)

37. "Mike Tyson needs a rabies vaccination. After all, if something is a boxer, then it's a dog. And, if it's a dog, then it needs a rabies vaccination. And, Mike Tyson is a boxer."

ANSWER: Equivocation (Two different meanings of "boxer")

38. "You really should buy this cologne: it's the latest; everyone's wearing it; and members of the opposite sex will not be able to resist you."

ANSWER: Popular Appeals including an Appeal to Novelty, a Bandwagon Fallacy, and a general Emotional Appeal for people to want to feel sexy.

39. "I've listened to these 'soft-on-crime' Democrats long enough. Now they want us to reduce military spending. If we do that, we will be totally unarmed, unprepared, and easy prey for any aggressor."

ANSWER: The phrase 'soft-on-crime' has no descriptive content at all and is a pure Emotional Appeals with no evidence to back it up. The author or speaker goes on to mention that the Democrats want to *reduce* military spending and then completely distorts that to mean *get rid of all* military spending. This is called the Straw Person Fallacy. The speaker then fallaciously extends the consequences of that position by a Misuse of Hypothesis.

40. "A and B and C are angles of this triangle. Each of the angles of a triangle are less than 180°. Therefore, A plus B plus C are less than 180°."

ANSWER: On the one hand we could argue that this is a composition fallacy: since each of the parts has a particular property, the whole that they go together must also have that property. However, one could also look at this one as an Equivocation Fallacy with the problem residing in the little word "Are." In the first instance, the word "are" is used as a copula to show that each of the angles of a triangle must be less than 180 degrees. In the second instance, the word "are" means "adds up to," as in "two plus two are four." Therefore, two different meanings of the word "are."

Essay Questions

41. Do you think that "Fallacies" are internal or external criticisms of arguments? Are there ways in which you could see them as partially both? Why?

42. In *Begging the Question* when a statement is offered as self-evident or as self-validating, are we necessarily involved in a Fallacy or not? What makes you think so? Suppose you meet up with an argument that comes in the form, "A and B and C and D are true. Therefore, A is true." Most logicians will say that this is a valid form of argumentation called "Simplification." For example, "Dave and Kelly and Tameka and Chien went to the Deadhead Club last night. Therefore, Dave went to the Deadhead Club last night." Would this constitute a form of *Begging the Question*? Why or why not?

43. Explain the difference between the fallacies of Division and Accident. Why are they considered to be "first cousins?"

44. Even if it is true that there can be no exhaustive list of fallacies, does this necessarily mean that there can be no completely comprehensive categorization of the *kinds* of fallacies that are possible? Be sure to justify whatever answer you take.

45. Explain why in logic and in critical thinking it is possible for an argument to be based on one or more fallacies and yet for the conclusion still to be true.

Chapter 6

The Categorical Syllogism

CHAPTER OUTLINE

6.1 The Categorical Syllogism
Exercises
6.2 The Rule Method for Testing Categorical Syllogisms
Exercises
6.3 The Venn Diagram Method for Testing Categorical Syllogisms
Summary
Exercises
Case Study

KEY TERMS

Categorical Logic - The study of arguments from the standpoint of the relationships between classes of entities or events.

Categorical Statement - A premise or conclusion in a categorical syllogism and in which members of one class are said to be included in or excluded from another class.

Categorical Syllogism - A two premise, one conclusion deductive argument in which all three statements are in standard categorical form.

Distribution - A property of a class or term referring to the members of that class individually. A term is said to be distributed when reference applies to each and every member of that class. The term is said to be undistributed when reference does not necessarily apply to every member, but only to some.

Existential Fallacy - Violation of the Corollary to Rule One of the Rule

Method for testing categorical syllogisms and which holds that whenever both premises are universal statements (A- or E-Form) and the conclusion is a particular statement (I- or O-Form) all three of the terms or classes must be known to have at least one member for the syllogism to be valid.

Fallacy of Faulty Exclusions - The violation of Rule Two of the Rule Method of testing categorical syllogisms and which holds that a valid categorical syllogism has either (A) no negative (E- or O-Form) statements or (B) one negative statement in the premises and one negative statement in the conclusion.

Fallacy of Illicit Distribution - The violation of Rule Three (B) of the Rule Method of testing the validity of categorical syllogisms and which holds that any term distributed in the conclusion must also be distributed in the premises.

Fallacy of the Undistributed Middle Term - The violation of Rule Three (A) of the Rule Method of testing categorical syllogisms and which holds that the Middle Term must be distributed at least once.

Formal Reasoning - Assessment of arguments on the basis of their structure and without regard to the actual truth or falsity of the premises.

Four Terms Fallacy - Violation of Rule One of the Rule Method for testing categorical syllogisms and which holds that a valid categorical syllogism has exactly three class terms each used in precisely the same sense in each of the statements in which it occurs.

Invalid Syllogism - A categorical syllogism in which the truth of the premises does not guarantee the truth of the conclusion.

Major Premise - The premise of a categorical syllogism containing the predicate class from the conclusion.

Major Term - The predicate class in the conclusion of a categorical syllogism.

Middle Term - The class term in a syllogism connecting the major and minor terms and which occurs only in the premises of the argument.

Minor Premise - The premise of a categorical syllogism containing the subject class from the conclusion.

Minor Term - The subject class in the conclusion of a categorical syllogism.

Particular Term - A term indicating at least one or more members of a class. It is represented by the quantifier "some" and can actually refer to any part of that whole, up to and including each and every member.

Predicate - The second class in a categorical statement and from which some portion of the subject class is being excluded or included.

Quantifier - A term which indicates which part of a class from none to some to all is being included or excluded from another class. The three standard quantifiers are all, some, and no.

Singular Term - An individual thing or event that is serving as an entire class, even though there is only one member. It is usually quantified by the terms all or no.

Subject - The class or category which is being included in or excluded from some relationship with a second class in a categorical statement.

Universal Term - A term indicating every member of the class, usually represented by the quantifier all or no.

Valid Syllogism - A categorical syllogism in
    which the truth of the premises
    guarantees the truth of the conclusion.

OVERVIEW

In Chapter Six we broach the topic of evaluating the structure of arguments for the first time. Because this is such a crucial subject matter for both logic and critical thinking, we spend some amount of time approaching the form or structure of arguments from several angles. Step Six of the Technique asks us to portray and assess the structure of a line of reasoning. Basically, this entails asking the question whether the premises in and of themselves provide irrevocable and conclusive grounds for believing in the conclusion.

Chapter Six focuses on one particular type of structure (or way of reading the structure) of arguments known as *categorical syllogisms*. The categorical syllogism is a two premise one conclusion line of reasoning in which each of the three statements has been cast in standard categorical form. A standard categorical form statement is an assertion that an individual or set of individuals or an entire class is included in or excluded from another group or set or class of individuals. The standard form categorical statement is quantified by the terms *all*, *some*, or *no*. There are two classes or categories in each categorical statement: the subject class and the predicate class.

Thus, any categorical syllogism has or should have three class terms. The *major term* of the syllogism is the predicate of the conclusion. The *major premise* is then the premise which contains the predicate term of the conclusion as one of its classes. The *minor term* of the syllogism is the subject class of the conclusion. The *minor premise* of the syllogism is then the premise in which the subject term of the conclusion is one of the classes. The *middle term* is the linking term that occurs in both of the premises but not in the conclusion.

A categorical syllogism is said to be valid when it establishes that the truth of its conclusion necessarily follows from the truth of its premises. There are three rules for determining validity plus one corollary to the first rule.

Rule One: A valid categorical syllogism has exactly three class terms, each occurring twice with precisely the same meaning in both of the statements in which it occurs. Violation of this rule constitutes the Four Terms Fallacy (even if there turn out to be six terms).

Rule Two: A valid categorical syllogism has the same number of negative (E- or O-Statements) in the premises as it has in the conclusion. Either there are no negative statements at all, or there is one in the premises and one in the conclusion.

Violation of Rule Two constitutes the Faulty Exclusions Fallacy.

Rule Three: In a valid categorical syllogism, (A) the middle term must be distributed at least once, and (B) any term that is distributed in the conclusion must be distributed in the premises as well. If a term is undistributed in the conclusion, it does not matter whether it is distributed or undistributed in the premises. Violation of Rule 3 (A) constitutes the Fallacy of the Undistributed Middle Term. Violation of Rule 3 (B) constitutes the Fallacy of Illicit Distribution.

Corollary: In a valid categorical syllogism, whenever both of the premises are universal
to Rule One statements (A- or E-Form) and the conclusion is a particular statement (an I- or O-Form), all three of the classes of the syllogism must be known to have at least one member. If any one (or more) of the classes turns out to be an empty set, the Existential Fallacy is committed.

Finally we show an alternative way of quickly assessing the validity of syllogisms by using diagraming techniques. In the latter part of the chapter, we present a way of utilizing Venn Diagrams to represent each of the classes of a syllogism. The idea is that when the two premises are diagrammed, the conclusion of a valid syllogism will "already be contained in" the diagram of the premises. If there is any way of diagramming the premises without the conclusion having to be true, then the syllogism will be invalid. In the Case Study, we present an alternative method, using Euler Diagrams instead of Venn ones.

Encourage the student to make use of the figures and flow charts in the chapter if they are helpful in getting them to apply the algorithms. Otherwise, encourage them to develop their own methods for applying the Rule and the Diagram techniques. These, too, have a way of showing themselves on many different kinds of standardized tests. To that end, we refine both of the diagramming techniques presented in this chapter later in Chapter Thirteen.

SOLUTIONS TO EXERCISE QUESTIONS

Answers to Exercises on Pages 118 and 119

Level A

1. * A *universal term* is a class or set which has been quantified, usually by the words "all" or "no," to indicate that each and every member of that set has or lacks a particular trait.
2. * A *particular term*, on the other hand, is a set or class in which only some of the members are referred to. The word "some" could refer to as few as one in a trillion or to as many as 999,999,999 out of a billion.
3. * The *Positive* Categorical Forms are the A- and I-Statements.

4. *   The *Negative* Categorical Forms are the E- and O-Statements.
5. *   The quantifier is "No."
6. *   The quantifier is "All" (or "Each" or "Every").
7. *   The O-Statement.
8. *   It is notoriously imprecise. It indicates at least one member out of the class in question, but it could go as high as all of them.
9. *   The *major term* in a categorical syllogism is the *predicate term* in the conclusion. It will also occur one time in the *major premise* of the argument.
10. * The *middle term* in a categorical syllogism is the class term that occurs in each of the premises, but does not occur in the conclusion.

Level B

		Quantifier	Subject	Relationship	Predicate
1. *	A-Statement	All	{Low-flying, High-speed Aircraft}	Are	{Planes which will have to use the city's alternative airport}
2.	I-Statement	Some	{Extremely low-budget Hollywood movies}	Are	{Films of distinctive quality and taste}
3. *	E-Statement	No	{Person who has filed a tax extension}	Is	{A person who is eligible for a refund at this time}
4.	O-Statement	Some	{Overpaid ball players}	Are Not	{Players who are fit to play on the second string of the better professional teams}

(This could also be done as an I-Statement, with the relationship being "Are" and the Predicate Term being "Players who are *not* fit to play second string on the better professional teams.")

	Quantifier	Subject	Relationship	Predicate
5. * I-Statement	Some	{Recipe cards that she uses}	Are	{Things that came from her Grandmother's side of the family}
6. E-Statement	No	{Medical procedures}	Are	{Completely risk-free procedures}
7. * A-Statement	All	{Street lights in town}	Are	{Things lit tonight}

It could also be done as an I-Statement:

	Quantifier	Subject	Relationship	Predicate
	Some	{Things lit tonight	Are	{Street lights in town}
8. 0-Statement	Some	{Excellent skiers from countries around the world}	Are Not	{Olympic Gold Medal hopefuls this year}
9. * I-Statement	Some	{Students who were thought to be too uninterested}	Are	{People who showed up for the rally held in the quad last night}
10. E-Statement	No	{Person who has not actually played a Rachmaninov piano concerto}	Is	{A person who should criticize Andre's performance tonight}

11.* A-Statement

Quantifier	Subject	Relationship	Predicate
All	{People who ever had a heart that was not made of cast-iron}	Are	{People who would be sorry for behaving that way}

12. Could be either:

(A) an I-Statement

Quantifier	Subject	Relationship	Predicate
Some	{Possible courses of action}	Are	{Things that have not been overlooked}

or (B) an O-Statement

Quantifier	Subject	Relationship	Predicate
Some	{Possible courses of action}	Are Not	{Things that have been overlooked}

13.* Again, can be done several ways:

(A) an A-Statement

Quantifier	Subject	Relationship	Predicate
All	{These shoes}	Are	{Shoes (or articles of clothing) that are way too tight}

or (B) an I-Statement

Quantifier	Subject	Relationship	Predicate
Some	{Shoes (particularly these)}	Are	{Shoes (or articles of clothing) that are way too tight}

14. This one may be done as either an E - or an A - Statement:

(A) an E-Statement

Quantifier	Subject	Relationship	Predicate
No	{Parking}	Is	{An activity allowed here}

or (B) an A-Statement

Quantifier	Subject	Relationship	Predicate
All	{Parking}	Is	{An activity which is not allowed here}

15.* Again, this one is possible several ways:

(A) an A-Statement	Quantifier All	Subject {ACME Industries}	Relationship Is	Predicate {A company that does not make the strongest widgets in the bus.}

or (B) an E-Statement	Quantifier No	Subject {Acme Industries}	Relationship Is	Predicate {A company that makes the strongest widgets in the bus}

(C)   Assuming there are other companies named ACME Industries, it may be possible to make this an I-Statement:

I-Statement	Quantifier Some	Subject {ACME Industries}	Relationship Is	Predicate {A company that does not make the strongest widgets in the bus}

(A) and (B) are better answers, for the most part.

16. A-Statement	Quantifier All	Subject {Sausage and peppers}	Relationship Is	Predicate {A wonderful Italian dish}

17.* I-Statement	Quantifier Some	Subject {Sausage and peppers}	Relationship Is	Predicate {A dish that is ready now}

18. O-Statement	Quantifier Some	Subject {Most intelligent and sensitive doctors}	Relationship Are Not	Predicate {Board-certified doctors}

19.* I-Statement	Quantifier Some	Subject {People I know}	Relationship Are	Predicate {People who attended the opening-day ceremonies at the stadium}

20. A Statement

Quantifier	Subject	Relationship	Predicate
All	{Dogs with long hair}	Are	{Animals that stay warm in winter}

(If we were only talking about "Most" or "Some" of them, then of course this would be an I-Statement. The only thing that would have to change would be the quantifier, from "All" to "Some.")

21.* O-Statement

Quantifier	Subject	Relationship	Predicate
Some	{People}	Are Not	{People who walk ten miles to school uphill in the snow anymore}

22. I-Statement

Quantifier	Subject	Relationship	Predicate
Some	{Examples here}	Are	{Things that have been exaggerated for heuristic purposes}

Answers to Exercises on Pages 131 and 132

Level A

1. * A *categorical statement* is a proposition which has been recast (without change of meaning) into a standard form which consists of a quantifier (all, some, or no), followed by a class term, then followed by a verb expressing the relationship (is included in or is excluded from), and finally followed by a predicate class term.
   A *categorical syllogism* is a two premise, one conclusion argument in which each of the statements is or has been recast in Standard Categorical Form.

2. * The Universal Categorical Statements in Standard Form are the A-Statements and the E-Statements.
   The Affirmative (or Positive) Forms are the A-Statements and the I-Statements.

3. * The Particular Categorical Statement Forms are the I-Statements and the O-Statements.
   The Negative Forms are the E-Statements and O-Statements.

4. * The three legitimate quantifiers are All, No, and Some

5. * When a term is *distributed*, it is quantified by the terms "All" or "No" insofar as we are alluding to each and every member of the class in question. *Undistributed Terms* are classes which are quantified by the term "Some" and are classes in which we are only referring to one or more of the members, but not necessarily to all of them.

6. * In Standard Categorical Form:

Negative Statements (E- and O-Forms) have Distributed Predicate Terms.

Universal Statements (A- and E-Forms) have Distributed Subject Terms.

7. *   The *Fallacy of Faulty Exclusions* is a violation of Rule Two of the Rule Method for Evaluating Categorical Syllogisms: this rule requires that there be the exact same number of Negative statements in the premises as there are Negative statements in the conclusion. So, in other words, a valid categorical syllogism will have either NO E- or O-Statements at all or one E- or O-Statement in the premise and one in the conclusion.

8. *   The *Four Terms Fallacy* is the violation of Rule One which requires that there be three and exactly three class terms each occurring twice with precisely the same meaning in each case.

9. *   The *Fallacy of Illicit Distribution* is the violation of Rule Three (B) which requires that any term which is distributed in the conclusion must also be distributed in the premise in which it occurs.

10. *   The *Fallacy of the Undistributed Middle Term* is the violation of Rule Three (A) requiring that the middle term, the one occurring in both of the premises and not in the conclusion, be distributed at least once.

11. *   The *Existential Fallacy* is a violation of the Corollary to Rule One, requiring that in syllogisms having two Universal (A- or E-Form) Statements in the premises and a Particular (I- or O-Form) Statement in the conclusion, one must examine each of the three classes to make sure that there is in fact in existence at least one member of the class. If any one of the classes is found to be empty or questionable, the Existential Fallacy is committed. If there are members of each class, the Rule is not violated.

12. *   *Proper Names and Singular Terms* in Categorical Syllogisms are to be treated as class terms which have one and only one member (unless, of course, they are a conjunction of proper names). Usually, these terms are quantified by a Universal "All" or "No," because we are referring to the entirety of that individual.

Level B

1. *

			D			U
P-1:	A	All Economic Theories		are		Theories About Humans in Society

			U		U
P-2:	I	Some Philosophical Theories	are		Theories About Humans in Society

---

			U		U
C:	I	Some Philosophical Theories	are		Economic Theories

> **MISTAKE BOX**
> Rule 1: ok
> Rule 2: ok   Invalid Argument:
> Rule 3(A): X   Undistributed Middle Term
> Rule 3(B): ok   (Theories About Human Beings in Society)
> Cor: ok

2.

			U		U		PITPS = People in the Political Spotlight
P-1:	I	Some	PITPS	are	PWCNTTT		PWCNTT = People Who Can Not Tell the Truth

			D		U		L = Liars
P-2:	A	All	PWCNTTT	are	L		

			U		U
C:	I	Some	L	are	PITPS

> **MISTAKE BOX**
> Rule 1: ok
> Rule 2: ok   **VALID ARGUMENT!**
> Rule 3(A): ok
> Rule 3(B): ok
> Cor: ok

3. *

			D		D
P-1:	E	No	Traffic Cops	are	One-Armed People

			U		D
P-2:	O	Some	V.P. Candidates	are not	One-Armed People

_____

			U		D
C:	O	Some	V.P. Candidates	are not	Traffic Cops

```
MISTAKE BOX
Rule 1:  ok
Rule 2:  X              INVALID ARGUMENT
Rule 3(A):  ok          Faulty Exclusions:
Rule 3(B):  ok          Three E/O Statements
Cor:  ok                Violates Rule Two
```

4.

			D		U
P-1:	A	All Persons Who Can Run A 3-Min. Mile		are	Potential Oly. GMWs

			D		U
P-2:	A	All Potential Oly. GMWs		are	Persons WW Make a Fortune in A.E.

_____

			U		U
C:	I	Some Pers. WW Make a Fortune in A.E.		are	Pers. Who C. Run 3-M M.

```
MISTAKE BOX
Rule 1:  ok
Rule 2:  ok
Rule 3(A):  ok          INVALID ARGUMENT:
Rule 3(B):  ok          EXISTENTIAL FALLACY
Cor:  X                 One of the classes—
                        "People who can run a 3 minute
                        mile" is an empty class.
```

5. *

			D		U
P-1:	A	All	Multigrain Cereals	are	Important Fiber Sources

			U		D
P-2:	O	Some	Kinds of Fruit	are not	Important Fiber Sources

_____

			D		U
C:	A	All	Multigrain Cereals	are	Kinds of Fruit

MISTAKE BOX
Rule 1: ok (MGC's, IFS's, and Kinds of Fruit)
Rule 2: X (only one E or O Statement)
Rule 3A: ok (IFS is dist at least once)
Rule 3B: ok (MGC is dist in Conc & in P-1)
Cor: ok

INVALID ARGUMENT:
FAULTY EXCLUSIONS,
(Only one E or O Statement in the
argument)

6.

			U		D	Key:
P-1:	O	Some	ADs	are not	LDs	AD = Automobile Drivers
			U		U	LD = Licensed Drivers
P-2:	I	Some	LDs	are	PWHNHAA (People who have never had an accident)	

			U		D
C:	O	Some	ADs	are not	PWHNHAA

MISTAKE BOX
Rule 1: ok (ADs, LDs, and PWHNHAA)
Rule 2: ok (one O in P-1, and one) in Conc)
Rule 3A: ok (Middle Term, LDs, is dist in P-1)
Rule 3B: X (PWHNHAA is dist in conc, not in P)
Cor: ok

INVALID ARGUMENT
ILLICIT DISTRIBUTION:
PWHNHAA is distributed in the
Conc., but not in P-2.

7. *

			U		U
P-1:	I	Some	ADs	are	LDs
			U		D
P-2:	O	Some	LDs	are not	PWHNHAA

			U		D
C:	O	Some	ADs	are not	PWHNHAA

MISTAKE BOX
Rule 1: ok (ADs, LDs, & PWHNHAA)
Rule 2: ok (one O in P-2; O in C)
Rule 3A: X (LDs is not dist)
Rule 3B: ok (PWHNHAA is dist in C
             and in P-2)
Cor: ok

INVALID ARGUMENT:
UNDISTRIBUTED MIDDLE TERM (Licensed
Drivers is not distributed in either premise)

8.

			U		D
P-1:	O	Some	Cigarettes	are not	Things Part. Good For Your Health

			D		U
P-2:	A	All	Cigarettes	are	Tobacco Products

			U		D
C:	O	Some	Tobacco Products	are not	Things Part. Good For Your Health

VALID ARGUMENT!
All Rules Satisfied

MISTAKE BOX
Rule 1: ok (Cigs, ThPartGFYH, and TobProds)
Rule 2: ok (one O-Stmt in P-1, one in Conc)
Rule 3A: ok (cigs is MT, distributed once)
Rule 3B: ok (TPGFYH is dist in conc & in P-1)
Cor: ok

9. *

			D		D
P-1:	E	No	TTTG	are	TGFY

			D		D
P-2:	E	No	TGFY	are	TTYL

Key:
TTTG = Things That Taste Good
TGFY = Things (That Are) Good For You
TTYL = Things That You Like

			D		D
C:	E	No	TTTG	are	TTYL

INVALID ARGUMENT:
FAULTY EXCLUSIONS—
THREE E OR O STATEMENTS

MISTAKE BOX
Rule 1: ok (TTTG, TGFY, and TTYL)
Rule 2: XX (Three E or O Statements!)
Rule 3A: ok (Middle Term, TGFY, is Dist in
                both premises.)
Rule 3B: ok (Both Terms are dist in C & P)
Cor: ok

10.

			U		D
P-1:	O	Some	C	are not	P

			D		U
P-2:	E	No	V	are	P

Key:
C = Cars
V = Vehicles That Have To Be Inspected
P = Pre-1985 Vehicles

			U		D
C:	O	Some	C	are not	V

INVALID ARGUMENT:
FAULTY EXCLUSIONS—
THREE E OR O STATEMENTS
(Violates Rule Two)

MISTAKE BOX
Rule 1: ok (C, V, and P)
Rule 2: X (Three E/O Statements!)
Rule 3A: ok (MidTerm, P, is dist in P-1)
Rule 3B: ok (V is Dist in conc and in P-2)
Cor: ok

11. *   First, put in standard form. Premise 1, "Not every Philosophy Course is a Skills Course," may be read as the negation ("NOT") of the A-Statement, All PC's are SC's. The direct opposite of an A-Statement is, not an E-Statement, but an O-Statement. So, P-1 should be expressed, "Some PC's are not SC's." Premise 2, "It is a Philosophy Course," is a categorical statement and as such is in A-Form: "All Logic Courses are Philosophy Courses." Finally, the Conclusion, "Logic is not a Skills Course," is actually an exclusion, saying that Logic is excluded from the class of Skills Courses. That is an E-Statement: "No Logic Course is a Skills Course."

The key for the classes then is   PC = Philosophy Course,
SC = Skills Course
LC = Logic Course

			U		D
P-1:	O	Some	PC	is not	SC
			D		U
P-2:	A	All	LC	is	PC
			D		D
C:	E	No	LC	is	SC

INVALID ARGUMENT;
UNDISTRIBUTED MIDDLE TERM—
The Class of "Philosophy Courses" is not distributed in either one of the premises.

MISTAKE BOX
Rule 1: ok (L, S, and PD)
Rule 2: ok (one O in P-1, E in Con)
Rule 3A: X (M.T., PC, undist twice!)
Rule 3B: ok (Both terms are dist in C
                    and also in the Prems.)
Cor: ok

12.

			D			D	Key:
P-1:	E	No	IP	are		PWSBCD	IP = Irresponsible People
			U			U	PWSBCD = People Who Should Be
P-2:	I	Some	R	are		IP	Camp Directors
			U			D	R = Republicans
C:	O	Some	R	are not		PWSBCD	

VALID ARGUMENT!
(ALL RULES OK)

MISTAKE BOX
Rule 1: ok (IP, PWSBCD, and R)
Rule 2: ok (E in P-1; O in Conc)
Rule 3A: ok (M.T., IP, is dist in P-1)
Rule 3B: ok (PWSBCD dist in P & C)
Cor: ok

13. * This one may be the subject of serious dispute. There are two distinct ways of doing it.
First:

			D			D	Key:
P-1:	E	No	TS	is		PWWMFOTB	TS = True Scotsman
			D			U	PWWMFOTB = People Who Would
P-2:	A	All	M	is		S	Make Fun of the Bagpipes
							M = Michael
			D			D	S = Scotsman
C:	E	No	M	is		PWWMFOTB	

VALID ARGUMENT:
FOUR TERMS FALLACY,
True Scotsmen, People Who
Would Make Fun Of The
Bagpipes, and Scotsmen

MISTAKE BOX
Rule 1: X (Four Terms: TS, PWWMFOTB, M, and S,
as per above key)
Rule 2: ok (E in Prems & E in Conc)
Rule 3A: ok (M.T. [TS] if any is dist)
Rule 3B: ok (Both dist in Conc & in P)
Cor. ok

The problem here is that some people may want to say that the categories of Scotsmen and
True Scotsmen are one and the same, making this a case of three classes or terms and, hence,
a perfectly valid line of reasoning. For either side of this dispute the arguer should try to show
(A) how the two classes of Scotsmen and True Scotsmen are in fact identical, that you could
not find a member of one class who was not also a member of the other, and conversely, or
(B) how the two classes of Scotsmen and True Scotsmen are actually different because you

can find examples of people who are by birth of Scottish descent (and hence, Scotsmen), but who do not think or act like Scotsmen (and hence are not "True Scotsmen"—whatever that is.)

14.

		D		U
P-1:	A	All AP	are	PWHAVSWOST
		D		U
P-2:	A	All AU	are	PWHAVSWOST

		D		U
C:	A	All AP	are	AU

Key:
AP = Artistic People
PWHAVSWOST = People Who Have A Very Special Way Of Seeing Things
AU - Autistic People

INVALID ARGUMENT:
UNDISTRIBUTED MIDDLE TERM—
"People Who Have A Very Special Way of Seeing Things"

MISTAKE BOX
Rule 1: ok (AP, PWHAVSWOST, and AU)
Rule 2: ok (no E or O Statements)
Rule 3A: X (M.T. undist both times)
Rule 3B: ok (AP is dist in C & in P-1)
Cor: ok

15. *

		D		U
P-1:	A	All PWPTIBO	are	E
		D		U
P-2:	A	All PWPTIOOBTO	are	A

		U		U
C:	I	Some E	are	A

Key:
PWPTIBO = People Who Put Their Interests Before Others
PWPTIOOBTO = People Who Put The Interests Of Others Before Their Own
E = Egoists
A = Altruists

INVALID ARGUMENT:
FOUR TERMS FALLACY, They are (1) People Who Put Their Own Interests First, (2) Egoists, (3) People Who Put The Interests of Others First, and (4) Altruists

MISTAKE BOX
Rule 1: X (Four Terms: PWPTIBO, E, PWPTIOOBTO, and A)
Rule 2: ok (No E or O Statements)
Rule 3A: There is no Middle Term
Rule 3B: ok (No dist terms in Conc)
Cor: ok (Both Prems are univ & C is a particular, BUT each class is known to have at least one member)

16.

			D		U	Key:
P-1:	A	All	TWD	are	TWDW	TWD = Things Worth Doing
			U		D	TWDW = Things Worth Doing Well
P-2:	O	Some	UT	are not	TWD	UT = Useless Tasks

			U		D
C:	O	Some	UT	are not	TWDW

INVALID ARGUMENT:
ILLICIT DISTRIBUTION,
"Things Worth Doing Well" is
distributed in the Conclusion but not
in Premise 1.

```
MISTAKE BOX
Rule 1:  ok (TWD, TWDW, and UT)
Rule 2:  ok (one O in Prem & in Conc)
Rule 3A:  ok (M.T., TWD, is distributed)
Rule 3B:  X (TWDW is dist in conc but not in P-1)
Cor:  ok
```

17. *

			D		D	Key:
P-1:	E	No	IS	are	GA	IS = Invalid Syllogisms
			D		D	GA = Good Arguments
P-2:	E	No	TAR	are	IS	TAR = True Act of Reasoning

			D		D
C:	E	No	TAR	are	GA

INVALID ARGUMENT:
FAULTY EXCLUSIONS, There are Three
Negative Statements Which Violates Rule 2.

```
MISTAKE BOX
Rule 1:  ok (IS, GA, and TAR)
Rule 2:  X (Three E Statements)
Rule 3A:  ok (IS is dist twice)
Rule 3B:  ok (both terms Dist in conc are
                   distributed in prems)
Cor:  ok (all are universal)
```

18.

			D		U	Key:
P-1:	A	All	PBIUS	are	TTAF	PBIUS = People Born In the U.S.
			D		U	TTAF = Things That Are Free
P-2:	A	All	TTAF	are	TTAC	TTAC = Things That Are Cheap

			D		U
C:	A	All	PBIUS	are	TTAC

MISTAKE BOX
Rule 1: Plugged in to a computer this would
probably be ok and look like three terms.
See below for more detailed explanation.
Rule 2: ok (No E or O Statements)
Rule 3A: ok? (TTAF is dist once)
Rule 3B: ok (PBIUS is dist in C & P)
Cor: ok (all universal statements)

This one can be handled in two ways. One, it can be looked upon as a VALID Argument form with a content problem: the Fallacy of EQUIVOCATION, insofar as the word "Free" is used in two different senses, the first of which is "having certain legal rights and liberties" and the second of which is "the absence of any monetary cost." Or, two, it can be seen as a FORMAL Problem consisting of the FOUR TERMS FALLACY, and, hence, we have an Invalid Argument.

19. *

			D		U
P-1:	A	All	TTAL	are	TWMSTM

			D		D
P-2:	E	No	YE	is	TWMSTM

			D		D
C:	E	No	YE	is	TTAL

Key:
TTAL = Things That are Logical
TWMSTM = Things Which Make
Sense To Me
YE = Your Explanation

VALID ARGUMENT!
(All Rules Satisfied)

MISTAKE BOX
Rule 1: ok (exactly 3 terms)
Rule 2: ok (one E in P and one in C)
Rule 3A: ok (TWMSTM is dist once)
Rule 3B: ok (both terms are dist in C
and also in the Prems)
Cor: ok (all statements are universals)

(This one may sound funny. What do you think is wrong with it? Hint: It is probably a content problem with one of the premises.)

20.

			D		U
P-1:	A	All	T	are	PEFTP
P-2:	A	All	D S	are	U USC

			D		U
C:	A	All	S	is	PEFTP

Key:
    T = Taxpayers
    PEFTP = People Eligible For This Pos.
    S = Solomon
    USC = U.S. Citizens

INVALID ARGUMENT:
FOUR TERMS FALLACY—
"Taxpayers", "People Eligible For This
Position", "Solomon", "U.S. Taxpayers"
There is also a violation of Rule 3 (A) insofar
as there is no middle term, so we cannot tell
whether it is distributed or not.

MISTAKE BOX
Rule 1: X (T, PEFTP, S, and USC)
Rule 2: ok (No Negative Stmts at all)
Rule 3A: X (There is NO Middle Term)
Rule 3B: ok (S is dist in the conc and also
                in P-2.)
Cor: ok

21. *

			D		U
P-1:	A	All	CTC	are	BSC
P-2:	E	No	D BSC	are	D WC

			U		D
C:	O	Some	CTC	are not	WC

Key:
    CTC = Critical Thinking Courses
    BSC = Basic Skills Courses
    WC = Worthless Courses

VALID ARGUMENT:
ALL RULES SATISFIED
(Including the Corollary)

MISTAKE BOX
Rule 1: ok (CTC, BSC, and WC)
Rule 2: ok (One neg. in P-2; one in C)
Rule 3A: ok (M.T. is BSC; dist in P-2)
Rule 3B: ok (WC is dist in C; also in P)
Cor: (Both Prems are universals, conc is a
          Particular, BUT, there are CTCs,
          BSCs, and WCs too, so OK.)

22.

			D	**D**		
P-1:	E	No	D	are	E	
			U	U		
P-2:	I	Some	E	are	F	

_____

			U	U	
C:	I	Some	F	are	D

Key:
   D = Didlips
   E = Eables
   F = Foints

INVALID ARGUMENT:
FAULTY EXCLUSIONS—
(Only One E Statement in the whole argument.)

```
MISTAKE BOX
Rule 1:  ok (Didlips, Eables, and Foints)
Rule 2:  X (only one E stmt—none in C)
Rule 3A:  ok (m.T. is Eables; dist in P-1)
Rule 3B:  ok (No term in Conc is dist)
Cor:  ok (Prems have one univ. and one part.)
```

Answers to Exercises on Pages 141 through 143

Level A

1. *   A Circle in a Venn Diagram represents a class or category. Think of it as the boundaries of a set whose members are all inside.

2. *   Venn Diagrams work best in displaying the relationship between three or fewer classes.

3. *   A portion of a Venn Diagram Circle is shaded in to show that there are no members in that particular part of the set.

4. *   The placement of an "X" in an area of a Venn Diagram indicates that there is at least one member known to exist in that region. For example, if there were two overlapping classes, marked S and P, and an "X" were drawn in that overlapping region, the "X" indicates that there is at least one S that is also a P (and, conversely, that there is at least one P that is also an S).

5. *   In a two-term Venn Diagram there are four areas which are represented.
     Let's use two overlapping circles to represent classes S and P.
     Area 1 = an S that is not a P
     Area 2 = an S that is a P
           (and a P that is an S)
     Area 3 = a P that is not an S
     Area 4 = something that is not an S
           or a P

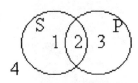

6. *   In a three-term Venn Diagram there are eight areas which are represented. (If you are in doubt see Figure 6.6 on page 135.)

7. *   This must be a typographical error. Otherwise it is analytically FALSE. Even if this one says the premises should be diagrammed before the conclusion, it would still be false because the conclusion is not supposed to be diagrammed at all. Remember that in a valid deductive argument, the conclusion is supposed to be contained in the premises to begin with. In a valid syllogism, then, one need diagram only the premises. The conclusion should already be apparent without having to draw anything.

8. *   True

9. *   False. It exists in one region or the other, but not necessarily in both.

10. *   True. But they will necessarily be invalid because, according to Rule One, a *Valid* Syllogism has exactly three class terms.

Level B

1. In order to facilitate working and understanding the diagram method of testing categorical syllogisms, we have included three diagrams for each problem to show the step-by-step process involved. The first diagram represents the drawing of the first universal premise in the argument. The second diagram represents *both* of the premises diagrammed at the same time. This is how the finished product should look, because the conclusion should already be contained in the premises of a valid deductive argument. The third diagram represents what the conclusion *should look like*.

1. *   Terms: ET = Economic Theories
                    TAHBIS = Theories About Human Beings In Society
                    PT - Philosophical Theories

Diagram 1: All ET are TAHBIS   Diagram 2: All ET are TAHBIS
                                                    and   Some PT are TAHBIS

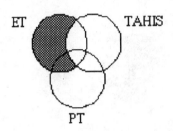   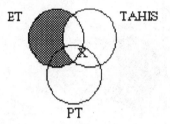

Diagram 3: The Conclusion—Some PT are ET

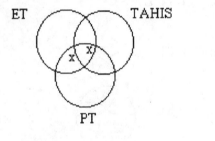   INVALID

Chapter 6

2. Terms: PITPS = People In The Political Spotlight
              PWCNTTT = People Who Can NOT Tell The Truth
              L = Liars

Diagram 1: All PWCNTTT are L   Diagram 2: All PWCNTTT are L
                                                              and Some PITPS are PWCNTTT

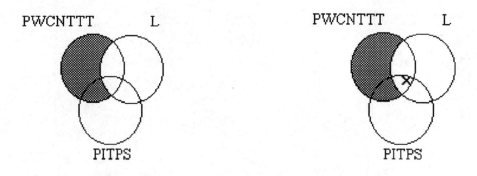

Diagram 3: The Conclusion—Some L are PITPS

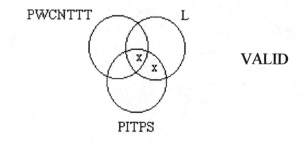   VALID

3. *   Terms: TC = Traffic Cops
                  OAP = One-Armed People
                  VPC = Vice Presidential Candidates

Diagram 1: No TC are OAP   Diagram 2: No TC are OAP
                                                     and Some VPC are not OAP

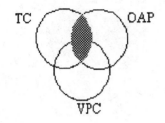   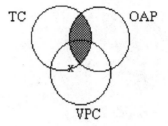

Diagram 3: The Conclusion—Some VPC are not TC

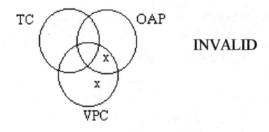   **INVALID**

4. Terms: PWCRATMM = People Who Can Run A Three Minute Mile
               POGMW = Potential Olympic Gold Medal Winner
               PWWMAFIAE = People Who Will Make A Fortune In Advertising Endorsements

Diagram 1: All PWCRATMM are POGMW   Diagram 2: All PWCRATMM are POGMW
                                                        and All POGMW are PWWMAFIAE

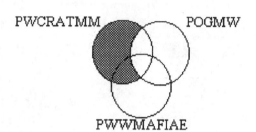

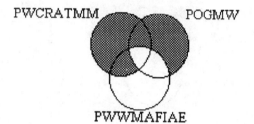

Diagram 3: The Conclusion—Some PWWMAFIAE are PWCRATMM

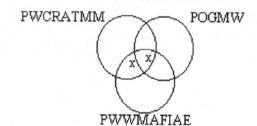

INVALID

5. *   Terms: MGC = MultiGrain Cereals
                  IFS = Important Fiber Sources
                  KOF = Kinds Of Fruit

Diagram 1: All MGC are IFS

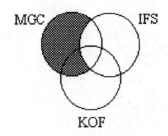

Diagram 2: All MGC are IFS
          and   Some KOF are not IFS

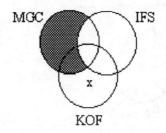

Diagram 3: The Conclusion—All MGC are KOF

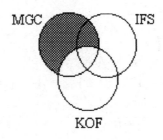

INVALID

Chapter 6

6. Terms: AD = Automobile Drivers
              LD = Licensed Drivers
              PWHNHAA = People Who Have Never Had An Accident

Diagram 1: Some AD are not LD

Diagram 2: Some AD are not LD
                   and   Some LD are PWHNHAA

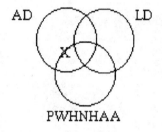

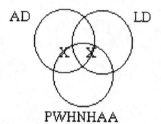

Diagram 3: The Conclusion—Some AD are not PWHNHAA

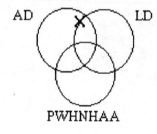

INVALID

7. *   Terms: AD = Automobile Drivers
                    LD = Licensed Drivers
                    PWHNHAA = People Who Have Never Had An Accident

Diagram 1: Some AD are LD   Diagram 2: Some AD are LD
                                                     and Some LD are not PWHNHAA

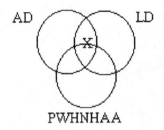

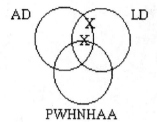

Diagram 3: The Conclusion—Some AD are not PWHNHAA

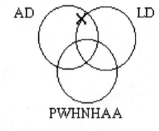   **INVALID**

Chapter 6

8. Terms: C = Cigarettes
        TPGFYH = Things Particularly Good For Your Health
        TP = Tobacco Products

Diagram 1: All C Are TP

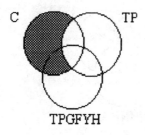

Diagram 2: All C Are TP
          and Some C Are Not TPGFYH

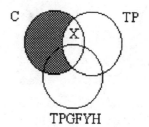

Diagram 3: The Conclusion—Some TP are not TPGFYH

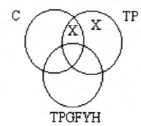

VALID

9. *   Terms: TTTG = Things That Taste Good
                    TTAGFY = Things That Are Good For You
                    TTYL = Things That You Like

Diagram 1: No TTTG Are TTAGFY   Diagram 2: No TTTG Are TTAGFY
                                                    and   No TTAGFY Are TTYL

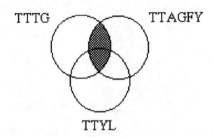   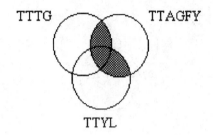

Diagram 3: The Conclusion—No TTTG Are TTYL

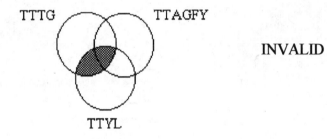   INVALID

125

10.   Terms: C=Cars
                 VTHTBI = Vehicles That Have To Be Inspected
                 PV = Pre-1985 Vehicles

Diagram 1: No VTHTBI Are PV

Diagram 2: No VTHTBI Are PV
            and   Some C Are Not PV

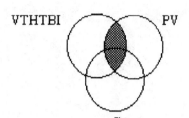

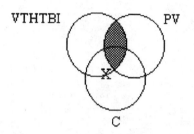

Diagram 3: The Conclusion—Some C Are Not VTHTBI

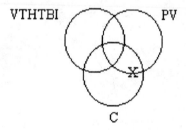

INVALID

11. *   Terms: PC = Philosophy Courses
                 SC = Skills Courses
                 LC = Logic Courses

Diagram 1: All LC Are PC

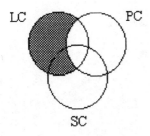

Diagram 2: All LC Are PC
        and   Some PC Are Not SC

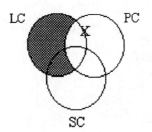

Diagram 3: The Conclusion—No LC Are SC

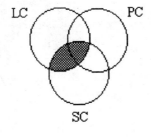

INVALID

Chapter 6

12.　Terms:　IP = Irresponsible People
　　　　　　　PWSBCD = People Who Should Be Camp Directors
　　　　　　　R = Republicans

Diagram 1:　No IP Are PWSBCD   Diagram 2:　No IP Are PWSBCD
　　　　　　　　　　　　　　　　　　　　　　　　　　　　　and　Some R Are IP

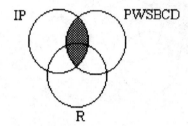   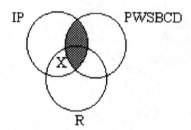

Diagram 3:　The Conclusion—Some R Are Not PWSBCD

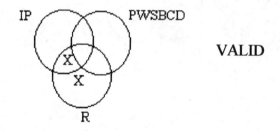   VALID

13. * If True Scotsmen and Scotsmen are two different classes then this one is invalid because of the FOUR TERMS FALLACY. To draw it would look something like Diagram 1. If True Scotsmen and Scotsmen are taken to be identical class terms in the final analysis, then the argument is a valid one as shown in Diagrams 2 through 4:

Diagram 1:
   TS = True Scotsmen
   PWWMFOTB = People Who Would Make
                       Fun Of The Bagpipes
   M = Michael
   S = Scotsman

Diagram 2:
   TS = S = True Scotsmen
   PWWMFOTB = People Who would
                       Make Fun Of The Bagpipes
   M = Michael

   No   TS Are PWWMFOTB

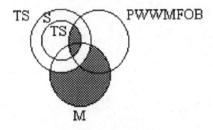

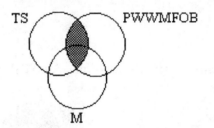

Diagram 3:   No TS Are PWWMFOTB
               All M Is TS

Diagram 4:   The Conclusion—
               No M Is PWWMFOTB

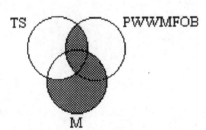

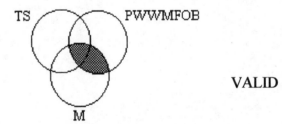

VALID

14.   Terms: ARP = Artistic People
       PWHAVSWOST = People Who Have A Very Special Way Of Seeing Things
       AUP = Autistic People

Diagram 1: All ARP Are PWHAVSWOST   Diagram 2: All ARP Are PWHAVSWOST
                                               and   All AUP Are PWHAVSWOST

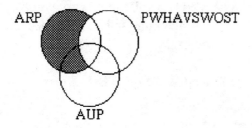   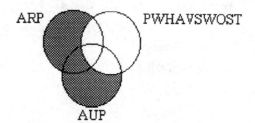

Diagram 3: The Conclusion—All ARP Are AUP

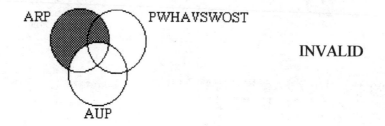

INVALID

15. *   Terms: PWPTIBO = People Who Put Their Interests Before Others
                    E = Egoists
                    PWPTIOOBTO = People Who Put The Interests Of Others Before Their Own
                    A = Altruists

Diagram 1: All PWPTIBO Are E   Diagram 2: All PWPTIBO Are E
                                                    and   All PWPTIOOBTO Are A

A FOUR TERM DIAGRAM CANNOT ADEQUATELY
BE DIAGRAMMED USING THE VENN TECHNIQUE.

Diagram 3: The Conclusion—Some E Are A

For example:

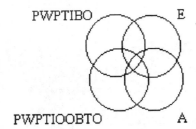

This diagram is incomplete for it leaves out two possibilities: (1) something that is in the classes of PWPTIBO and A, but not in the classes of PWPTIOOBTO and E; and (2) something being included in E and PWPTIOOBTO but excluded from PWPTIBO and A.

Chapter 6

16.   Terms: TWD = Things Worth Doing
                 TWDW = Things Worth Doing Well
                 ULT = Useless Tasks

Diagram 1: All TWD Are TWDW   Diagram 2: All TWD Are TWDW
                                          and   Some UT Are Not TWD

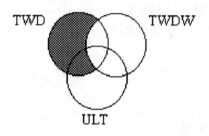   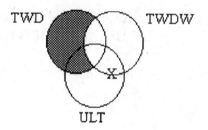

Diagram 3: The Conclusion—Some ULT Are Not TWDW

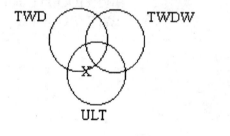   INVALID

17. *   Terms: IS = Invalid Syllogisms
                    SA = Sound Arguments
                    TAOR = True Act Of Reasoning

Diagram 1: No IS Are SA

Diagram 2: No IS Are SA
            and   No TAOR Is IS

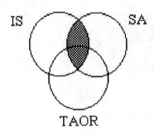

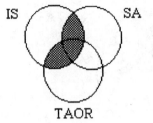

Diagram 3: The Conclusion—No TAOR Is SA

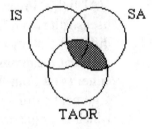

INVALID

133

Chapter 6

18.   Terms: PBIUS = People Born In The United States
                    TTAF = Things That Are Free
                    TTAC = Things That Are Cheap

Diagram 1: All PBIUS Are TTAF   Diagram 2: All PBIUS Are TTAF
                                                            and   All TTAF Are TTAC

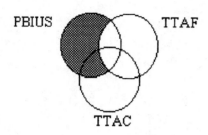   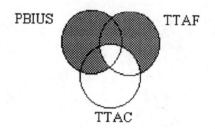

Diagram 3: The Conclusion—All PBIUS Are TTAC

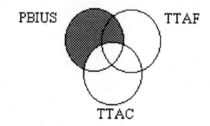

VALID! (However, if TTAF is a term that is
used with two different meanings in the two
different statements, or if TTAC has two
different meanings, or both, then we have
either (a) 2 Four Terms Fallacy, or (b) a valid
argument form with an Equivocation Fallacy,
which is a content problem.)

19. *   Terms: TTAL = Things That Are Logical
                    TTMSTM = Things That Make Sense To Me
                    YE = Your Explanation

Diagram 1: All TTAL Are TTMSTM

Diagram 2: All TTAL Are TTMSTM
            and   No YE Is TTMSTM

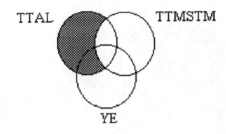

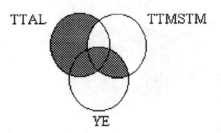

Diagram 3: The Conclusion—No YE Is TTAL

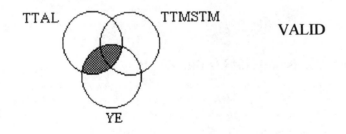

VALID

135

20.   Terms: T = Taxpayers
                   PEFTP = People Eligible For This Position
                   USC = U.S. Citizens
                   S = Solomon

Diagram 1: All T Are PEFTP

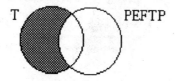

Diagram 2: All T Are PEFTP
            and   All S Is USC

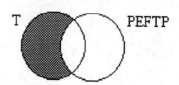

Where to draw the next two classes:

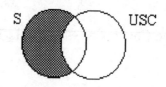

Diagram 3: The Conclusion—All S Is PEFTP

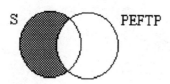

INVALID: Four Terms Fallacy

21. *   Terms: CTC = Critical Thinking Courses
                   BSC = Basic Skills Courses
                   WC = Worthless Courses

Diagram 1: All CTC Are BSC

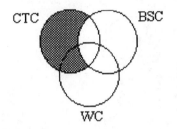

Diagram 2: All CTC Are BSC
            and   No BSC Are WC

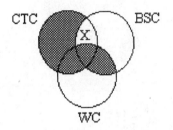

Diagram 3: The Conclusion—Some CTC Are Not WC

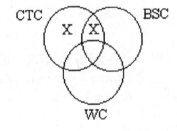

VALID: (Since there actually are
members of CTC, BSC, and WC)

Chapter 6

22.　　Terms:　　D = Didlips
　　　　　　　　E = Eables
　　　　　　　　F = Foints

Diagram 1: No D Are E

Diagram 2: No D Are E
　　　　　　　and　Some E Are F

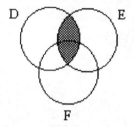

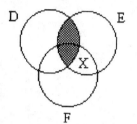

Diagram 3: The Conclusion—Some F Are D

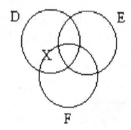

INVALID: (Note that the conclusion,
"Some F's are not D's," would be validly
drawn here.)

TEST BANK

Multiple Choice Questions

1. A Categorical syllogism having an affirmative (positive) conclusion
   A. cannot be valid unless the conclusion is a universal statement.
   B. may be valid if one of the premises is a negative statement.
   C. must have its middle term distributed in both premises.
   D. cannot be valid unless it has a negative statement in the premises.
   E. None of the above.
   F. Both A and C above.

   ANSWER: E

2. If a categorical syllogism has a negative conclusion, it
   A. cannot be valid unless it has one and only one negative premise.
   B. cannot be valid, at all.
   C. must have a particular statement in the conclusion.
   D. can be valid only if both premises are universal statements.
   E. Both A and D above.

   ANSWER: A

3. In a categorical syllogism, when both of the premises are universal statements and the conclusion is a particular statement,
   A. the Existential Fallacy is always committed.
   B. the argument can be valid as long as one of the premises is a negative statement.
   C. the argument can be valid as long as each of the classes is known to have at least one member.
   D. the argument cannot be made valid without obverting at least one of the statements.
   E. None of the above.

   ANSWER: C

4. A categorical syllogism with two particular statements as premises
   A. cannot be made valid at all.
   B. can be valid, but only if the conclusion is a particular statement.
   C. can be valid, but only if the conclusion is a universal statement.
   D. can be valid, but only if the conclusion is a negative statement.
   E. can be valid, but only if the conclusion is an affirmative statement.

   ANSWER: A

5. The statement "Some A's are B's"
   A. implies the statement "Some A's are not B's."
   B. implies that there really are A's and B's.
   C. does not imply anything in ordinary language, although it does in categorical logic.
   D. has at least one distributed term in the subject or predicate position.
   E. Both A and C above.

   ANSWER: B

6. A categorical syllogism with two universal, affirmative premises
   A. automatically has its middle term distributed at least once.
   B. will always generate a validly drawn conclusion.
   C. must be known to have a member of each of the classes involved.
   D. does not imply anything about the existence of members of the classes.
   E. cannot generate a validly drawn conclusion.

   ANSWER: D

7. In a valid categorical syllogism, when one of the premises is an E-Statement,
   A. the middle term will automatically be distributed at least once.
   B. the conclusion will have to be a universal, affirmative statement.
   C. the other premise will have to be an affirmative statement.
   D. the conclusion cannot have any distributed terms in it.
   E. Both A and C above.

   ANSWER: E

Questions 8 through 10 concern the following problem:

GIVEN: All O's are D's
          No R's are D's
          Some D's are A's
          Some N's are O's
          Some A's are R's

8. Given the truth of the above statements, which of the following must be true?
   A. Some N's are D's.
   B. Some O's are not N's.
   C. Some A's are N's.
   D. Some R's are not A's.
   E. Some O's are A's.

ANSWER: A

9. If all N's are A's, which of the following can be inferred?
    A. Some R's are N's.
    B. All A's are D's.
    C. Some O's are A's.
    D. All R's are D's.
    E. Some R's are O's.

ANSWER: C

10. If all T's are O's, which of the following is NOT possible?
    A. All T's are A's.
    B. Some T's are D's.
    C. All T's are N's.
    D. No T's are A's.
    E. No T's are D's.

ANSWER: E

Putting Ordinary Language in Standard Categorical Form

For each of the statements below numbered 11 through 20, rephrase them in standard categorical form, making sure to show the quantifier, the subject and predicate classes exactly, and the relationship. Also, show the distribution for each of the terms involved.

11. Quite a number of people watched the State of the Union Address.

    ANSWER: U   U
        Some [people] are [those who watched the State of the Union Address]

12. *Things Fall Apart* is a great book.

    ANSWER: D   U
        All (of) [*Things Fall Apart*] is [a great book]

13. Only an expert systems analyst could run such a program.

    ANSWER: D   U
        All [persons who could run such a program] are [expert systems analysts]

14. Nothing that comes easy is truly appreciated.

141

ANSWER: D   D

No [Thing that comes easy] is [a thing that is truly appreciated]

15. Not every resort had a significant snowfall yesterday.

ANSWER: U   D

Some [resorts] are not [places that had significant snowfalls yesterday]

16. Bean burritos are healthier for you than cheese enchiladas are.

ANSWER: D   U

All [bean burritos] are [a food that is healthier for you than cheese enchiladas are]

(A case can be made for seeing this one as an I-Statement because, while this is probably true for most bean burritos, it may not be true for all of them, but only for some of them.)

17. If you love jazz, then you will love Gato's new CD.

ANSWER: D   U

All [those who love jazz] are [those who will love Gato's new CD]

18. Just about every piece of art in the Uffizi is a priceless masterpiece.

ANSWER: U   U

Some [pieces of art in the Uffizi] are [priceless masterpieces]

19. Most post War novels do not have much depth.

ANSWER: U   D

Some [post War novels] are not [works that have much depth]
(or it could be done)
               U   U

Some [post War novels] are [works that do not have much depth]

20. Where there is a will there is a way. (difficult!)

ANSWER: D   U

All [times there is a will] are [times there is a way]

Extra Credit Problem: We will meet next Tuesday unless it snows.

ANSWER: D   U
      All [non-snowing next Tuesdays] are [days we will meet]

Evaluating Categorical Syllogisms

Take each of the five arguments below, put it into standard form and test it for validity, using the Rule Method. If it is invalid, show why. If you only put down whether it is valid or invalid and don't say anything else, even if you are correct, you will get only partial or no credit. Als, if the only thing you can find wrong with the argument is that it seems to have four terms, be real sure that you are being fair to the argument, and be sure that you state *exactly* what the four terms are.

21. Most of this November's election winners are not Democratic candidates. Natty Bumpo is a Democratic candidate. Therefore, Natty Bumpo is not one of this November's election winners.

     ANSWER: Invalid: violates Rule 3(B), Illicit Distribution of the class of "This November's Election Winners"

22. Nothing that is doubtful is certain. Some propositions are doubtful. Therefore, some propositions are certain.

     ANSWER: Invalid: violates Rule 2, Faulty Exclusions because there is only one E or O Statement in the argument.

23. Anything that makes sense is logical. But, this test is not logical. That's why this test does not make sense.

     ANSWER: Valid Argument: all the rules are met
                       The classes are   (1) things that make sense
                                        (2) things that are logical
                                        (3) this test

24. Monika and Jameel must have an excellent relationship because they have no trouble communicating with each other and all those who have an excellent relationship have no trouble communicating with each other.

     ANSWER: Invalid: violates Rule 3(A), Undistributed Middle Term, "People who have no trouble communicating with each other"

25. You are bound to make the swimming team, because only excellent swimmers will make the swimming team and you're definitely an excellent swimmer.

> ANSWER: Invalid: violates Rule 3(A), Undistributed Middle Term, "Excellent swimmers." (Many will miss the translation of the premise, "only excellent swimmers will make the swimming team"—which should be "All those who make the swimming team are excellent swimmers."

26. Male students who make poor grades need to study more than women do. And, Bo is a male student who makes poor grades. Therefore, he needs to study more than he needs women.

> ANSWER: Invalid: violates Rule 1, Four Terms Fallacy: classes are
> (1) Bo
> (2) Male Students Who Make Poor Grades
> (3) People Who Need To Study More Than Women Do
> (4) People Who Need To Study More Than They Need Women

27. This piece of sculpture cannot be a work of the artist, Moore, because it is done in plaster and Moore only worked in bronze and stone.

> ANSWER: Valid Argument: all the rules are met
> The classes are (1) this piece of sculpture
> (2) works done by the artist, Moore
> (3) pieces of sculpture done in bronze or stone
> Note: This will require you to retranslate the premise that states "All of this piece of sculpture is a work done in plaster" to "None of this piece of sculpture is a piece done in bronze or stone" (Otherwise they will come up with four terms and faulty exclusions.)

28. No one who didn't study hard for this test will do well on it. But, all people who do well on this test will do well on the next test too. Thus, no people who didn't study hard for this test will do well on the next test.

> ANSWER: Invalid: violates Rule 3(B), Illicit Distribution of the class of "Those Who Will Do Well On The Next Test"

29. All A's are B's. Some A's are not C's. So, some of the C's are not B's.

> ANSWER: Invalid: violates Rule 3(B), Illicit Distribution of the class of B's.

30. No A's are B's. Some A's are not C's. So, some of the B's are not C's.

> ANSWER: Invalid: violates Rule 2, Faulty Exclusions because there are three negative (E- or O-Form) statements.

Diagramming Categorical Syllogisms

For questions 31 through 40, go back through the exercises 21 through 30 and diagram each of the arguments using the Venn (or the Euler) Method.

Essay Questions

41. Explain the concept of *distribution*. What is its significance for categorical reasoning and syllogistic logic?

42. What are some of the crucial differences in syllogistic reasoning between the universal quantifiers "all" and "no" and the particular quantifier "some?"

43. What is indicated by the placement of an "X" in the Venn Diagram method of testing for the validity of categorical syllogisms?

44. What is meant by an "empty class" and how does it affect syllogistic thinking if at all?

45. Class thinking and categorical logic require us to break the world down into definite classes of objects, events, and ideas. The ability to distinguish is also the ability to discriminate. What do you take to be the principal strengths and weaknesses in this way of thinking and *why* do you think so?

Chapter 7

The Syllogism Refined

CHAPTER OUTLINE

7.1 Immediate Inferences
Exercises
7.2 Enthymemes and Sorites
Summary
Exercises
Case Study

KEY TERMS

Contradictions - Two statements with the same subject and predicate, one of which must be true and the other false. Categorical contradictions are either A-Form versus O-Form or E-Form versus I-Form.

Contraries - Two statements with the same subject and predicate, one A-Form and the other E-Form, both of which cannot be true at the same time but which may both be false.

Conversion - Switching the subject and predicate terms of a categorical statement while preserving the truth of the original statement.

Enthymeme - A syllogism missing a premise or a conclusion.

Immediate Inference - A conclusion drawn from a single statement, or the drawing of such a missing conclusion.

Mediate Inference - A conclusion such as that of a syllogism reached by connecting two of the terms through a third or "mediate" term that bridges the gap or links the two previous terms.

Obversion - Changing affirmatives to

negatives or negative statements to affirmative ones while preserving the truth of the original statement.

Sorites - An argument composed of a string of categorical syllogisms with the conclusion of one becoming a premise for the next. Because sorites usually do not state the implied conclusions, they are also examples of enthymemes.

Square of Opposition - A diagram or figure showing the truth-relationships between different forms of the same categorical statement. One may also use it to determine distribution of the different classes or terms.

Subalterns - Two statements with the same subject and predicate classes, one of which is a universal statement (A- or E-Form), the other of which is a particular statement (I- or O-Form). If the universal statement is known to be true, and the classes are known to contain at least one member, then the particular statement must also be true.

Subcontraries - Two statements with the same subject and predicate classes, one of which is an I-Form and one of which is an O-Form, both of which may turn out to be true, but both of which cannot turn out to be false, unless the classes turn out to be empty ones.

OVERVIEW

Step Six of the Technique concerns evaluating the structure or form of an argument in terms of its validity. That is, do the premises of the argument absolutely and unequivocally guarantee the truth of the conclusion? In order to deepen the discussion of one method for evaluating the form of an argument and that began in Chapter Six, the Categorical Syllogism, Chapter Seven proceeds to open up a range of possibilities not considered previously.

This seems to be a point at which many students become lost. Whereas they can generally grasp the algorithms of evaluating categorical syllogisms when all of the parts are given, they find themselves at sea when it comes to recognizing what is missing. We have tried to come up with a number of techniques to facilitate this, yet experience seems to bear out that there is little substitute for practice.

So, we begin by explaining what an immediate inference is—namely, the drawing of a conclusion or implication from a single premise or statement. While this may be helpful in any number of areas, we focus in on those that are most relevant in the realm of categorical reasoning. First, the Square of Opposition provides an overall reference point for reminding us of which statement forms are compatible or incompatible with which other statement forms. It helps us visualize which forms are contradictory to one another and which ones are contrary to each other. Subcontraries, statements which can both be true at the same time but which cannot both be false at the same time are also illustrated. The relationship of subalternation and superalternation may also be shown on the square. In fact, one may use it as a reminder of which terms are distributed and which terms are undistributed in each of the four forms of categorical statements.

We proceed to fill in the blanks by looking in depth at three forms of immediate inference:

1. Inferences from known truth conditions

   For example, when we know that one standard form is false (or true), then we know something else about at least one other form. If we find that it is false, that All A's are B's, then we know immediately that Some A's are not B's.

2. Conversion

   There are occasions when we will need to reverse or switch the subject and the predicate classes of a categorical statement. We may do so preserving the truth value of the original statement, quite easily in the case of I-Form and E-Form statements. O-Form statements cannot be legitimately converted at all. And, A-Form statements may be converted into I-Form statements as long as we know that there are actually members of both the subject and the predicate classes.

3. Obversion

   There are even more occasions when we may need to change the relationship of a categorical statement in order to change or reduce the number of terms in a syllogism. By obverting we can change affirmative statements to negative ones and negative statements to affirmative ones at the same time changing the predicate class to its obverse or complimentary class.

These three forms of inference allow us to handle situations we could not previously handle in Chapter Six. We round out the chapter with a discussion of enthymemes and sorites. Enthymemes are particularly important because they deepen our technique for spotting missing premises (hidden assumptions) and unstated conclusions (implications). And, while sorites may not be as prevalent in ordinary reasoning, they do have a way of popping up in non-standard guises. For example, people do often justify their reasoning in quasi-deductive form, but leave out points that either they feel are obvious and don't bear reiterating, or they do not want to become obvious because they are quite assailable.

One of the most important things you can do with this chapter is to give the students enough examples for them to play with and practice upon until they begin to see the how, the when, and the why, for using immediate inferences.

Chapter 7

SOLUTIONS TO EXERCISE QUESTIONS

Answers to Exercises on Pages 163 through 165

Level A

1. *   An *immediate inference* is the drawing of a necessary conclusion from a single premise. It is called "immediate" because there are no "mediating" terms, such as the middle term in a syllogism, needed to get from one point to the next.

2. *   The statement, "All P's are Q's," would not necessarily imply that "Some P's must be Q's" in the event that there were no such thing as either P's or Q's (in other words that either P or Q or both were an empty class).

3. *   Whenever an E-Statement is known to be false, we know immediately that the I-Form of that statement must be true. We cannot immediately determine whether the A-Form or the O-Form of that statement is either true or false, but we do know that one of them must be true and the other has to be false.

4. *   If the O-Form is true, the A-Form of that same categorical statement must be false, because these two forms are always contradictory.

5. *   The immediate inference of *conversion* is the legitimate form of switching the subject and predicate classes of a categorical proposition. The E-Form and the I-Form Statements may be converted (have their subjects and predicates switched) without changing the Form of the Statement at all. The A-Statements may be converted but with two limitations: (1) they must be known to have at least one member of both the subject and the predicate class, and (2) they must be converted to I-Form Statements. (Just because All A's are B's does not necessarily mean that All B's are A's.) Finally, it must be remembered that the O-Form Statements may not be converted at all.

6. *   The E-Statement and the I-Statement Forms may be converted into the same statement forms—note that the distribution of each of their terms remains the same; that is, in the E-Form, the subject and predicate are both distributed (we are talking about all of the members of each class) and in the I-Statement, both subject and predicate are undistributed both times (since we are only referring to some of the members of each class).

7. *   The immediate inference known as *obversion* is the changing of a categorical statement from positive to negative or negative to positive, with a corresponding change in the predicate class to its obverse or complementary class. All four of the categorical statement forms may be legitimately obverted.

8. *   As mentioned in the preceding answer, any standard form categorical statement may be obverted. This is done by first changing the statement form from affirmative to negative or negative to affirmative. There will be a corresponding change in the quantifier (unless we are dealing with the particular statement forms). The subject term cannot be changed in any way. The predicate class is "obverted" by changing to its complementary class.

9. *   From an A-Statement to the E-Statement:

E No Wizards are People Who Do Not Know Magic
10. * It would remain an E-Statement with changed subject and predicate terms:
E No People Who Know Magic are Wizards

Level B

1. * A. True
   E. False
   I. True (As long as there were persons in attendance and persons carrying wallets.)
   O. False
2. E. True
   A. False
   I. False
   O. True (As long as there were cookies and things made with chocolate chips.)
3. * I. True
   A. ?
   E. False
   O. ?
4. O. True
   A. False
   E. ?
   I. ?
5. * A. True
   E. False
   I. True (As long as there are salespersons and people who meet their quotas.)
   O. False

Try Supposing that the Statement Forms in 6 Through 10 are false:

6. E. False
   A. ?
   I. True
   O. ?
7. * I. False
   A. False
   E. True
   O. True
8. O. False
   A. True
   E. False
   I. True
9. * A. False
   E. ?
   I. ?

O. True
10.   O. False
A. True
E. False
I. True

Converting:

11. *   E-Statement   D   D
      No Skydivers are Sculptors

12.   I-Statement   U   U
      Some Coniferous Things are Trees

13. *   I-Statement   U   U
      Some Lovable Creatures are Kittens

14.   Cannot be converted as an O-Statement. (If you did this one, you had to obvert it first: Some cans are things that are not recyclable. Then you could convert it as an I-Statement to "Some things that are not recyclable are cans.")

15. *   Again, cannot be converted as an O-Statement. As in the previous example, if it were obverted then converted as an I-Statement, the result would be "Some people who do not love modern dance are people who love classical ballet."

16.   E-Statement   D   D
      No Cars That Had Automatic Transmissions Model-T Cars

17. *   Cannot be converted as an O-Statement. But, like numbers 14 and 15 above, this one could be converted AS AN I-STATEMENT (which would involve either retranslating or obverting first).
      I-Statement   U   U
      Some People Who Were Not Admitted Are People Who Came Late To The Theater

18.   I-Statement   U   U
      Some Days I am Extremely Productive are Days I Don't Have To Go To Work

19. *   I-Statement   U   U
      Some Things That Are Good For A Number of Purposes are Handtools

20.   I-Statement   U   U
      Some Things That Seek to Influence The Viewer are TV Commercials

Obverting:

                             D   D
21. *   A becomes E   No Doughnuts are Non-Tasty Treats
                             D   U
22.   E becomes A   All Pterodactyls are Non-Lazy Beasts
                           U   D
23. *   I becomes O   Some Articles of Clothing are not Non-Useless (Useful?) Things
                           U   U
24.   O becomes I   Some Bananas are Unripe Things

25. * A becomes E   No Scientific Experiment is an Unrepeatable Event
D   D

26. E becomes A   All Polluted Cities are Undesirable Habitats
D   U

27. * I becomes O   Some Children are not People Who Were Uncurious
U   D

28. O becomes I   Some Automobiles are Non-Electrically Powered Vehicles
U   U

29. * E becomes A   All People Who Heard the Lecture are People Who Did Not Remain Unmoved
D   U

30. Several ways of working this problem are possible. They all depend upon how this sentence is translated in the first place. If it is taken as an A-Statement (All First Place Blue Ribbons are Things That Were Not Achieved By Everyone), then it becomes an E-Statement. If it is taken as an O-Statement (Some People are not Those Who Achieved Blue Ribbons), then it becomes an I-Statement.

Level C

1. * Key: MB = Mortal Beings;   IMB = ImMortal Beings
       PB = Perfect Beings;   IPB = ImPerfect Beings
       HB = Human Beings;   NHB = NonHuman Beings

		D		U				D		D
A	All	MB	are	IPB	→	obverts to E	No MB	are	non-XPB
E	No	HB	are	IMB	→	obverts to A	All HB	are	non-XMB

		D		U				D		D
A	All	PB	are	NHB	→	obverts to E	No PB	are	non-XHB

```
┌─────────────────────────────────┐        ┌──────────────────────────────────┐
│ MISTAKE BOX #1                  │   →    │ MISTAKE BOX #2                   │
│ Rule 1:  X (6 Terms!)           │        │ Rule 1:  ok (MB, PB, and HB)     │
│ Rule 2:  X (only 1 E/O Stmt)    │        │ Rule 2:  ok (one E in P; one in C)│
│ Rule 3A: X (no Middle Term)     │        │ Rule 3A: ok (MT is MB; dist in P-1)│
│ Rule 3B: X (no PB in prems)     │        │ Rule 3B: ok (both terms in C are dist│
│ Cor:  ok                        │        │                 in the premises) │
│                                 │        │ Cor:  ok (all stmts are universals)│
└─────────────────────────────────┘        └──────────────────────────────────┘
```

VALID ARGUMENT! Meets all Rules

2. Key: R = Residents   NonR = Non-Residents
          C = Citizens   NonC = Non-Citizens
          V = Voters   NonV = Non-Voters

		D		D					D		U
E	No	NonR	are	C	obverts to →	A	All	NonR	are	NonC
		D		U					D		D
A	All	NonC	are NonV	obverts to →	E	No	NonC	are	N~~on-N~~onV

		D		U					D		D
A	All	V	are	R	obverts to →	E	No	V	are	NonR

→

MISTAKE BOX #1
Rule 1: X (Six Terms)
Rule 2: X (only one E Stmt)
Rule 3A: X (No Middle Term)
Rule 3B: X (V is dist in C but
                no V in Prem)
Cor: ok (all stmts are univ.)

MISTAKE BOX #2
Rule 1: ok (Non R, NonC, and V)
Rule 2: ok (one E in Prem, one in C)
Rule 3A: ok (M.T. is NonC, dist in P2)
Rule 3B: ok (both terms dist in C are
                distributed in Premises)
Cor: ok (All stmts are universals)

VALID ARGUMENT! (Note this one could
have been worked many other ways as well;
e.g., it could have been reduced to the terms
V, C, and R.)

3. *   Key: J = Joe   PWF401 = People Who Flunked the 401 Class
              PI402 = People in 402 Class   PWP401 = People Who Passed the 401 Class

	D		U				D		U
A	All PI402	are	PWP401	stays same →	A	All PI402	are		PWP401

	D		D				D		D
E	No J	is	PI402	stays the same →	E	No J	is		PI402

	D		U				D		D	(D)
A	All J	is	PWF401	obverts to →	E	No J	is	PWDNF401	(=? PWP401)

MISTAKE BOX#1
Rule 1: X (Four Terms)
Rule 2: X (Only one E Stmt)
Rule 3A: ok (PI402 is dist, twice)
Rule 3B: ok (Joe is dist in C & in P)
Cor: ok (All are universal Stmts)

→

MISTAKE BOX #2
Rule 1: ok (*See Below for Disc.)
Rule 2: ok (one in P; one in C)
Rule 3A: ok (PI402 is MT, is dist)
Rule 3B: X (Now both terms in C are
          dist, but PWP401 is undist in
          the premise)
Cor: ok (All Ps and C are univs)

INVALID ARGUMENT! Breaks Rules 1 & 2

→ STILL INVALID ARGUMENT!
(Either it breaks Rule 3B as shown above or
there are still 4 terms because "People Who
Did Not Fail 401" is not exactly the same
class as "People Who Passed 401."
*—For instance, there may be someone who
did not take the class or who audited it. They
would be included in the class of
PWDNF401, but not in the class of
PWP401.)

4. The first statement, "It is simply false that all architects are good engineers," is logically equivalent to saying that the A-Statement, All A's are GE's, is false. If the A-Form of a statement is false, then the O-Form must be true. Hence, statement (A) is Some "A's are not GE's." The second statement, "But it is true that they all know something about construction," when put in standard form is "All Architects are People Who Know Something About Construction." The conclusion is given: "Some people who know something about construction are not good engineers." Putting the whole argument together in standard form, we have:

```
                          U                    D
P-1:    O  Some   Architects are not Good Engineers
                          D                            U
P-2:    A  All        Architects are People Who Know Something About Construction
```
_____

```
                              U                                           D
C:      O  Some   People Who Know Something About Construction are not Good Engs
```

MISTAKE BOX
Rule 1: ok (Three Classes: Architects, Good Engineers, and PWKSAC)
Rule 2: ok (One O Statement in Premises and one in the Conclusion)
Rule 3A: ok (Middle Term is Architects; it is distributed in P-2)
Rule 3B: ok (Good Engineers is dist in the conclusion and in P-1)
Cor: ok (One Universal and one particular in the premises)

VALID ARGUMENT! All Rules Met

5. * Key: IFT = Inflammable Things   UST = Unsafe Things
          ST = Safe Things   NET = NonExplosive Things
          ET = Explosive Things   FT = Flammable Things

			D (IFT)		U (UST)				D (IFT)		D (nXnNST)
P-1:	A	All	IFT	are	UST	obverts to →	E	No	IFT	are	nXnNST

			D (ET)		U (FT)				D (ST)		U (FT)
P-2:	A	All	ET	are	FT	stays same →	A	All	ST	are	FT

			D (ST)		U (NET)				D (ST)		D (nXnnXnET)
C:	A	All	ST	are	NET	obverts to →	E	No	ST	are	nXnnXnET

MISTAKE BOX #1
Rule 1: X (6 Terms—see above)
Rule 2: ok (all A-Statements)
Rule 3A: ok or No M.T.?
Rule 3B: ST is dist in Conc, not in P
Cor: ok (All are universals)

→

MISTAKE BOX #2
Rule 1: ok or X (see below)
Rule 2: ok (One E in P-1, one in C)
Rule 3A: ok or No M.T. (see below)
Rule 3B: ok (both terms dist in C
                      are dist in Premises)
Cor: ok (All are universals)

After obversion the argument appears to be "ok," except for the fact that there seem to be four terms. We have seen that "non-non-Explosive Things" is precisely the same class as "Explosive Things." And, "non-unSafe Things" is equivalent to "Safe Things." The problem appears to remain with Flammable Things and Inflammable Things. First, ask yourself: would you rather run into a truck with the label "Flammable Stuff On Board!" or one with the label "Inflammable Stuff On Board!?" Hopefully, you answered, "Neither!" If you look them up in an English dictionary, you will find that both classes have exactly the same meaning: "substances that will catch fire or burn." So there really are only three classes in this argument, and it is a VALID one.

6. Key: TP = This Painting   PBMS = Paintings By the Master Steen
         WCP = Water Color Paintings   PDIO = Paintings Done In Oil

		D	U				D	D
P-1:	A All	TP	is WCP	*obverts to →	E No		TP	is PDIO

		D	U				D	U
P-2:	A All	PMBS	are PDIO	stays same →	A All		PBMS	are PDIO

		D	D				D	D
C:	E No	TP	is PBMS	stays same →	E No		TP	is PBMS

```
MISTAKE BOX #1
Rule 1:  X (Four Terms—TP, WCP,
            PDIO, and PBMS)
Rule 2:  X (Only one E Statement)
Rule 3A:  X (There is no M.T.)
Rule 3B:  ok (Both Terms in C are
            Dist in Premises)
Cor:  ok (All Univ Stmts)
```

→

```
MISTAKE BOX #2
Rule 1:  ok (Three Terms Now—
            TP, PDIO, PMBS)
Rule 2:  ok (One E in C; one
            in P-1)
Rule 3A:  ok (PDIO is dist in
            P-1 now)
Rule 3B:  ok (Both Terms in C
            are Dis. in Prem)
Cor:  ok (All Universals)
```

* Actually this is not so much a process of obversion as it is another process of immediate inference. "Paintings done in oil" is not the obverse class or complementary class of "Watercolor paintings." There could be paintings that are neither. Rather the first premise of the argument relies on an unstated premise to generate another conclusion: (P-1) This Painting is a Water Color Painting. (A-1) No Water Color Paintings are Paintings Done in Oil. Therefore, (C) This Painting is not a Painting Done in Oil. And, it is this conclusion which becomes our new P-1. As long as the assumption is true, this is a VALID argument.

Answers to Exercises on Pages 167 through 169

Level A

1.*   False. Either a Premise *or* a Conclusion may be left out of an enthymeme.
2. *   True. Often, that is why they are left out.
3. *   True. This is a very reliable way of determining exactly what is missing.
4. *   True. And, they have premises or conclusions which are not stated.
5. *   True
6. *   True

7. *   True, with an unstated conclusion that she must not be a good actress.
8. *   True. We are missing the obvious intermediary conclusion that Sam and Sally are persons.
9. *   False. It is an example of an invalid categorical syllogism. But no parts are missing.
10. * False again.

Level B

1. *   Given: (P-1) Andy is a Politician, and (C) He (Andy) is looking out for himself. What is missing is a (P-2) to the effect that Politicians always look out for themselves. To put this in standard form:

			D			U	
(P-1):	A	All	Andy	is	a	Politician	

			D			U	
(Missing P-2):	A	All	Politicians	are	People Who Look Out For Themselves		

			D			U	
(C):	A	All	Andy	is	A	Person Who Is Looking Out For Themselves	

> MISTAKE BOX
> Rule 1: ok (3 Terms - Andy, Politicians, People Who Look Out For Themselves)
> Rule 2: ok (All A-Statements)
> Rule 3A: ok (Middle Term, "Politicians," is distributed in P-2)
> Rule 3B: ok ("Andy" is distributed in the conclusion, and in P-1)
> Cor: ok (All Statements are Universals)

VALID ARGUMENT!

2.   Given: (P-1) This stuff is a natural food; (C) This stuff must be good for us. What is missing is an unstated premise, (P-2), "All natural foods are things that are good for us." In standard form we have the three classes already given: TS = This Stuff; NF = Natural Foods; TTAGFU = Things That Are Good For Us:

			D		U	
(P-1):	A	All	TS	is	NF	

			D		U	
(Missing P-2):	A	All	NF	are	TTAGFU	

			D		U	
(C):	A	All	TS	is	TTAGFU	

VALID ARGUMENT!

> MISTAKE BOX
> Rule 1: ok (3 Terms)
> Rule 2: ok (All A Stmts)
> Rule 3A: ok (M.T. is NF, dist in P-2)
> Rule 3B: ok (TS is dist in C and in P-1)
> Cor: ok (All Universal Stmts)

3. *   Given: (P-1) You just passed that trooper at 90 mph; (C) You are going to get a ticket. Missing here is a premise, (P-2), People Who Pass Troopers at 90 mph are People Who are Going to Get Tickets. This is one way of depicting the three classes (though there are other equally viable ones): Y = You; PWPTA = People Who Pass Troopers At 90 MPH; PWAGTGT = People Who Are Going To Get A Ticket.

```
                        D              U
(P-1):      A   All     Y       are    PWPTA90
                        D              U
(Missing P-2): A All    PWPTA90   are PWAGTGT
_____
                        D              U
(C):        A   All     Y       are    PWAGTGT
```

MISTAKE BOX:
Rule 1: ok (See 3 Cls above)
Rule 2: ok (All A-Stmts)
Rule 3A: ok (MT, PWPTA90 is dist in P-2)
Rule 3B: ok (Y is dist in C and in P-1)
Cor: ok (All Universals)

VALID ARGUMENT!

4.   Given: (P-1) These bushes do not have any thorns; (C) These bushes are not rose bushes. Missing in this case is a premise, (P-2), that all rose bushes have thorns (or that No bushes that do not have thorns are rose bushes). Let's use: TB = These Bushes; RB = Rose Bushes; and BTHT = Bushes That Have Thorns.

```
                        D       D
(P-1):      E   No      TB      are BTHT
                        D       U
(Missing P-2): A All    RB      are BTHT
_____
                        D       D
(C):        E   No      TB      are RB
```

MISTAKE BOX
Rule 1: ok (3 Terms, See Above)
Rule 2: ok (1 E in P; 1 in Conc)
Rule 3A: ok (BTHT is M.T., dist in P1)
Rule 3B: ok (Both terms in C are dist, and both are dist in Ps)
Cor: ok (All Universal Statements)

VALID ARGUMENT!

5. *   Given: (P-1) Dr. K is not listed in the ERP; (C) Dr. K cannot be a reputable teacher. Missing is a premise which could be stated "None of those who are not listed in the ERP are reputable teachers" or "All reputable Teachers are listed in the ERP." Our key will be: DK = Dr. K; RT = Reputable Teachers; and TLIERP = Teachers Listed in the ERP.

			D		D
(P-1):	E	No	DK	is	TLIERP
			D		U
(Missing P-2):	A	All	RT	are	TLIERP

			D		D
(C):	E	No	DK	is	RT

MISTAKE BOX
Rule 1: ok (3 Terms Listed Above)
Rule 2: ok (1 E in P; 1 in Conc.)
Rule 3A: ok (TLIERP is dist in P-1)
Rule 3B: ok (Both terms in Conc are dist, and also in Prem)
Cor: ok (All Universals)

VALID ARGUMENT!

6. Given: (P-1) Vegetarians do not eat BiggaBurgers; and (P-2) This [Burger] is a BiggaBurger. What is missing is an implied but unstated conclusion: (C) Vegetarians will not eat this [Burger]. Key: TB = This Burger; BB = BiggaBurgers; TVWNE = Things Vegetarians Will Not Eat.

			D		U
(P-1):	A	All	BB	are	TVWNE
			D		U
(P-2):	A	All	TB	is	BB

			D		U
(Missing C):	A	All	TB	is	TVWNE

MISTAKE BOX
Rule 1: ok (3 Terms Shown Above)
Rule 2: ok (All A-Statements)
Rule 3A: ok (M.T. is BB, dist in P1)
Rule 3B: ok (TB is dist in C & P2)
Cor: ok (All Stmts are Univsls)

VALID ARGUMENT!

7. * Given: (P-1) The "Journal" is an awful paper, and (P-2) That paper is not the "Journal." If it is being implied that (C) Therefore, that paper is not an awful paper, there may be a problem. The classes or terms are TJ = The "Journal," TP = That Paper, and AP = Awful Papers.

			D		U
(P-1):	A	All	TJ	is	AP
			D		D
(P-2):	E	No	TP	is	TJ

			D		D
(Missing C):	E	No	TP	is	AP

MISTAKE BOX
Rule 1: ok (3 Terms: TJ, TP, and AP)
Rule 2: ok (one E in P and one in C)
Rule 3A: ok (M.T., TJ, is dist twice)
Rule 3B: X (TP is dist in C and in P2 But AP is dist in C, not in P-1)
Cor: ok (all Statements are universal)

INVALID ARGUMENT! Illicit Distribution (of the term "Awful Papers"—in other words, there could be other awful papers besides the Journal)

8.   This one is tougher. We are given: (P-1) A lot of houses are for sale. (C) Interest Rates must be down. We are missing a premise. If we take the phrase "a lot of" in P-1 to mean "Some" as we have been doing a lot of the time, we are going to end up with four terms: (i) houses, (ii) things that are for sale, (iii) interest rates, and (iv) things that are down. What do P-1 and P-2 have in common? Well, for one thing, we are drawing the conclusion that interest rates must be down right now because right now, a lot of houses are for sale. It is the "right now" or time element, or possibly the space element—insofar as we are talking about a particular place—that links the premise with the conclusion. Let's try it this way:

                                   D   U

(P-1): A All   [Right Now] is [A Time A Lot of Houses Are For Sale]

                                    D   U

(Missing P-2): A All   [Times A Lot of Houses Are For Sale]   are   [Times IRAD]

                                   D   U

(C):   A All   [Right Now] is [Time Interest Rates Are Down]

```
MISTAKE BOX
Rule 1:  ok (3 Terms—RN, TALOHAFS, TIRAD
Rule 2:  ok (All A-Statements)
Rule 3A:  ok (M.T. is TALOHAFS, is dist in P-2)
Rule 3B:  ok (Right Now is dist in C and in P-1)
Cor:  ok (All Statements are Universals)
```

VALID ARGUMENT!
Missing P-2

9. *   The conclusion is that it will rain today, based upon the evidence that I just washed my car. The missing premise that would guarantee this otherwise illogical conclusion is probably based upon the Fallacy of Assuming the Cause, but from a strictly formal point of view, it is that "whenever I wash my car, it rains." Putting that argument in standard categorical form, it looks like this—

		D		U
P-1:	A All	Today	is	A Time I Just Washed My Car
		D		U
P-2:	A All	Times I Just Washed My Car Are	Times It Will Rain [UNSTATED]

_____

		D		U
C:	A All	Today	is	A Time It Will Rain

MISTAKE BOX
Rule 1: ok (Today, Times I Washed My Car, Times It will Rain)
Rule 2: ok (No E or O Statements at all)
Rule 3A: ok (Middle Term is "Times I Washed My Car;" Distributed in P-2)
Rule 3B: ok ("Today" is Distributed in Conc. and in P-1)
Cor: ok (All statements are universals)

VALID ARGUMENT! All Rules Satisfied; Missing a Premise as Noted Above

10. The conclusion is that I will get a bad grade in that class based upon the premise that class is a Geology class. This one can be done several ways too. The missing premise is that I always get bad grades in Geology classes. In standard form the argument is—

		D		U
P-1:	A All	This Class Is	A Geology Class
		D		U
P-2:	A All	Geology Classes Are	Classes In Which I Get Bad Grades [UNSTATED]

_____

		D		U
C:	A All	This Class Is	A Class In Which I Will Get A Bad Grade

---

MISTAKE BOX
Rule 1: ok (This Class, Geology Classes, Classes I Get Bad Grades In)
Rule 2: ok (No negative statements at all)
Rule 3A: ok (Middle Term, "Geology Classes," is distributed in P-2)
Rule 3B: ok ("This Class" is distributed in the conclusion and in P-1)
Cor: ok (All statements are universals)

VALID ARGUMENT! All Rules Satisfied; Missing A Premise As Indicated

SORITES

11. * All   Ronnie is a Lawyer
       All   Lawyers are People Who Argue Well
       All   Ronnie is a Person Who Argues Well   (MISSING CONCLUSION)

   All   Ronnie is a Person Who Argues Well
   All   Ronnie is a Person Who Makes A Lot Of Money
   All   People Who Argue Well Are People Who Make A Lot Of Money

Note: The First Argument with the Missing conclusion is a valid line of reasoning. All of the Rules are met. The Second Argument, which begins by using the Missing Conclusion from the first argument is INVALID, because of the Fallacy of Illicit Distribution—People Who Argue Well is distributed in the conclusion but not in Premise 1. It is a kind of Hasty Generalization to assume that because Ronnie argues well and makes a lot of money that everyone who argues well makes a lot of money. Notice also that if the conclusion had been "So, Ronnie makes a lot of money," and the last statement, "Anyone who argues well makes a lot of money," the argument would have been a VALID one.

12.   All   good actors are people who can play any role
      All   Nancy is a good actor
      All   Nancy is a person who can play any role   (MISSING CONCLUSION)

          VALID ARGUMENT

   All   Nancy is a person who can play any role   (From Previous Conclusion)
   All   persons who can play any role are persons who lie well
   All   Nancy is a person who lies well

          VALID ARGUMENT (All Rules Are Satisfied)

13. * All   Times It Rains Are Times The Streets Get Wet
       All   Times The Streets Get Wet Are Times More Accidents Occur
       All   Times It Rains Are Times More Accidents Occur   (MISSING CONCLUSION)

          VALID ARGUMENT

   All   Times It Rains Are Times More Accidents Occur   (From Previous Conclusion)
   All   Times More Accidents Occur Are Times The P.D. Has Much More Work
   All   Times It Rains Are Times The Police Department Has Much More Work

          VALID ARGUMENT

14.　All　Geology Classes Are Classes Requiring Much Memorization
　　　No　Classes Requiring Much Memorization Are Classes I Do Well In
　　　No　Geology Classes Are Classes I Do Well In　(MISSING CONCLUSION)

　　　　VALID ARGUMENT

　　　All　This Particular Geology Class Is A Geology Class
　　　No　Geology Classes Are Classes I Do Well In　(Previous Conclusion)
　　　No　This Particular Geology Class Is A Class I Will Do Well In

　　　　VALID ARGUMENT

15. *　All　Persons Watching Television Are Persons Having Deadened Imaginative Powers
　　　All　Peter Is A Person Having Deadened Imaginative Powers
　　　All　Peter Is A Person Who Watches Too Much Television

　　　　INVALID ARGUMENT:　At Least Two Problems Here—
　　　　(A)　FOUR TERMS FALLACY: Persons Watching Television, Persons Having
　　　　　　　Deadened Imaginative Powers, Peter, and People Who Watch Too Much
　　　　　　　Television. Even if this were rewritten as three terms, it would still be
　　　　(B)　FALLACY OF THE UNDISTRIBUTED MIDDLE TERM: The Class of
　　　　　　　Persons having Deadened Imaginative Powers is the Middle Term and It Is
　　　　　　　Undistributed Both Times

TEST BANK

Multiple Choice Questions

1. The obverse class of "stupid test questions" is
   A. non-stupid test questions
   B. non-non stupid test questions
   C. stupid non-test questions
   D. non-stupid non-test questions
   E. non-stupid non-test non-questions

   ANSWER: A

2. An immediate inference from the statement "it is false that no S's are P's is
   A. All S's are P's
   B. Some S's are not P's
   C. All P's are S's

165

    D. Some P's are S's

    E. No P's are S's either

ANSWER: D

3. An enthymeme is a syllogism with
   A. a missing premise
   B. a missing conclusion
   C. either A or B
   D. neither A nor B
   E. both A and B

ANSWER: C

4. Two statements are said to be contrary when
   A. they contradict one another
   B. one must be true and the other one false; or conversely
   C. both of them can be true but both of them can't be false
   D. both of them can be false but both of them can't be true
   E. none of the above

ANSWER: D

5. The A-Statement "All A's are B's" implies the I-Statement "Some A's are B's"
   A. all the time, just like it says in the Square of Opposition
   B. in ordinary language, but not in Standard Categorical Form
   C. as long as there is at least one A and one B
   D. as long as the middle term is distributed at least once
   E. none of the above

ANSWER: C

6. When the statement "No A's are B's" is converted, the result is
   A. All A's are non-B's
   B. No B's are A's
   C. Some A's are not B's
   D. Some B's are not A's
   E. No non-B's are non-A's

ANSWER: B

7. Suppose the statement "Some A's are not B's" is true. What inference follows from this?

A. All A's are non-B's
B. Some A's are B's
C. Some B's are not A's
D. Some non-B's are A's
E. Either B or C

ANSWER: D

8. Sorites are
   A. a kind of truth-arrangement
   B. a chain of enthymemes with premises or conclusions omitted
   C. invalid forms of argumentation
   D. formal fallacies
   E. none of the above

ANSWER: B

9. In an enthymeme,
   A. either a premise or a conclusion is missing.
   B. you should be able to determine the two classes in the missing statement by observing the classes in the two statements which are given.
   C. it cannot be determined which statement form (A, E, I, or O) is missing simply by looking at the other two statement forms.
   D. it is always possible to make the argument valid.
   E. both A and B above.

ANSWER: E

10. When one converts the categorical statement, "Some A's are not B's," the result is
    A. Some A's are not non-B's
    B. Some B's are not A's
    C. All B's are not some A's
    D. No B's are A's either
    E. This form cannot be validly converted

ANSWER: E

Immediate Inferences

For each statement given below, perform the immediate inference(s) required. Show your work where applicable.

Chapter 7

A. Determine the truth value of the statements below from the truth value of the GIVEN statement:

GIVEN: "It is definitely false that all Alps are Bavarians."

11. No Andes are Bavarians

ANSWER: Undeterminable or ?

12. Some Andes are Bavarians

ANSWER: Undeterminable or ?

13. Some Andes are not Bavarians

ANSWER: True

GIVEN: "It has to be the case that some philosophy professors are absent-minded."

14. All philosophy professors are absent-minded

ANSWER: Undeterminable or ?

15. No philosophy professors are absent-minded

ANSWER: False

16. Some philosophy professors are not absent-minded

ANSWER: Undeterminable or ?

B. Convert the following two statements and show what statement form results:

17. All nursing students are required to take organic chemistry.

ANSWER: I-Statement: Some People required to take organic chemistry are Nursing Students.

18. No sneaky people are honest.

ANSWER: E-Statement: No Honest People are Sneaky People.

C. Obvert the following two statements and show what statement forms result:

19. No hints were helpful.

    ANSWER: A-Statement: All hints are things that were non-helpful.

20. Some exercises were not aerobic.

    ANSWER: I-Statement: Some exercises are things that were non-aerobic.

Arguments Requiring Immediate Inferences

Determine the validity of the following arguments, performing whatever immediate inferences you need to (and SHOW what the inference was), using whatever standard form you wish:

21. No safe rivers are uncharted waters because all navigable waters are charted waters and no non-navigable waters are safe rivers.

    ANSWER: Valid Argument! If one converts the second premise to "No safe rivers are non-navigable waters," and then obverts it to "All safe rivers are navigable waters. And, one also obverts the conclusion to "All safe rivers are charted waters," then we have three A-Statements and three classes or terms.

22. No welders materials are non-metals, but some metals are rare and costly substances. So, some welders materials must be rare and costly substances.

    ANSWER: This argument is still invalid, even after we obvert the first premise to "All welders materials are metals" because now we have an undistributed middle term, "metals."

Enthymemes

Two of the three enthymemes below will expand into valid syllogisms, and one will not. For the two that will, state whether a premise or a conclusion is missing and exactly what it is. For the one that cannot be made valid, explain why:

23. ACME Insurance Corp. must be a greedy organization, because they are only interested in making money and cutting health services.

    ANSWER: This syllogism is valid; it is missing an assumed premise, "All corporations that are only interested in making money and cutting health services are greedy organizations."

169

24. Logic classes that rely on old textbooks can't be very practical. But our class doesn't rely on an old textbook.

    ANSWER: This syllogism is missing the conclusion: therefore, "Our logic class is a practical class." But, it cannot be validly drawn because we must violate either rule 2 by having two negative statements in the premises or rule 3(B) by having an illicitly distributed class of "practical classes."

25. She works hard for the money, and people who work hard for the money will get what they want in the end.

    ANSWER: This is a valid syllogism missing the conclusion that "she will get what she wants in the end."

Essay Questions

26. Explain what an enthymeme is. How does it relate to step three of the Technique, spotting assumptions and implications?

27. Why are immediate inferences important in categorical reasoning in particular and in critical thinking generally?

28. What is being assumed about "obverse" classes in categorical logic?

29. How can we intertranslate between different kinds of complex statements, so that hypothetical, alternative, disjunctive, compound, and negated statements may all be rephrased in standard categorical form?

30. What is a "sorites?" When might one ever encounter such a form of reasoning in ordinary day to day life?

Chapter 8

Symbolizing Statements

CHAPTER OUTLINE

8.1 Symbolizing Conjunctions and Disjunctions
Exercises
8.2 Symbolizing Negations and Conditionals
Exercises
8.3 Symbolizing Biconditionals
Summary
Exercises
Case Study

KEY TERMS

Antecedent - The "if" part of a conditional statement. Symbolized, it is placed to the left of the arrow.

Biconditional - Represented by a ↔, a biconditional asserts that one component is true if and only if the other one is true.

Conditional - Represented by a →, a conditional or hypothetical statement asserts that if the first component (or antecedent) is true, then the second component (or consequent) is also true.

Conjunction - Represented by the symbol &, a conjunction asserts that the two conjoined statements are both true (or both retain their given truth value).

Consequent - The "then" part of a conditional statement. Symbolized, it is always placed to the right of the arrow.

Disjunction - Represented by the symbol ▼, a disjunction asserts that one of the two component statements is true. If it is possible that both statements are true, then the disjunction is said to be *inclusive*. If only one of the statements can be true, the disjunction is said to be *exclusive*.

Logical Connective - A term that connects statements together into a complex statement or that changes the truth value of a statement.

Necessary Condition - A condition that must be present for another to occur. It is symbolized as the consequent of a conditional. It may be thought of as a prerequisite or a *sine qua non*.

Negation - Represented by a ~, a negative asserts that the following statement is *false*.

Propositional Logic - The study of relationships among specific assertions and denials and the assessment of the validity or invalidity of resulting argument forms.

Sufficient Condition - A condition the presence of which is all that is needed to conclude that another condition is also present. It is symbolized as the antecedent of a conditional statement.

Symbolic Logic - The use of symbols to designate the logical connections between statements in order to assess the validity of arguments.

Truth Value - The given assignment of a value of "true" or "false" to a given statement.

OVERVIEW

Chapter Eight marks a change in the direction of analyzing and evaluating the structure of arguments. Although we are still very much in the heart of Step Six of the Critical Technique, we are embarking on another way of portraying the same structures and consequently about to deal with another set of rules for evaluating those structures.

Instead of dealing with the relationships between classes of objects, events, or ideas as we did in the previous two chapters, we turn to consider the different ways that simple statements (in their entirety) may be logically connected to or with other simple statements. This in turn allows us to construct lines of reasoning and to determine the validity of those argument forms composed of the resulting statements.

Simple statements are symbolized by a capital letter. The symbols that link the simple statements into a complex one are known as logical or truth-functional connectives. These symbols correspond to the ordinary English language words "and", "either...or", "not", "if...then", and "if and only if." Complex statements connected by the word "and" are known as conjunctions and the simple statements that connected are called conjuncts. They are symbolized by an ampersand or "&."

Disjunctions are complex statements whose simple statements (called disjuncts) are connected by the phrase "either...or." They are symbolized by the wedge or "▼." Negations are simple statements to which the equivalent expression "it is false that" or "not" is added. The tilde or "~"

symbolizes the negation. Unlike any of the other connectives, the tilde goes before the statement it modifies. The other connective symbols all come in between the two statements being linked.

"If...then" statements are called conditionals. They are symbolized by arrows that always point to the right: "→." In a conditional, the antecedent or statement to the left of the arrow is the sufficient condition for the consequent, which is always placed to the right of the arrow. The consequent is said to be the necessary condition for the antecedent. A Biconditional is a special form of the conditional in which each of the simple statements is both a necessary and a sufficient condition for the other. Biconditionals are symbolized by the double arrow: "↔."

These logical connectives are known as truth-functional connectives, because we can study and determine the truth value conditions for the entire complex statement from a knowledge of the known or supposed truth values for each of the component statements. Conjunctions, for example, are true only when both of the conjuncts are true, and are false in every other case. Disjunctions, on the other hand, are false only when both of the disjuncts are false, and are true in every other case. Negations simply have truth values opposite in truth value to the negated statement without the tilde. Conditionals are false only when the antecedent is true and the consequent is false. They are true in all other cases. This point may be the hardest one for students of this chapter to grasp. One way of explaining it that seems to work fairly well is to use the example of a guarantee or warranty we used on pages 186 and 187 of the text.

There are four possible combinations of truth values for the components of a conditional statement:
  (1) The antecedent could be true and the consequent could be true.
  (2) The antecedent could be true and the consequent could be false.
  (3) The antecedent could be false and the consequent could be true.
  (4) The antecedent could be false and the consequent could be false.

Suppose we had a guarantee for a product we just purchased and that guarantee read something to the effect: "If this product breaks in the next two years, then we will fix or replace it for free." There are two statements within this complex conditional statement. The antecedent is "this product breaks in the next two years." The consequent is "we will fix or replace it for free." The antecedent could be true or false; the product in fact breaks, or it does not break. And, the consequent could be true or false; they could fix or replace it for free or they might not do so. Now refer to the four possibilities above.

In case (1), the product breaks and they fix it for free. In that case they have "made good" on their guarantee and the truth value of the entire complex is also true. In case (3), the product does not break, but they fix or replace it for free anyway. Perhaps there was a product recall or a defect. But, whatever the reason, the entire complex is still true, for they have stood behind and made good on their guarantee. In case (4), the product does not break and they do not fix or replace it for free. Even in this case, they could claim that their guarantee was still good, because IF anything HAD happened, then they WOULD have done something about it. So, the entire complex is still true, even when both of the conditions are false.

The only time the conditional is false is in case (2) when the antecedent is true, the product breaks, but the consequent is false, they do not fix or replace it for free.

Finally, in the case of the biconditional, the entire complex statement is true when both elements are true. It is also true when both elements are false. The biconditional is false when its two components have opposing truth values; i.e., one is true and the other false, or conversely.

SOLUTIONS TO EXERCISE QUESTIONS

Answers to Exercises on Pages 182 and 183

Level A

1. *   A *conjunction* is a "truth-functional connective" represented by the symbol "&", asserting that two claims are being put together as one compound claim in which both parts are true.
2. *   A *disjunction* is a "truth-functional connective" represented by the symbol "▼", and asserting that two component claims are being put together as one complex claim in which at least one of the two components is true.
3. *   An *inclusive* disjunction is a complex "either-or" claim with two components such that *at least one* but possibly *both* statements are true. An *exclusive* disjunction is a complex "either-or" claim with two component statements, only *one* of which can be true.
4. *   The *truth value* of a statement is the artificial assignment of a value, either "true" or "false", to a statement in order to determine what consequences follow for the values of more complex statements or arguments.
5. *   Both conjuncts must be true.
6. *   Both disjuncts must be false.
7. *   False. (Both of them must be true.)
8. *   True
9. *   True
10. *   True
11. *   False
12. *   False
13. *   False
14. *   True
15. *   False
16. *   True

Level B

1. *   S ▼ T
2.   R & W
3. *   B & Y
4.   G ▼ O
5. *   F & B
6.   (F & F) = False
7. *   (T ▼ F) = True
8.   (T ▼ F) & (T & T) = (T & T) = True
9. *   (F ▼ T) = True
10.   (F & T) = False

<u>Answers to Exercises on Pages 191 and 192</u>

Level A

1. *   A *negation* is a "truth-functional connective" that does not really link anything but which changes the truth value of the statement or statement complex if modifies. It is symbolized by a tilde or "~".
2. *   A *conditional* statement is a complex claim expressing a hypothetical relationship between the truth values of its two component claims. It is a truth-functional relationship symbolized by an arrow or "→".
3. *   In a conditional statement neither the antecedent (the "IF" part) nor the consequent (the "THEN" part) is being asserted as categorically true, but rather the first condition is sufficient for us to know that the second condition is true, and the second condition is a necessary condition in the sense that if it, the consequent, were not true, then the antecedent could not be true either.
4. *   A hypothetical or conditional statement is false, just in case the antecedent is true and the consequent is false. For all other truth values of the antecedent and consequent, the complex statement (the conditional itself) is true.
5. *   True
6. *   False. (The antecedent *is* false, but the consequent is not.)
7. *   False. (It is always the consequent of a conditional.)
8. *   False. (It is the antecedent—unless the condition turns out to be a *necessary and sufficient* one, as we shall see.)
9. *   False. (The phrase "only if" denotes a *necessary* condition.)
10. * False. (Strictly speaking, it is not a "connector" at all. It serves as a truth-functional connective to change the truth value of the statement it modifies.)
11. * True
12. * False. The statement, "Jim decided to accept the new job," is being asserted as true

independent of other considerations, including the pay. (By the way, this is true if there are any job offers out there.)

Level B

1. *   C → G
2.   ~T → ~C
3. *   R → S   (or, if S = you *do* smoke, then [R → ~S])
4.   S → H   (or, where S = you *have* sugar, then ~S → H)
5. *   M → L
6.   T → ~I
7. *   H → E
8.   ~CB → W
9. *   ~P → R
10.   C → W
11. * (T → F) = False
12.   (F → T) = True
13. * ~(T & F) = ~(~) = True
14.   (T → F) = False
15. * (F → F) = True

Answers to Exercises on Pages 196 through 198

Level A

1. *   A *biconditional* is also a "truth-functional connective;" in this case, a special form of the conditional in which each simple statement is both the necessary and the sufficient condition for the other. It is symbolized by the double arrow, "↔".

2. *   A *necessary* condition is a *sine qua non*, a *prerequisite*, an *essential* condition, without which the antecedent of a conditional statement would be false. It is always the consequent of the complex hypothetical or conditional statement and symbolized to the right of the arrow, "→".

3. *   A *sufficient* condition is the antecedent or first half of a conditional or hypothetical statement. It is symbolized before or to the left of the arrow, "→", to show that it is *one* adequate way (not necessarily the *only* one) of insuring that the consequent must be true.

4. *   A conditional statement only asserts that the consequent is a necessary condition for the antecedent (or that the antecedent is a sufficient condition for the consequent) whereas in a *biconditional statement* each condition is both *sufficient* and *necessary* for the other condition. Put simply, if A is true, then B must be true too <u>AND</u> if A is false, then B must be false too. In a regular conditional statement, if A is true, B must be true too, but if A is

false, B may be true or false.

5. *   True
6. *   False. (Each has two components.)
7. *   False. (It may only indicate a necessary condition.)
8. *   False. (It would be "(V & N) → L." It matters a great deal *where* the parentheses are put.)

Level B

1. *   D → L
2.   J → C
3. *   C → E
4.   P → L
5. *   ~J → ~R
6.   J → R
7. *   ~E → ~J
8.   ~C → ~G
9. *   M → D
10.   O → R
11. *   ~(~O & ~G)
12.   ~(K ▼ E)
13. *   (P ▼ R) & ~(P & R)
14.   (Y & I) ▼ (~Y & ~I) or (Y ↔ I)
15. *   ~(→ R)
16.   S ↔ [~(L & J)]
17. *   [~(C ▼ P)] → U
18.   M ▼ ~R
19. *   ~R & ~W
20.   ~R & W
21. *   (G ▼ D) & P
22.   (~W & ~F) & ~P
23. *   (W ▼ F) & F
24.   (P & R) ▼ (T & L)
25. *   (P ▼ R) & (T ▼ L)
26.   (S → C) → P
27. *   W → F
28.   S & (C → P)
29. *   C & (P → S)
30.   W ↔ F
31. *   (L → D) → (C → R)
32.   L → D

177

33. *   ~D → (P & R)
34.   (F → ~I) & (M → J)
35. *   (A → B) → (C → D)
36.   D → S
37. *   P → T
38.   S → W
39. *   J → V
40.   K → H
41. *   Either yellow or blue is Lisa's favorite color.
42.   Either yellow is Lisa's favorite color or blue is not Lisa's favorite color.
43. *   If blue is Lisa's favorite color, then yellow is not Lisa's favorite color.
44.   Blue is Lisa's favorite color, and yellow is not Lisa's favorite color.
45. *   Blue is Lisa's favorite color, if and only if yellow is not Lisa's favorite color.
46.   Blue is Lisa's favorite color, and, if blue is Lisa's favorite color, then yellow is not Lisa's favorite color.
47. *   If I wash my car, then it is raining.
48.   If it is raining, then I wash my car. (I will wash my car, if it is raining.)
49. *   I am washing my car and it is raining.
50.   Either I am not washing my car or it is raining.
51. *   It rains if and only if I wash my car.
52.   It is not raining if and only if I am not washing my car.

TEST BANK

Multiple Choice Questions

1. A disjunction happens to be false when
    A. both of the disjuncts are false
    B. either one of the disjuncts are false
    C. just one of the disjuncts is false
    D. neither one of the disjuncts is false
    E. either B or C above

    ANSWER: A

2. A conjunction happens to be true when
    A. either one of the conjuncts is also true
    B. neither one of the conjuncts is true
    C. both of the conjuncts are true
    D. none of the above

E. either A or C above

ANSWER: C

3. A conditional statement is true whenever
   A. the antecedent is true
   B. the consequent is true
   C. the antecedent is false
   D. the consequent is false
   E. either B or C above

   ANSWER: E

4. The truth values for the biconditional are
   A. true whenever both conditions are true and false whenever they are both false
   B. false whenever both conditions are false or have the same truth value and true whenever they are both true
   C. always true unless the two conditions are both false
   D. always false unless both conditions are true
   E. true whenever both conditions have the same truth value and false whenever both conditions have different truth values

   ANSWER: E

5. Take the complex statement [A ▼ B) → C]. Suppose that A is false; B is true; and C is false. What is the resulting truth value for the whole entire complex statement?
   A. True
   B. False
   C. Cannot be determined from the information given so far
   D. It depends upon the context in which the statement occurs
   E. None of the above

   ANSWER: B

6. All of the following have the same truth value and meaning in logic except which one?
   A. If something is intelligent, then it has life.
   B. It cannot be intelligent unless it has life.
   C. All things that are intelligent are things that have life.
   D. Only things that are intelligent are things that have life.
   E. A thing has life provided that it is intelligent.

   ANSWER: D

7. In ordinary language each of the following expressions may have a slightly different meaning, but in logic each one of these means the same thing except which one?
    A. A is true even though B is true.
    B. A is true if B is true.
    C. A is true despite the fact that B is true.
    D. A is true, whereas B is true.
    E. A is not false. Still, B is true anyway.

    ANSWER: B

8. A sufficient condition is
    A. a prerequisite for the other condition in a conditional statement
    B. the antecedent of a conditional statement
    C. follows the word "only" or "then" in a hypothetical or conditional statement
    D. one way of justifying belief in the truth of the consequent
    E. the only way of justifying belief in the truth of the consequent of a conditional statement

    ANSWER: D

Translating Ordinary Language Into Symbols

Questions 9 through 20 involve translating the statements given in ordinary language into symbolic form. Use the first letter of the underlined words to stand for, or symbolize, the appropriate statement.

9. Most people would like to have either <u>money</u> or <u>power</u>, and they would also like to have <u>health</u> and freedom.

    ANSWER: (M ▼ P) & (H & F)

10. If you can <u>make</u> the meeting tomorrow, then you will either <u>gain</u> valuable information about a new client or <u>keep</u> from wasting time on an unclosable deal.

    ANSWER: M → (G ▼ K)

11. A political party will <u>win</u> an election, just in case it both <u>captures</u> a majority of the votes and <u>seduces</u> the media into supporting its causes.

    ANSWER: W ↔ (C & S)

12. You can't make an <u>omelet</u> without breaking a few eggs, and you can't get to the <u>top</u> without

breaking a few <u>legs</u>.

ANSWER: (~E → ~O) & (~L → ~T)

13. If <u>Austria</u> and <u>Bulgaria</u> enter the confrontation, then either <u>Czechoslovakia</u> or <u>Denmark</u> withdraw.

ANSWER: (A & B) → (C ▼ D)

14. If either <u>Albania</u> or <u>Bosnia</u> should become involved, then it will not be the case that both <u>Crimea</u> and <u>Dhoumbia</u> remain neutral.

ANSWER: (A ▼ B) → ~(C & D)

15. A person can <u>legally</u> drive, if and only if they have <u>passed</u> the driving test and have a <u>valid</u> current driver's license.

ANSWER: L ↔ (P & V)

16. If a person does not have a pilot's <u>license</u>, then that person cannot legally <u>fly</u>, unless, of course, they are with a flight <u>instructor</u>.

ANSWER: ~I → (~L → ~F)

17. Only the <u>good</u> <u>die young</u>.

ANSWER: D → G

18. You can't both <u>beat</u> them and <u>join</u> them without having a lot of <u>money</u> or <u>political</u> power.

ANSWER: [~(M ▼ P)] → [~(B & J)]

19. Having a great deal of <u>confidence</u> as well as a staff of <u>excellent</u> advisors is a necessary condition for <u>political</u> success.

ANSWER: P → (C & E)

20. If an <u>apple</u> is a kind of <u>fruit</u>, then it <u>keeps</u> the doctor away unless it is <u>poisoned</u> or <u>rancid</u>.

ANSWER: (A → F) → [~(P ▼ R) → K]

Chapter 8

For questions 21 through 25, translate the following symbolized statements into meaningful English sentences where

    A = Argentina becomes involved
    B = Brazil becomes involved
    C = Columbia has mobilized her forces
    D = Peru has mobilized her forces

21. (A ▼ B) → (C & D)

    ANSWER: If either Argentina or Brazil becomes involved, then both Columbia and Peru have mobilized their forces.

22. (A & B) ▼ (C & D)

    ANSWER: Either Argentina and Brazil become involved or Columbia and Peru have mobilized their forces.

23. (A ▼ B) & (C ▼ D)

    ANSWER: It is both the case that either Argentina or Brazil has become involved and either Columbia or Peru has mobilized her forces.

24. ~(A & B) → (~C ▼ ~D)

    ANSWER: If it is not the case that Argentina and Brazil become involved, then either Columbia will not mobilize her forces or Peru will not mobilize her forces.

25. (~A & ~B) ▼ (~C → D)

    ANSWER: Either Argentina and Brazil have not become involved or if Columbia does not mobilize her forces, then Peru will mobilize hers.

For questions 26 through 30, determine the truth value of the whole complex statement when the following symbolized statements have the truth values assigned below:

    A = True; B = True; C = True
    P = False; Q = False; R = False
    X = Undetermined; Y = Undetermined; Z = Undetermined

26. (A → P) ▼ (B → Q)

    ANSWER: F ▼ F = False

27. $[(A \blacktriangledown P) \& (B \blacktriangledown Q)] \rightarrow C$

   ANSWER: $[(T \& T) \rightarrow T] = \text{True}$

28. $[(X \rightarrow A) \& (R \rightarrow Z)]$

   ANSWER: $T \& T = \text{True}$

29. $[(B \blacktriangledown Y) \& (R \& Z)] \rightarrow X$

   ANSWER: $[(T \& F) \rightarrow ?] = F \rightarrow ? = \text{True!}$

30. $[(A \rightarrow B) \& (C \rightarrow {\sim}P)] \rightarrow {\sim}(Q \rightarrow {\sim}R)$

   ANSWER: $[(T \& T) \rightarrow {\sim}T\,] = T \rightarrow F = \text{False}$

Essay Questions

31. What is the difference between a necessary condition and a sufficient condition? Give an example of each in order to illustrate your explanation.

32. What is the difference between a conditional statement and a biconditional statement?

33. What is the difference between the "inclusive" sense of a disjunction and the "exclusive" sense? How would you show the difference between the two symbolically?

34. Explain the truth values for the conditional statement. Why is the conditional considered to be true whenever the antecedent is false?

Chapter 9

Argument Forms

CHAPTER OUTLINE

9.1 Conditional Argument Forms
Exercises
9.2 Conjunctive and Disjunctive Argument Forms
Summary
Exercises
Case Study

KEY TERMS

Affirming the Consequent - An invalid argument of the form $A \rightarrow B$, B therefore A.

Affirming a Disjunct - An invalid argument of the form $A \blacktriangledown B$, A, therefore ~B.

Broken Chain - An invalid argument form in which the consequent of neither conditional premise is identical to the antecedent of the other. For instance, $A \rightarrow B$, $C \rightarrow D$, so $A \rightarrow D$.

Chain Argument - A valid argument of the form $A \rightarrow B$, $B \rightarrow C$, so $A \rightarrow C$.

Complex Dilemma - A valid argument of the form $A \blacktriangledown B$, $A \rightarrow C$, $B \rightarrow D$, therefore $C \blacktriangledown D$.

Conjunctive Argument - A valid argument of the form ~(A & B), A, so ~B.

Denying a Conjunct - An invalid argument of the form ~(A & B), ~A. so B.

Denying the Antecedent - An invalid of the form $A \rightarrow B$, ~A, so ~B.

Disjunctive Argument - A valid argument of the form $A \blacktriangledown B$, ~A, so B.

Invalid Arguments - Deductive arguments in which the conclusion is not necessarily true even if all the premises should turn out to be true.

Modus Ponens - A valid argument of the form A → B, A, therefore B.

Modus Tollens - A valid argument of the form A → B, ~B, therefore ~A.

Simple Dilemma - A valid argument of the form A ▼ B, A → C, B → C, therefore C.

Sound Argument - A valid argument in which all of the premises are in fact true. The conclusion of a sound argument *must* be true.

Valid Arguments - Deductive arguments in which if and only if all the premises turn out to be true, does the conclusion *have* to be true too.

OVERVIEW

Chapter Nine is the continuation of the discussion of symbolic logic begun in Chapter Eight and concerned with portraying the structure or form of reasoning in order to determine its validity. Because Step Six of the Technique is so crucial to an accurate assessment of any form of reasoning and because it is not a skill generally developed over the course of normal day to day experience, we spend a little extra time and effort in studying it that it might become a part of our reasoning habits.

Again, the logical form of an argument is in part determined by the types of statements that constitute the premises and the conclusion, and their relationships within the argument. To that end, Chapter Nine deals with both valid argument forms and with their associated fallacies. Conditional statements generate the valid argument forms *modus ponens*, *modus tollens*, and *the chain argument*. Invalid forms or fallacies associated with the conditional statement are known as *affirming the consequent*, *denying the antecedent*, and *the broken chain*.

When the conjunction is employed, it is usually in the form of a negated conjunction or a *not both* statement that supplies the first premise of the argument. The valid form associated with a conjunction is known as a *conjunctive argument* and the fallacy associated with this form is called *denying a conjunct*.

The disjunction yields several forms of argument. One valid form is known as the *disjunctive argument*, where two alternatives are put forward, at least one of which must be true and the minor premise denies one of those alternatives. The conclusion that the other alternative must be true is validly drawn. The fallacy associated with this form of reasoning is called *affirming a disjunct*. The problem is that in an *inclusive* sense of the disjunction, the fact that one of the alternatives turns out to be true does not necessarily mean that the other alternative has to be false. It could be true too.

Two other valid forms of reasoning involve both the disjunction and the conditional statement forms. The first is called the *simple dilemma* and it involves two different conditional statements, both of which have the same consequent. A third premise is added that either the antecedent of one of those conditionals is true or the antecedent of the other conditional statement is true. The conclusion is validly drawn that the consequent of the conditional statements must be true. The second valid form is called the *complex dilemma* and it involves two different conditional statements with two different consequents. A third premise is the disjunction of the antecedents of both conditional statements. The conclusion is validly drawn that either one consequent or the other consequent of the conditional statements must be true.

In all of these cases, in the valid argument forms, the truth of the premises absolutely guarantees the truth of the conclusion. It would be a contradiction to say that the premises all might be true but the conclusion could still be false. In the case of the invalid argument forms, the conclusions are put forth as if the premises guaranteed them, when in fact they do not do so. (Table 9-1 on page 219 summarizes the valid argument forms and their associated fallacies.)

SOLUTIONS TO EXERCISE QUESTIONS

Answers to Exercises on Pages 211 through 213

Level A

1. *   A *valid argument* is a deductive line of reasoning in which if and only if all of the premises are true, the conclusion must be true too. An *invalid argument* is a line of reasoning put forward *as if* the premises absolutely guaranteed the truth of the conclusion when in fact they do not do so. Because of a flaw in the structure of the reasoning in invalid arguments, the conclusion may turn out to be false even when all of the premises are true.

2. *   Yes. Because the Modus Ponens argument form is a valid one, in the case of an argument having this form and also having true premises, the conclusion must necessarily be true.

3. *   No. Because arguments having the form of denying the antecedent are invalid, even if the premises of such an argument form were true, the conclusion would not *have to be* true.

4. *   False. If one or more of the premises are false, the conclusion could be false too.

5. *   False. The conclusions of invalid argument forms may be true anyway, but for entirely different reasons, for example.

6. *   True

7.   True

8. *   True

9. *   False. It may be either true or false; the point is that an invalid argument form does not guarantee *anything* about the truth or falsity of the conclusion.

10. *   True

Level B

Chapter 9

1. *   W → C   Valid:
        W   MODUS PONENS
        _____
        C

2.   S → L   Invalid:
        L   Affirming the Consequent
        _____
        S

3. *   ~E → I   Invalid:
        E (because S) Denying the Antecedent
        _____
        ~I

4.   W → S   Invalid:
        ~W   Denying the Antecedent
        _____
        ~S

5. *   ~T → ~P   Valid:
        Y → ~T   Chain Argument
        _____
        Y → ~P

6.   P → T   Valid:
        ~T   MODUS TOLLENS
        _____
        ~P

7. *   ~C → ~G   Valid:
        ~C   MODUS PONENS
        _____
        ~G

8.   ~J → ~L   Invalid:
        ~L (Because F) Affirming The Consequent
        _____
        ~J

188

9. *   ~T → ~P   Invalid:
         T   Denying The Antecedent
       _____
         P

10.   P → ~L   Valid:
         L   MODUS TOLLENS
       _____
         ~P

11. *   ~E → ~G   Valid:
         ~E   MODUS PONENS
       _____
         ~G

12.   ~J → ~E   Invalid:
         ~E   Affirming The Consequent
       _____
         ~J

13. *   V → (L & C)   Invalid: It is an inductive argument as it stands and it is
        (L & C) → (P & I)   fallacious. If the conclusion had been, "If we let the
        (P & I) → A   communists win in Vietnam, then Australia won't be
       _____   far behind," the form would have been a valid one
         S   (Chain Argument), although the content
                                            fallacy—SLIPPERY SLOPE—would still remain.

14.   E ▼ A   Invalid:
         E   Affirming A Disjunct
       _____
         ~A

                       (Put in Conditional Form it would still be Invalid:)
         ~E → A   Invalid:
          E   Denying The Antecedent
       _____
         ~A

15. *   E → S   Invalid:
         S   Affirming The Consequent
       _____
         E

Chapter 9

16. $G \rightarrow W$ Valid:
        ~W   MODUS TOLLENS
        _____
        ~G   (Possibly a content fallacy of <u>MISUSE OF HYPOTHESIS</u> Contrary to Fact)

<u>Answers to Exercises on Pages 218 through 223</u>

Level A

1. *   A *Disjunctive Argument* is a valid form of reasoning which has the structure:
        A ▼ B, ~A; therefore B.
        For example: Either Gore will write a sequel, or Hillary gets involved.
                       <u>Gore is not going to write a sequel.</u>
        So: Hillary gets involved.

2. *   A *Conjunctive Argument* is a valid reasoning form having the structure:
        ~(A & B), A; therefore ~B.
        For example: The Bosnians and the Serbs cannot both win.
                       <u>The Serbs win.</u>
        Therefore: The Bosnians cannot win.

3. *   In a *Disjunctive Argument* the reasoning is valid because if it is true both that (A) one of the two possibilities must be true, and (B) one of them turns out to be false, then (C) the other one HAS TO BE true [otherwise (A) was false]. Whereas in the argument forms which Affirm a Disjunct, when one of two possibilities must be true and one of the two turns out to be true, then we cannot draw any necessary inference about the truth or falsity of the other possibility.

4. *   *Conjunctive Arguments* are valid forms of reasoning that two things cannot both be true at the same time and that since one of them is true, the other one cannot possibly be true too. Arguments which Deny a Conjunct are invalid because the reasoning is that since two things cannot both be true at the same time and that since one of them is false, the other one must be true. The problem here is that it is possible that *neither* of the two possibilities is true.

5. *   A *Simple Dilemma* takes the form A → C. B → C, and A ▼ B; therefore C.
        The conclusion of a simple dilemma is a simple statement (such as "C"), whereas the conclusion of a complex dilemma is a complex statement which is a disjunction, because the *Complex Dilemma* takes the form A → C, B → D, and A ▼ B; therefore C ▼ D.
        A Simple Dilemma might occur in reasoning such as this—
        If market conditions improve, then we will make money on this fund.
        If market conditions remain stable, we will make money on this fund.
        <u>Market conditions will either improve or remain stable.</u>
        So: We will make money on this fund.

A Complex Dilemma might occur in reasoning such as this—
If we utilize behavior modification, then we may have some undesirable side effects.
If we utilize a Freudian approach, then we may reinforce unwanted neuroses.
We will utilize either behavior modification or a Freudian approach.
So: We may have either some undesirable side effects or reinforce unwanted neuroses.

6. * True
7. * True
8. * False (Both contain disjunctions.)
9. * True
10. * False

Level B

1. * ~(C & S)   Valid:
      C   Conjunctive Argument

    ————
    ~S

2.   ~(G & B)   Invalid:
     ~G   Denying A Conjunct

    ————
    B

3. * ~(R & C)   Invalid:
    ~C   Denying A Conjunct

    ————
    R

4.   ~(~W & P)   Valid:
     P   Conjunctive Argument

    ————
    W

5. * ~(S & H)   Invalid:
    ~H   Denying A Conjunct

    ————
    S

6.   M ▼ L   Valid:
    ~M   Disjunctive Argument

    ————
    L

7. *   L ▼ M   Valid:
        L → D   Simple Dilemma
        M → D
        _____
        D

8.   B ▼ W   Valid:
        ~B   Disjunctive Argument
        _____
        W

9. *   C ▼ T   Invalid:
        T   Affirming A Disjunct
        _____
        ~C

10.   H ▼ A   Invalid:
        H   Affirming A Disjunct
        _____
        ~A

11. *   M ▼ L   Invalid:
        L   Affirming A Disjunct
        _____
        ~M

Level C

1. *   D → C   Valid:
        D   MODUS PONENS
        _____
        C

2.   D → C   Invalid:
        C   Affirming The Consequent
        _____
        D

3. *   N → M   Valid:

~M (assumed) MODUS TOLLENS

_____

~N

4.   A ▼ C   Valid:

A → M   Simple Dilemma

C → M

_____

M

5. *   F → I   Valid:

I → W   Chain Argument

_____

F → W

6.   (A & W) → E Invalid:

E   Affirming The Consequent

_____

(A & W)

7. *   DWI → F   Valid:

DWI   MODUS PONENS

_____

F

8.   ~(C → F)   Neither Valid nor Invalid:

~(D → W)   This is an Inductive Argument

_____

U & I   It is a generalization from two cases.

9. *   C → (A & E) Invalid:

(A & E)   Affirming The Consequent

_____

C

10.   S → D   Valid:

~S → D   Simple Dilemma

S ▼ ~S (Assumed)

_____

D

11. *   L → H   Valid:
        H → F   Chain Argument
        _____
        L → F   (Content Fallacy of Assuming the Cause)

12.   L → E   Valid Argument:
        E → D   There are two parts to this argument: the first is composed of the first two
        ~D   premises forming a Chair Argument to generate the conclusion, L → D.
        _____   Then, the third premise (~D) together with this implied conclusion, yield a
        ~L   valid argument by MODUS TOLLENS with the conclusion, ~L.

13. *   ProChoice → Paid Dues   Valid Argument:
        ProChoice   MODUS PONENS
        _____

        Paid Dues

14.   ~DC → ~W   Invalid Argument:
        ~W → ~PT   Two arguments here: the first is a Chain Argument leading to the
        ~PT   conclusion, ~DC → ~PT. This part is valid. The second part
        _____   ~DC → ~PT and ~PT, therefore ~DC, is invalid by Affirming The
        ~DC   Consequent.

15. *   H → R   Invalid Argument:
        ~H   Denying The Antecedent
        _____

        ~R

16.   S → ~L (assumed) Valid Argument:
        S   MODUS PONENS
        _____

        ~L   Fielder is assuming what we stated in the first premise: that if he
                          was asleep then the music wasn't too loud. (Or, put another way: if
                          the music were too loud, then he would not have been able to
                          sleep.)

(Do not forget that there is more than one way to work these Level C Exercises)

TEST BANK

Multiple Choice Questions

1. All of the following are forms of Modus Ponens except which one?
    A. $A \rightarrow B$, A; therefore B
    B. $\sim A \rightarrow B$, ~A; therefore B
    C. $\sim A \rightarrow \sim B$, A; therefore ~B
    D. $A \rightarrow \sim B$, A; therefore ~B
    E. $\sim A \rightarrow \sim B$, ~A; therefore ~B

    ANSWER: C

2. Each of the following argument forms is fallacious except which one?
    A. $A \rightarrow B$, B: therefore A
    B. $A \rightarrow \sim B$, B; therefore ~A
    C. $\sim A \rightarrow \sim B$, ~B; therefore ~A
    D. $\sim A \rightarrow B$, B; therefore ~A
    E. $A \rightarrow \sim B$, ~A; therefore B

    ANSWER: B

3. A conjunctive argument form
    A. maintains that the two component statements cannot both be true at the same time.
    B. is only valid if both of the component statements are true.
    C. is never a valid form regardless of content.
    D. is valid whenever either one of the component statements is true.
    E. assumes that the two components cannot both be false at the same time.

    ANSWER: A

4. Affirming a disjunct
    A. is a valid form of the either-or argument.
    B. relies on the assumption that both disjuncts cannot be true at the same time.
    C. is an invalid argument form because it fails to consider the possibility that both disjuncts could be false.
    D. is an invalid argument form because it fails to consider the possibility that both disjuncts could be true.
    E. is a valid form of argument as long as both of the premises are true.

    ANSWER: D

5. The inclusive form of disjunction
    A. is actually symbolized the same as the exclusive form of disjunction.
    B. is symbolized the same way as the denial of a conjunction.
    C. requires that one of the disjuncts be affirmed in order to complete a valid argument form.
    D. is symbolized using an arrow rather than a wedge.
    E. is symbolized differently from the exclusive form of disjunction.

ANSWER: E

Short Answer Questions

Symbolize each of the following arguments, then state which rule it exemplifies and whether it is a valid or invalid argument form.

6. If the TIGERS win this game, then they will win the PENNANT. Too bad, the TIGERS lost. Therefore, they cannot win the PENNANT.

ANSWER: T → P
            ~T
            _____
            ~P   INVALID: Denies the Antecedent

7. You can't both ITEMIZE deductions and USE the short form. But, you didn't USE the short form. Therefore, you must have ITEMIZED deductions.

ANSWER: ~(I & U)
            ~U
            _____
            I   INVALID: Denying a Conjunct

8. You can either ATTEND the 10:00 interview or GO to the review session. Since you ATTENDED the 10:00 interview, you must not have GONE to the review session.

ANSWER: A ▼ G
            A
            _____
            ~G   INVALID: Affirming a Disjunct

9. If you are PRESIDENT of the United States, then you are THIRTY-FIVE years of age or older. Sam is younger than THIRTY-FIVE. So, she cannot possibly be the PRESIDENT of the United States.

ANSWER: P ➔ T
           ~T
           _____
           ~P   VALID: Modus Tollens

10. You cannot both TRANSFER this term and SATISFY the residency requirement. Since you are TRANSFERRING this term, you therefore cannot SATISFY the residency requirement.

ANSWER: ~(T & S)
             T
           _____
             ~S   VALID: Conjunctive Argument

11. Either you are taking CHEMISTRY or you're in my SOCIOLOGY class. Since I know you're in my SOCIOLOGY class, you must not be taking CHEMISTRY.

ANSWER;   C ▼S
           S
           _____
           ~C   INVALID: Affirming a Disjunct

12. Whenever you PUSH your exercising to the limit, you are immunologically COMPROMISED. And, if you're immunologically COMPROMISED, then you RUN the risk of serious illness. So, it follows that if you PUSH your exercising to the limit, you RUN the risk of serious illness.

ANSWER: P ➔ C
           C ➔ R
           _____
           P ➔ R   VALID: Chain Argument

13. Sara must have done WELL on the test because if she did WELL on it, then she would have FINISHED early, and she definitely FINISHED early.

ANSWER: W ➔ F
           F
           _____
           W   INVALID: Affirming the Consequent

14. Nick cannot possibly be GUILTY, unless his ALIBI is false. But, it turns out that his ALIBI is actually true. So, he can't possibly be GUILTY.

197

ANSWER: ~(~A) → ~G   Or   A → ~G
           A

_____

     ~G   VALID: Modus Ponens

15. If you can VOTE in a national election, then you must be a UNITED States citizen. And, if you are a United States TAXPAYER, then you must have FILED a Form 1040. Therefore, if you can VOTE in a national election, then you must have FILED a Form 1040.

ANSWER: V → U
           T → F

_____

     V → F   INVALID: Broken Chain

16. Either a new AIRLINE has been found to move into the metro airport or Acme Airlines FARES would have gone up even more. Thus, a new AIRLINE must have been found to move into the metro airport, since Acme Airlines FARE have not gone up at all.

ANSWER: A ▼ F
           ~F

_____

     A   VALID: Disjunctive Argument

17. If you haven't TAUGHT me anything of value, then I should not have to PAY. But, if you have TAUGHT me anything of value, then (I should win my dispute and) I should not have to PAY. Either you have TAUGHT me something of value or you have not TAUGHT me something of value. So, no matter what, I should not have to PAY.

ANSWER: ~T → ~P
         T → ~P
         T ▼ ~T

_____

     ~P   VALID: Simple Dilemma (Perhaps a content fallacy of Limited
                                Options or Fallacious Extension)

18. This must be an extraordinarily serious EMERGENCY, because there have been FIVE alarms, and only in the case of extraordinarily serious EMERGENCIES do they take this action (i.e., sound FIVE alarms).

ANSWER: F → E

F

_____

E   VALID: Modus Ponens

More Difficult Short Answer Questions

Treat each of the arguments below "enthymematically," supplying the missing premise or conclusion that would make it valid. Then, state which rule is being applied.

19. Kant must have been an idealist. Basically, either a person is a realist or they are an idealist.

    ANSWER: A valid argument by Disjunctive Argument missing a premise that Kant was not a realist.

20. I'll go to the concert with you only if the subdudes are playing. But, the subdudes are not in fact playing.

    ANSWER: A valid argument by Modus Tollens missing a conclusion that therefore I will not go to the concert with you.

21. You can't both be hairy-chested and a dweeb. So, Emilio cannot possibly be a dweeb.

    ANSWER: A valid argument by Conjunctive Argument missing a premise that Emilio is hairy-chested.

Each of the arguments below closely resembles one of the argument forms we have studied, but does not precisely commit any one of the fallacies we have studied. Explain what is wrong with the reasoning.

22. If it rains for the next three days we are going to be in for some terrible flooding. The weather forecast looks awfully bleak. Therefore, we are going to be in for some terrible flooding.

    ANSWER: This argument resembles the valid form of Modus Ponens, although it is more likely that there is not a clear cut case of affirming the antecedent but rather an unclear relationship between the two premises. That is, the second premise does not exactly repeat the antecedent of the conditional statement.

23. If a person makes over $50,000 in annual income, then they will have to file both state and federal income tax forms here. And, since you had over $50,000 in annual income this year, you are going to owe the state and the federal government a lot of income tax.

> ANSWER: This argument's structure also closely resembles the valid form of Modus Ponens; the second premise clearly affirms the antecedent of the first premise which is a hypothetical or conditional statement. The problem is that the conclusion of the reasoning does not exactly match the consequent.

Essay Questions

24. Explain the argument form known as Modus Ponens. Give an example of it. If arguments of this form have premises which are all true, must the conclusion also be true? Why or why not?

25. Explain the argument form known as denying the antecedent. Give an example of this form. Suppose an argument of this form has premises that are all true. Does the conclusion also have to be true? Why or why not?

26. What are the main differences and similarities between necessary and sufficient conditions?

27. Explain what a complex dilemma is and whether it is a valid or invalid form of reasoning.

28. What is the difference between affirming the consequent and Modus Tollens? Why is one of them a valid form of argumentation when the other one is fallacious?

29. Explain the concept of validity. What is the difference between validity and truth?

30. What is the difference between a sound argument and a valid argument? What is the connection between the two?

Chapter 10

Truth Tables, Equivalence and Validity

CHAPTER OUTLINE

10.1 Testing for Logical Equivalence
Exercises
10.2 Testing for Validity
Summary
Exercises
Case Study

KEY TERMS

Addition - The rule of combining a disjunct to a statement already known to be true.

Combination - The joining of two statements into a single conjunction.

Derivation - The extraction of a conclusion from the premises according to rules of logic.

Formal Equivalence - Statements are said to be formally equivalent when they have identical truth values. This is also known as *logical equivalence*.

Simplification - The assertion of one of a pair of conjuncts. In other words if A and B are true, then A is true.

Truth Table - A method for determining the truth value of complex statements. It can be used to establish whether or not two complex statements are logically equivalent or to determine if an argument is valid or invalid.

Valid Deductive Argument - One that guarantees the truth of its conclusions. In other words, if the premises of the argument are true, then its conclusion *must* also be true.

Chapter 10

OVERVIEW

In broadening our strategies under Step Six of the Critical Technique, the Truth Table method becomes a very useful tool. It can be helpful in establishing the logical equivalence between different statements, and it can be used to test arguments for validity. When using a truth table, the idea is to look at the possible combinations of truth values of all of the variables, and then to solve for the truth values of the premises as well as the conclusion. Once this is done, if there are no lines in which all of the premises yield a truth value of true while the conclusion turns out to be false, then the argument is considered to be a valid one. This is because the truth of the premises is shown to guarantee the truth of the conclusion. If there is at least one line in which all of the premises yield a value of true while the conclusion yields a value of false, then the argument is shown to be invalid.

Included at the end of the discussion of using truth tables to show logical equivalence is a discussion of another method for "translating" complex statement forms governed by a given logical connective into statement forms governed by other logical connectives. This requires, among other things, negating the elements according to the rules spelled out at the end of 10.1 and recapitulated in the conversion pyramid shown in Figure 10.1. Accordingly a Categorical Statement Form (from Chapters 6 and 7), such as "All A is B", is logically equivalent to the Conditional statement, "If A, then B", which is logically equivalent to the Disjunctive statement, "Either not A, or B", which is logically equivalent to the Conjunctive statement, "Not both A and not B."

Also discussed in the chapter is the derivation of statements from arguments. This allows us to utilize all of the valid argument forms discussed in Chapters 6, 7, 8, and 9, along with the translation of logical equivalences and three new rules: combination, simplification, and addition. Combination is simply the ability to put together into a complex statement two statements that are independently known to be true. For instance, if it is known that P is true, and it is also known that Q is true, then it is legitimate to infer that P and Q are true. Simplification allows us to do the opposite: if a conjunction is known to be true, then each of the conjuncts may stand on its own independently from the other. That is, if A and B are true, then A is true, and so is B. Finally, addition is the "curious" rule that for any statement known to be true, we may legitimately add a disjunct; any disjunct! If it is true that the sun is shining, then it is just as true that either the sun is shining or Moses supposes his toes are roses. Why this is helpful is not immediately apparent, but consider the following example:

Suppose we know that A is true. And, we also know that if either A is true or F is true, then T must also be true. At this point we have no means of validly establishing the truth of T. But, with the rule for addition, we may legitimately infer from A that therefore either A or F is true. Once we have established A or F, we can use this statement with our rule for Modus Ponens to generate the conclusion T.

SOLUTIONS TO EXERCISE QUESTIONS

<u>Answers to Exercises on Pages 236 through 238</u>

Level A

1. *   True
2. *   True
3. *   True
4. *   False. The inference is equally valid in both directions.
5. *   False. A → B is logically equivalent to ~(A & ~B).
6. *   False. "It's raining and the streets are wet" is logically equivalent to the statement "It is not the case that either it is not raining or the streets are not wet."
7. *   False. "It's raining and the streets are wet" is logically equivalent to "It is not the case that if it is raining then the streets are not wet."
8. *   True. (If I understand this question?)
9. *   False. It is logically equivalent to "It is not the case that neither Perot nor Bush lost the election of 1992."
10. * True

Level B

1. *

A	B	~A	(~A & B)	(A → B)	(~A & B) ↔ (A → B)
T	T	F	F	T	F
T	F	F	F	F	T
F	T	T	T	T	T
F	F	T	F	T	F

They are NOT logically equivalent expressions.

2.

P	Q	~Q	(P ▼ ~Q)	(P → ~Q)	(P ▼ ~Q) ↔ (P → ~Q)
T	T	F	T	F	F
T	F	T	T	T	T
F	T	F	F	T	F
F	F	T	T	T	T

They are NOT logically equivalent expressions.

3. *

R	S	~R	~S	(R → ~S)	(~R ▼ ~S)	(R → ~S) ↔ (~R ▼ ~S)
T	T	F	F	F	F	T
T	F	F	T	T	T	T
F	T	T	F	T	T	T
F	F	T	T	T	T	T

These two expressions ARE logically equivalent.

4.

T	V	~V	~(T ▼ ~V)		(T → V)	~(T ▼ ~V) ↔ (T → V)
T	T	F	F	T	T	F
T	F	T	F	T	F	T
F	T	F	T	F	T	T
F	F	T	F	T	T	F

They are NOT logically equivalent.

5. *

M	N	M → N	~(M → N)	(M & N)	~(M → N) ↔ (M & N)
T	T	T	F	T	F
T	F	F	T	F	F
F	T	T	F	F	T
F	F	T	F	F	T

They are NOT logically equivalent.

6.   (a) ~L & ~J
      (b) ~(L & J)

L	J	~L	~J	(~L & ~J)	(L & J)	~(L & J)	(~L & ~J) ↔ ~(L & J)
T	T	F	F	F	T	F	T
T	F	F	T	F	F	T	F
F	T	T	F	F	F	T	F
F	F	T	T	T	F	T	T

They are NOT logically equivalent expressions.

7. * (a) B → F
   (b) ~B → ~F

B	F	~B	~F	(B → F)	(~B → ~F)	(B → F) ↔ (~B → ~F)
T	T	F	F	T	T	T
T	F	F	T	F	T	F
F	T	T	F	T	F	F
F	F	T	T	T	T	T

They are NOT logically equivalent expressions.

8. (a) P → F
   (b) ~P ▼ F

P	F	~P	P → F	~P ▼ F	(P → F) ↔ (~P ▼ F)
T	T	F	T	T	T
T	F	F	F	F	T
F	T	T	T	T	T
F	F	T	T	T	T

These two expressions ARE logically equivalent.

9. * (a) ~L → ~A
   (b) L → A

A	L	~A	~L	(~L → ~A)	(L → A)	(~L → ~A) ↔ (L → A)
T	T	F	F	T	T	T
T	F	F	T	F	T	F
F	T	T	F	T	F	F
F	F	T	T	T	T	T

They are NOT logically equivalent expressions.

10. (a) L ↔ J
    (b) ~1 ↔ ~J

L	J	~L	~J	L ↔ J	~L ↔ ~J	(L ↔ J) ↔ (~L ↔ ~J)
T	T	F	F	T	T	T
T	F	F	T	F	F	T
F	T	T	F	F	F	T
F	F	T	T	T	T	T

These two statements ARE logically equivalent.

11. *   (a) ~J → L
    (b) ~L → J

~J	L	~L	J	~J → L	~L → J	(~J → L) ↔ (~L → J)
T	T	F	F	T	T	T
T	F	T	F	F	F	T
F	T	F	T	T	T	T
F	F	T	T	T	T	T

The two statements ARE logically equivalent.

12.   (a) G → W
    (b) ~G ▼ W

G	W	~G	G → W	~G ▼ W	(G → W) ↔ (~G ▼ W)
T	T	F	T	T	T
T	F	F	F	F	T
F	T	T	T	T	T
F	F	T	T	T	T

The two statements ARE logically equivalent.

13. *   (a) ~ (B & T)
    (b) ~B ▼ T

B	T	~B	~(B & T)		~B ▼ T	~(B & T) ↔ (~B ▼ T)
T	T	F	F	T	T	F
T	F	F	T	F	F	F
F	T	T	T	F	T	T
F	F	T	T	F	T	T

The two expressions are NOT logically equivalent.

14.   (a) S → ~F
    (b) ~(S & F)

S	F	~F	(S → ~F)	~(S & F)		(S → ~F) ↔ ~(S & F)
T	T	F	F	F	T	T
T	F	T	T	T	F	T
F	T	F	T	T	F	T
F	F	T	T	T	F	T

The two statements ARE logically equivalent.

15. *   ~A → B

16.   A → ~B
17. *   ~(A → B)
18.   ~A → ~B
19. *   S ▼ I = ~S → I (If you don't stop, I'll shoot.)
20.   L ▼ E = ~L → E (If you don't love America, then leave it.)
21. *   L ▼ ~J = ~L → ~J (If Lisa does not go to the concert, then Jill will not go.)
22.   ~L ▼ ~J = L → ~J (If Lisa goes to the concert, then Jill will not go.)
23. *   C ▼ L = ~C → L (If you don't take calculus to fulfill this requirement then you need to
                        take logic to do so.)
24.   ~P ▼ ~Q
25. *   P ▼ ~Q
26.   ~(~P ▼ ~Q)
27. *   ~(P ▼ ~Q)
28.   S ▼ D
29. *   ~B ▼ F
30.   R ▼ O
31. *   O ▼ R
32.   B ▼ ~F

Answers to Exercises on Pages 248 through 251

Level A

1. *   A *valid deductive argument* is a line of reasoning in which the truth of the premises would
       absolutely guarantee the truth of the conclusion, or, put more formally, it is one in which
       the conclusion must be true if and only if the premises are true.
2. *   A *Truth Table* is a method of assigning all possible truth values to the simple statements
       which comprise a complex statement in order to determine the truth values of that
       complex statement. Truth tables may be used to establish the logical equivalence between
       different statements, to determine the validity of arguments, to establish whether certain
       statement forms are tautologies, contradictions, or contingent statements, or even to solve
       certain kinds of logical puzzles and games.
3. *   To this point we have looked at several other methods: one, for example, are the Proofs
       and Derivations from the Rules found in Chapters Eight and Nine; another are the Rule
       Method and the Diagram Method for evaluating Categorical Syllogisms found in Chapters
       Six and Seven.
4. *   False. Validity is shown by constructing a truth table in which there are NO lines in which
       all of the premises are true and the conclusion is false.
5. *   True
6. *   True
7. *   True

8. *   False. It is the Rule by which two statements known to be true are joined together in a *conjunction*.
9. *   True
10. * False. It is the Rule by which a *conjunction* is simplified into one of its component conjuncts.

Level B

1. *   R → ~S
        ~S
        _____
        R

R	~S	R → ~S	R
T	T	T	T
T	F	F	T
F	T	T	F
F	F	T	F

Line 3 shows an instance where both premises are true and the conclusion is false. Thus, the argument is VALID.

2.   W → R
        W
        _____
        R

W	R	W → R	R
T	T	T	T
T	F	F	F
F	T	T	T
F	F	T	F

Whenever the premises are all true (line 1) the conclusion is true too. The argument is VALID. Whenever the conclusion is false, at least one of the premises is false too.

3. *   W → S
        W
        _____
        S

W	S	W → S	S
T	T	T	T
T	F	F	F
F	T	T	T
F	F	T	F

The argument is VALID: in all instances where premises are true (line 1), the conclusion is true too. And, anytime the conclusion is false (as in lines 2 and 4) at least one of the premises is false too.

4. (a) A ▼ P
    (b) A → ~E
    (c) P → ~E
    _____
    (d) ~E

A	P	~E	(A ▼ P)	(A → ~E)	(P → ~E)	~E
T	T	T	T	T	T	T
T	T	F	T	F	F	F
T	F	T	T	T	T	T
T	F	F	T	F	T	F
F	T	T	T	T	T	T
F	T	F	T	T	F	F
F	F	T	F	T	T	T
F	F	F	F	T	T	F

The argument is VALID. Whenever all the premises are true, the conclusion is true too; and in all instances in which the conclusion is false, at least one of the premises is false too.

5. * (a) B → W
      (b) T → W
      (c) B ▼ T
      _____
      (d) W

B	T	W	(B → W)	(T → W)	(B ▼ T)	W
T	T	T	T	T	T	T
T	T	F	F	F	T	F
T	F	T	T	T	T	T
T	F	F	F	T	T	F
F	T	T	T	T	T	T
F	T	F	T	F	T	F
F	F	T	T	T	F	T
F	F	F	T	T	F	F

The argument is VALID. Whenever all the premises are true, the conclusion is true too (lines 1, 3, and 5); and in all instances in which the conclusion is false (lines 2, 4, 6, and 8) at least one of the premises is false.

209

6.   (a) P → G
       (b) ~P
       _____
       (c) ~G

P	G	~P	(P → G)	~G
T	T	F	T	F
T	F	F	F	T
F	T	T	T	F
F	F	T	T	T

This argument is INVALID. In line 3, both of the premises are true, but the conclusion is false.

7. *   (a) ~(A & P)
        (b) P → C
        (c) ~C
        _____
        (d) A

A	P	C	(A&P)	~(A & P)	(P → C)	~C	A
T	T	T	T	F	T	F	T
T	T	F	T	F	F	T	T
T	F	T	F	T	T	F	T
T	F	F	F	T	T	T	T
F	T	T	F	T	T	F	F
F	T	F	F	T	F	T	F
F	F	T	F	T	T	F	F
F	F	F	F	T	T	T	F

The argument is INVALID, because in line 8 of the table, all of the premises are true, but the conclusion is false.

8. (a) ~(C & W)
    (b) W

    _____
    (c) ~P & ~C

P	C	W	(P & C)	(C & W)	~(P & C)	~(C & W)	W	(~P & ~C)	
T	T	T	T	T	F	F	T	F	
T	T	F	T	F	F	T	F	F	
T	F	T	F	F	T	T	T	F	*
T	F	F	F	F	T	T	F	F	
F	T	T	F	T	T	F	T	F	
F	T	F	F	F	T	T	F	F	
F	F	T	F	F	T	T	T	T	
F	F	F	F	F	T	T	F	T	

The argument is INVALID. In line 3 all three of the premises are true, but the conclusion is false.

9. * (a) P → T
      (b) E → M
      (c) ~T & ~M

    _____
    (d) ~P & ~E

P	T	E	M	(P → T)	(E → M)	(~T & ~M)	(~P & ~E)
T	T	T	T	T	T	F	F
T	T	T	F	T	F	F	F
T	T	F	T	T	T	F	F
T	T	F	F	T	T	F	F
T	F	T	T	F	T	F	F
T	F	T	F	F	F	T	F
T	F	F	T	F	T	F	F
T	F	F	F	F	T	T	F
F	T	T	T	T	T	F	F
F	T	T	F	T	F	F	F
F	T	F	T	T	T	F	T
F	T	F	F	T	T	F	T
F	F	T	T	T	T	F	F
F	F	T	F	T	F	T	F
F	F	F	T	T	T	F	T
F	F	F	F	T	T	T	T

This argument is VALID: in all cases where the three premises are true (line 16), the conclusion is also true. And, in all instances where the conclusion is false (lines 1 through 10 and 13 and 14), at least one of the premises is also false.

10.   (a) H ▼ O
       (b) H → A
       (c) O → L
       (d) ~A & ~L
_____
       (e) ~H & ~O

H	O	A	L	(H ▼ O)	(H → A)	(O → L)	(~A & ~L)	(~H & ~O)
T	T	T	T	T	T	T	F	F
T	T	T	F	T	T	F	F	F
T	T	F	T	T	F	T	F	F
T	T	F	F	T	F	F	T	F
T	F	T	T	T	T	T	F	F
T	F	T	F	T	T	T	F	F
T	F	F	T	T	F	T	F	F
T	F	F	F	T	F	T	T	F
F	T	T	T	T	T	T	F	F
F	T	T	F	T	T	F	F	F
F	T	F	T	T	T	T	F	F
F	T	F	F	T	T	F	T	F
F	F	T	T	F	T	T	F	T
F	F	T	F	F	T	T	F	T
F	F	F	T	F	T	T	F	T
F	F	F	F	F	T	T	T	T

The argument is VALID! There are no instances where the premises are all true and the conclusion is false.

11. *   (1) A → B   given
          (2) B → C   given
          (3) ~C   given
          _____
So,   (4) ~A   To Prove
          (5) ~B   Lines (2) and (3), Modus Tollens
          (6) ~A   Lines (1) and (5), Modus Tollens

12.   (1) ~(P & Q)   given
         (2) R   given
         (3) R → Q   given; Therefore: ~R (To Prove)
         _____
         (4) ~Q   Lines (1) and (2), Conjunctive Argument
         (5) ~R   Lines (3) and (4), Modus Tollens

13. *   (1) R → S   given
         (2) R ▼ T   given
         (3) ~T   given; Therefore: S   (To Prove)
         _____
         (4) R   Lines (2) and (3), Disjunctive Argument
         (5) S   Lines (1) and (4), Modus Ponens

14.   (1) Z ▼ X   given
         (2) X → Y   given
         (3) Z → Y   given
         (4) Y → N   given; Therefore: N   (To Prove)
         _____
         (5) Y   Lines (1), (2), and (3), Simple Dilemma
         (6) N   Lines (4) and (5), Modus Ponens

15. *   (1) R → W   given
         (2) W → S   given
         (3) R   given; Therefore: S   (To Prove)
         _____
         (4) W   Lines (1) and (3), Modus Ponens
         (5) S   Lines (2) and (4), Modus Ponens

16.   (1) ~(P & L)   given
         (2) P   given
         (3) J → L   given; Therefore: ~J (To Prove)
         _____
         (4) ~L   Lines (1) and (2), Conjunctive Argument
         (5) ~J   Lines (3) and (4), Modus Tollens

17. *   (1) R → W   given
         (2) W → S   given
         (3) ~S   given; Therefore: ~W   (To Prove)
         _____
         (4) ~W   Lines (2) and (3), Modus Tollens

18.   (1) O ▼ A   given
       (2) ~A   given
       (3) O → L   given; Therefore: L & O (To Prove)

       _____

       (4) O   Lines (1) and (2), Disjunctive Argument
       (5) L   Lines (3) and (4), Modus Ponens
       (6) L & O   Lines (4) and (5), Combination

Level C

1. *   (1) D → C   given
        (2) D   given; Therefore: C   (To Prove)

        _____

        (3) C   Lines (1) and (2), Modus Ponens

D	C	D → C	C
T	T	T	T
T	F	F	F
F	T	T	T
F	F	T	F

The argument is VALID: There are no instances where the conclusion is false and both of the premises are true. In case both of the premises are true (Line 1), the conclusion is also true.

2.   (1) D → C   given
       (2) C   given; Therefore: D   (To Prove)

       _____

       Invalid: Affirming the Consequent

D	C	D → C	D
T	T	T	T
T	F	F	T
F	T	T	F
F	F	T	F

The argument is INVALID. In the third line, both of the premises are true, but the conclusion is false.

3. *   (1) N → M   given
       (2) ~M   given; Therefore: ~N   (To Prove)

       _____

       (3) ~N   Lines (1) and (2), Modus Tollens

N	M	N → M	~M	~N
T	T	T	F	F
T	F	F	T	F
F	T	T	F	T
F	F	T	T	T

The argument is VALID: In all cases where the conclusion is false (Lines 1 and 2), at least one of the premises is false also. And, in all cases in which the premises are both true, the conclusion is also true (Line 4).

4.   (1) A ▼ J   given
       (2) A → ~P   given
       (3) ~P → G   given
       (4) J → C   given
       (5) C → G   given; Therefore: G (To Prove)

       _____

       (6) ~P ▼ C   Lines (1), (2), and (4), Complex Dilemma
       (7) G   Lines (6), (3), and (5), Simple Dilemma

A	J	~P	G	C	A ▼ J	A → ~P	~P → G	J → C	C → G	G
T	T	T	T	T	T	T	T	T	T	T
T	T	T	T	F	T	T	T	F	T	T
T	T	T	F	T	T	T	F	T	F	F
T	T	T	F	F	T	T	F	F	T	F
T	T	F	T	T	T	F	T	T	T	T
T	T	F	T	F	T	F	T	F	T	T
T	T	F	F	T	T	F	F	T	F	F
T	T	F	F	F	T	F	F	F	T	F
T	F	T	T	T	T	T	T	T	T	T
T	F	T	T	F	T	T	T	T	T	T
T	F	T	F	T	T	T	F	T	F	F
T	F	T	F	F	T	T	F	T	T	F
T	F	F	T	T	T	F	T	T	T	T
T	F	F	T	F	T	F	T	T	T	T
T	F	F	F	T	T	F	T	T	F	F
T	F	F	F	F	T	F	T	T	T	F
F	T	T	T	T	T	T	T	T	T	T

215

F	T	T	T	F	T	T	T	F	T	T
F	T	T	F	T	T	T	F	T	F	F
F	T	T	F	F	T	T	F	F	T	F
F	T	F	T	T	T	T	T	T	T	T
F	T	F	T	F	T	T	T	F	T	T
F	T	F	F	T	T	T	T	T	F	F
F	T	F	F	F	T	T	T	T	T	F
F	F	T	T	T	F	T	T	T	T	T
F	F	T	T	F	F	T	T	T	T	T
F	F	T	F	T	F	T	F	T	F	F
F	F	T	F	F	F	T	F	T	T	F
F	F	F	T	T	F	T	T	T	T	T
F	F	F	T	F	F	T	T	T	T	T
F	F	F	F	T	F	T	T	T	F	F
F	F	F	F	F	F	T	T	T	T	F

The argument is VALID! When all of the premises are true (Lines 1, 9, 10, 17, and 21), the conclusion is true too. When the conclusion is false (Lines 3, 4, 7, 8, 11, 12, 15, 16, 19, 20, 23, 24, 27, 28, 31, 32), at least one of the premises is false too.

5. *   A = You Fear Something, B = You are Fighting Something, C = Something Weakens you, and D = Higher Levels are Inaccessible

     (1) A → B   given

     (2) B → C   given

     (3) C → D   given [If we take the indicator words at face the third premise could be read as A → (C & D) or (A → C) & D.]

     (4) A → D   (To Prove)

     (5) A → C   Lines 1 and 2, Chain Argument

     (6) A → D   Lines 5 and 3, Chain Argument

A	B	C	D	(A → B)	(B → C)	(C → D)	(A → D)
T	T	T	T	T	T	T	T
T	T	T	F	T	T	F	F
T	T	F	T	T	F	T	T
T	T	F	F	T	F	T	F
T	F	T	T	F	T	T	T
T	F	T	F	F	T	F	F
T	F	F	T	F	T	T	T
T	F	F	F	F	T	T	F
F	T	T	T	T	T	T	T
F	T	T	F	T	T	F	T
F	T	F	T	T	F	T	T
F	T	F	F	T	F	T	T
F	F	T	T	T	T	T	T
F	F	T	F	T	T	F	T
F	F	F	T	T	T	T	T
F	F	F	F	T	T	T	T

The argument is VALID: In all cases where the three premises are true, the conclusion is also true. And, anytime the conclusion is false, at least one of the premises is also false.

NOTE: Also, this way of construing the argument relies on the assumption that "something that weakens you makes you impotent."

6.   (1)   W → E   given

     (2) ~E   given; To Prove: ~W

     (3) ~W   Lines 1 and 2, Modus Tollens

W	E	(W → E)	~E	~W
T	T	T	F	F
T	F	F	T	F
F	T	T	F	T
F	F	T	T	T

The argument is VALID: When all of the premises are true (Line 4), the conclusion is true too. When the conclusion is false (Lines 1 and 2), at least one of the premises is false too.

7. *   M = The Male skeleton is missing a rib. A = The skeleton is Adam's.
    (1) M   given
    (2) A → M   To Prove: A

_____

Invalid: Fallacy of Affirming the Consequent

M	A	A → M	M	
T	T	T	T	The argument is INVALID: In line 2, the conclusion is false, but both of the premises are true.
T	F	T	F	
F	T	F	T	
F	F	T	F	

8.   (1) D → S   given
    (2) ~D → C   given
    (3) D ▼ ~D assumed
    (4) S → L   assumed
    (5) C → L   assumed; To Prove: L

_____

    (6) S ▼ C   Lines 1, 2, and 3, Complex Dilemma
    (7) L   Lines 4, 5, and 6, Simple Dilemma

D	S	C	L	(D → S)	(~D → C)	(D ▼ ~D)	(S → L)	(C → L)	L
T	T	T	T	T	T	T	T	T	T
T	T	T	F	T	T	T	F	F	F
T	T	F	T	T	T	T	T	T	T
T	T	F	F	T	T	T	F	T	F
T	F	T	T	F	T	T	T	T	T
T	F	T	F	F	T	T	T	F	F
T	F	F	T	F	T	T	T	T	T
T	F	F	F	F	T	T	T	T	F
F	T	T	T	T	T	T	T	T	T
F	T	T	F	T	T	T	F	F	F
F	T	F	T	T	F	T	T	T	T
F	T	F	F	T	F	T	F	T	F
F	F	T	T	T	T	T	T	T	T
F	F	T	F	T	T	T	T	F	F
F	F	F	T	T	F	T	T	T	T
F	F	F	F	T	F	T	T	T	F

The argument is VALID: In Lines 1, 3, 9, and 13, all the premises are true and the conclusion is true too. In all cases where the conclusion is false (Lines 2, 4, 6, 8, 10, 12, 14, and 16), at least one of the premises is false.

9. *   (1) L → H   given
       (2) H → F   given; To Prove: L → F

       ─────────────
       (3) L → F   Lines 1 and 2, Chain Argument

L	H	F	(L → H)	(H → F)	(L → F)
T	T	T	T	T	T
T	T	F	T	F	F
T	F	T	F	T	T
T	F	F	F	T	F
F	T	T	T	T	T
F	T	F	T	F	T
F	F	T	T	T	T
F	F	F	T	T	T

The argument is VALID: In all cases where the premises are all true (Lines 1, 5, 7, and 8), the conclusion is also true. In all cases where the conclusion is false (lines 2 and 4), at least one of the premises is also false.

10.   (1) L → ~S   assumption
       (2) S   given; To Prove: ~L

       ─────────────
       (3) ~L   Lines 1 and 2, Modus Tollens

L	~S	S	(L → ~S)	~L
T	T	F	T	F
T	F	T	F	F
F	T	F	T	T
F	F	T	T	T

The argument is VALID: When the conclusion is false (Lines 1 and 2), at least one of the premises is false. And, when all the premises are true (Line 4), the conclusion is true too.

TEST BANK

Multiple Choice Questions

1. Truth tables are useful tools in
   A. determining which statements are believable and which are not.
   B. determining the validity of purportedly deductive arguments.
   C. determining the logical equivalence of different statements forms.
   D. All of the above.
   E. Only B and C above.

   ANSWER: E

2. DeMorgan's Law is primarily used to
   A. convert conditional statements into disjunctive ones.
   B. convert conjunctive statements into disjunctive ones.
   C. convert conjunctive statements into conditional ones.
   D. convert categorical statements into conditional ones.
   E. convert conditional statements into either conjunctive or disjunctive ones.

   ANSWER: B

3. The truth table for the conditional statement, (A → B), is logically equivalent to the conjunction:
   A. ~(~A & ~B)
   B.   ~A & ~B
   C. ~(A & ~B)
   D.   ~A ▼ B
   E. ~(A & B)

   ANSWER: C

4. How does a truth table show if two statements are logically equivalent?
   A. If the lines marked "true" on the truth table all match each other.
   B. If the lines marked "false" on the truth table all match each other.
   C. Either A or B above.
   D. Neither A nor B above.
   E. Both A and B above.

   ANSWER: E

5. How does a truth table show that an argument is invalid?
   A. If any line in the truth table shows a value of "false" for all of the premises.
   B. If any line in the truth table shows "false" for all of the premises and "false" for the conclusion.
   C. If there are no lines in the truth table where all of the premises are true and the conclusion is true.
   D. If any line in the truth table shows a value of "true" for all of the premises and "false" for the conclusion.
   E. Both B and C above.

   ANSWER: D

6. The logical rule known as *Addition* is
   A. the legitimate inference that if a statement is true, so is its disjunction with any other statement.
   B. the legitimate inference that if a statement is true, we can add any other statement to it as a conjunction.
   C. the legitimate inference that any two lines in a derivation may be added together to form a larger conjunction.
   D. the legitimate inference that any simple statement within a complex conjunction may be represented on a line by itself.
   E. None of the above.

   ANSWER: A

7. The logical rule of *Combination* allows for
   A. two statements within a conjunction to be ordered in either possible way (i.e., A & B is also legitimately expressed B & A).
   B. any two statements which occur independently in a proof or derivation to be added together into a conjunction of both statements.
   C. is actually a Fallacy of combining or conjoining together two statements, one of which is false.
   D. the permutation of any two mutually exclusive statements.
   E. the legitimate inference that if any particular statement form is true, so is the combination of that statement with any other statement form.

   ANSWER: B

8. Which of the following argument forms best exemplifies the logical rule of *Simplification*?
   A. (A and B) is true, so either A has to be true or B has to be true.
   B. (A or B) is true, so either A has to be true or B has to be true, but not both.
   C. (A and B) is true, so B has to be true.

D. (A or B) is true, so A and B cannot both be true.
E. None of the above.

ANSWER: C

9. Which three statements below are all logically equivalent?
A. P → Q;   ~P ▼ Q;   ~(P & ~Q)
B. P → Q;   P ▼ Q;   ~(~P & ~Q)
C. P → Q;   ~P ▼ ~Q; ~(P & Q)
D. P → Q;   ~P ▼ ~Q; ~(P & ~Q)
E. P → Q;   P ▼ ~Q;   ~(Q & ~P)

ANSWER: A

10. The conjunction ~(~P & ~Q) is logically equivalent to which of the following disjunctions:
A. ~P ▼ ~Q
B. ~(P ▼ Q)
C. ~(~P ▼ ~Q)
D. P ▼ Q
E. None of the above.

ANSWER: D

Short Answer Questions

Determine whether the following statement forms are logically equivalent by using truth tables:

11. A ▼ ~B   and   A → ~B

ANSWER:

A	B	A▼ ~B	A → ~B
T	T	T	F
T	F	T	T
F	T	F	T
F	F	T	T

The two statements are not logically equivalent.

12. ~C ▼ D   and   C → D

ANSWER:

C	D	~C ▼ D	C → D
T	T	T	T
T	F	F	F
F	T	T	T
F	F	T	T

The two statements ARE logically equivalent.

13. ~(E ▼ ~F)   and   E → F

ANSWER:

E	F	~(E ▼ ~F)	E → F
T	T	F T	T
T	F	F T	F
F	T	T F	T
F	F	F T	T

The two statements are not logically equivalent.

14. ~(~G & ~H)   and   G ▼ V

ANSWER:

G	H	~(~G & ~H)	G ▼ H
T	T	T F	T
T	F	T F	T
F	T	T F	T
F	F	F T	F

The two statements ARE logically equivalent.

Transform the following disjunctions into conditional statements:

15. ~I ▼ ~J

ANSWER: I → ~J

16. (K → L) ▼ (M & N)

ANSWER: ~(K → L) → (M & N)

17. Either the stock market will stabilize or interest rates will climb.

   ANSWER: If the stock market doesn't stabilize, then interest rates will climb.

Transform the following conditional statements into disjunctions:

18. (N → O) → P

   ANSWER: ~(~N ▼ O) ▼ P

19. If you know the answer, you will write it down.

   ANSWER: Either you do not know the answer or you will write it down.

20. If you can't stand the heat, then don't go in the kitchen.

   ANSWER: Either you can stand the heat or you don't go in the kitchen.

Using truth tables, determine whether the following arguments are valid or not:

21. A → B; A → C, ~B ▼ ~C.   Therefore: ~A

   ANSWER:

A	B	C	A → B	A → C	~B ▼ ~C	~A
T	T	T	T	T	F	F
T	T	F	T	F	T	F
T	F	T	F	T	T	F
T	F	F	F	F	T	F
F	T	T	T	T	F	T
F	T	F	T	T	T	T
F	F	T	T	T	T	T
F	F	F	T	T	T	T

   VALID: In all cases where the conclusion is false (Lines 1, 2, 3, and 4), at least one of the premises is false; and, in all cases where the premises are all true (Lines 6, 7, and 8), the conclusion is also true.

22. ~(P → Q); P   Therefore: Q

ANSWER:

P	Q	~(P → Q)	P	Q
T	T	F T	T	T
T	F	T F	T	F
F	T	F T	F	T
F	F	F T	F	F

INVALID: In Line 2 the premises are both true, but the conclusion is false.

23. If you major in mathematics, you will have to do a lot of analytical reasoning. If you major in philosophy, you will have to do a lot of analytical reasoning. Since you do not want to do a lot of analytical reasoning, you should not major in either math or philosophy.

ANSWER:

M → A,   P → A,   ~A;   Therefore: ~(M ▼ P)

M	P	A	~A	M → A	P → A	~(M ▼ P)
T	T	T	F	T	T	F T
T	T	F	F	F	F	F T
T	F	T	F	T	T	F T
T	F	F	F	F	T	F T
F	T	T	T	T	T	F T
F	T	F	T	T	F	F T
F	F	T	T	T	T	T F
F	F	F	T	T	T	T F

INVALID: In Line 5 all of the premises are true but the conclusion is false.

Express the following conjunctions, first as disjunctions, then as conditional statements:

24. C & ~D

ANSWER: ~(~C ▼ D), ~(C → D)

25. ~(~E & F)

ANSWER: E ▼ ~F, ~E → ~F

26. You cannot both graduate this term and have less than 128 semester hour credits.

    ANSWER: Either you are not graduating this term, or you do not have less than 128 semester hour credits.

                      If you are graduating this term, then you do not have less than 128 semester hour credits.

Essay Questions

27. Explain what the rule of simplification is and how it works (give an example).

28. Explain what the rule of addition is and why it yields legitimate conclusions.

29. What are the two major functions of truth tables and why do they "work?"

30. Explain the nature of "truth functionality."

Chapter 11

Statement Forms:
Contraries, Contradictions, and Tautologies

CHAPTER OUTLINE

11.1 Contraries
Exercises
11.2 Contradictions
Exercises
11.3 Tautologies and Contingent Statements
Summary
Exercises
Case Study

KEY TERMS

Contingent Statements - Propositions that under some truth conditions are true and under other conditions are false statements. All simple statements are treated as contingent statements.

Contradiction - The conjunction of two statements related in such a way that exactly one must be true and the other must be false. The column under a contradiction in a truth table yields all lines with the value "false."

Contrary Statements - Two propositions that cannot both be true at the same time but that may both be false simultaneously.

Inconsistent Statements - A pair of assertions which cannot be true at the same time. The two species of inconsistent statements are contrary statements and contradictory statements.

Chapter 11

Tautology - The disjunction of a statement
and its negation; it is always true. Its
column in a truth table yields every line
with a value of "true."

OVERVIEW

The elements of Step Six of the Technique are rounded out, tied together, and completed with a discussion of certain complex statement forms. Certain particular types of statements are distinguished by their *contents*; others, by their *forms*. *Contrary statements* are those complexes of simple statements that, because of their meaning (or content), cannot both be true at the same time, although they both very well may be false at the same time.

A type of inconsistency is also exhibited on the formal level in the case of *contradictions*, which we may determine without even looking at or understanding the content or meaning. This is because each of the two statements in a contradiction is the logical negation of the other. Hence, contradictions must always be false. A truth table reveals that each line under the column of a contradiction has a truth value of "false."

Just as there are statements which must always be false, so there are statements which must always, by their form, be true. These are called *tautologies*. They are expressed as the disjunction of a statement and its negation: "Either A is true or it is not true." Although they are always true, tautologies actually tell us nothing at all because they have to be true regardless of their content.

The most common form of statement is the *contingent statement*. These are statements that under certain truth conditions turn out to be true, and under other conditions turn out to be false. In a truth table for a contingent statement, then, there is at least one line with a value of true and at least one line with a value of false under the column for a contingent statement.

If you have covered Chapters Six and Seven prior to Chapter Eleven, then it might be instructive for you to tie together the concepts in this latter chapter with those covered, particularly in 7.1 with the Square of Opposition and which categorical statements are inconsistent, which are contradictory, which are contrary, and which are subcontrary. Moreover, the ideas from both of these chapters may be picked up again profitably in Chapter Thirteen in the section concerning Liar's Paradox puzzles and problems. When working these kinds of riddles, it is quite helpful to be able to discern contradictory and contrary statements.

SOLUTIONS TO EXERCISE QUESTIONS

Answers to Exercises on Pages 260 and 261

Level A

1. *   Two statements are said to be *contrary* when both of them cannot possibly be true at the same time, but both could conceivably be false at the same time.

2. *   ~(A & B) This says that both A and B cannot be true simultaneously. At least one of them, possibly both, have to be false.

3. *   There are a number of answers which could be given to this question:
   (A) Because *any* conclusion follows from inconsistent premises or beliefs, it would be possible to justify anything one wanted, which makes reasoning little more than a rubber stamp for whatever we were predisposed unreflectively to believe in the first place.
   (B) A second problematic area would be the upshot of trying to follow inconsistent orders or directions. Because obedience to one means disobedience to another, the only way to keep from violating contradictory instructions may be to do nothing (which may itself be another form of violating them).

4. *   Advantages of being able to spot inconsistent statements include:
   (A) Being able to readjust our belief system and to grow with increased knowledge.
   (B) Being able to critically evaluate other people's reasoning so that you force them to reexamine and readjust their own lines of thinking and behavioral tendencies.
   (C) Being able to recognize when someone else is trying to sell you fallacious goods, so that you have good grounds for refusing to "buy" them.

5. *   Basically TRUE. At least from the large perspective, insofar as we are trying to determine if both claims can be simultaneously true and if they can be simultaneously false. As we get into details, inconsistent propositional statements are determined either by truth tables or by the rules governing their usage, while categorical inconsistencies are determined by the Square of Opposition and the Rules for Immediate Inference (See Chapter 7).

6. *   True. They just cannot be true simultaneously.

7. *   False

8. *   False. We may do it, but it is part of the meaning of "reasonable" in Western Logic that a statement and its contrary or contradiction cannot both be true at the same time.

9. *   True. Because it leaves open the possibility that both could be false.

10. *   True

Level B

1. *   It is possible to believe in both God and the Devil, especially when the two are not conceived as exactly contradictory to one another (e.g., as having exactly similar powers except one is all good and the other, all evil).

2.   These two statements are *Contraries* if the "Brenda" in (a) is the same person as the

"Brenda" in (b) and if a person can only have *one* favorite color.

3. * These two statements are *Contrary*, if a state can have only one capital.

4. These are not necessarily inconsistent since each state has two Senators.

5. * These two are *Contradictory* if they refer to the same place and time.

6. Again, these two are *Contradictory* if they refer to the same time of his life. Often we do change our beliefs as we grow, and these two statements may be accurate if they describe different periods in Marx's life.

7. * These may both be true.

8. These two appear to be inconsistent statements, but could be considered as compatible if she loves some rap artists and intensely dislikes others.

9. * *Inconsistent* Statements.

10. *Inconsistent* Statements.

Level C

1. * For example, go back to Case Study Two on Pages 36 through 38 and look at the claims made by Dennis Meadows and Lawrence Summers. Which ones of these are inconsistent?

Answers to Exercises on Pages 266 and 267

Level A

1. * A logical *Contradiction* is the conjunction of two statements related such that one must be true while the other is false and conversely, if the second is true, the first must be false. Such a conjunction shown in a truth table will result in all "false" values in the column under the conjunct.

2. * Both contrary and contradictory pairs cannot be true simultaneously. However, contrary statement pairs *can* both be false (All chewing gum is sugarless/No chewing gum is sugarless), whereas contradictory statement pairs cannot both be false either. (If one is false, the other must necessarily be true.)

3. * When the conjunction of those two statements is displayed in a truth table, every line under that column will be "false."

4. * One way is to derive a statement and its opposite or negation from the given set of premises. That statement and its contradiction may be simple (A & ~A) or complex [~(A → B) & (A → B)].

5. * True

6. * False. The second statement must necessarily be false if the first one is true.

7. * False. A truth table will show that line 3 has a value of "true."

8. * False. It would be a tautology.

9. * False. All contradictory statements are also inconsistent insofar as one of the two has to be false.

10. * False. This may generate some controversy, but most likely the disagreement will be

verbal: if the statement "it is sunny" is exactly equivalent in meaning to "it is not raining," then the two statements will be seen as contradictory. On the other hand, because this can be seen as a matter of *content* rather than *form*, some people will maintain that they have seen it raining when in fact the sun was still shining. Since both can be true, they are not even inconsistent.

Level B

1. *   Contradictory
2.   Inconsistent
3. *   Inconsistent
4.   Inconsistent
5. *   Contradictory
6.   Inconsistent
7. *   Inconsistent
8.   Maybe neither.
9. *   Contradictory
10.   Contradictory
11. * (1) R → W   given
       (2) ~(W & S)   given
       (3) S   given
       (4) R   given

       ───────────
       (5) ~W   Lines 2 and 3, Conjunctive Argument
       (6) ~R   Lines 1 and 5, Modus Tollens
       (7) R & ~R   Lines 4 and 6, Conjunction

12.   (1) L ▼ J   given
       (2) ~P → ~L   given
       (3) P   given
       (4) ~J   given

       ───────────
       (5) L   Lines 1, 4 Disjunctive Argument
       (6) P   Lines 2, 5 Modus Ponens
       No contradiction here: Pam's going to the party; so is Lucy; but Joe is not.

13. * (1) E ▼ A   given
    (2) A → L   given
    (3) E → M   given
    (4) L   given
    (5) E   given

---

    (6) M   Lines 3, 5 Modus Ponens

Not contradictory, perhaps she feels both logical and majestic while listening to Beethoven.

14. (1) ~(B & I)   given
    (2) B   given
    (3) ~I → ~D given
    (4) D   given

---

    (5) ~I   Lines 1 and 2, Conjunctive Argument
    (6) I   Lines 3 and 4, Modus Tollens
    (7) I & ~I   Lines 5 and 6, Conjunction

Yes, a contraction results.

Answers to Exercises on Pages 269 and 270

Level A

1. * A *Tautology* is a complex statement usually expressed as a disjunction of a statement and its negation such that a truth table column yields all "true"values.

2. * Under any and all conditions, a tautology is true by virtue of its form alone and regardless of its content.

3. * Actually, contradictions and tautologies are direct opposites insofar as one is a conjunction of two statements which is always false while the other is a disjunction of two statements which is always true. The tautology may be expressed as the denial of the contradiction and, conversely, contradiction may be expressed as the denial of the tautology.

4. * A *Contingent Statement* is one which yields a mixture of true and false values in a truth table. Basically, it is either a simple statement (they are all contingent statements) or a complex statement that under some truth conditions is true and under other truth conditions is false. We must look at the content of the statement itself to determine whether it is true or false.

5. * A *Tautology* differs from a *Contingent Statement* in two important ways. First, all of the truth values for the tautology are "true," whereas they are not all true for a contingent statement. And, second, a tautology is determined by its form alone whereas a contingent

statement is determined by its content.

6. * False. (Because of its form.)

7. * True. (Sort of: that is, its truth values may under certain conditions be true, but under other conditions be false.)

8. * True

9. * True

10. * False. (The contingent statement is the most common.)

Level B

1. *   R ▼ ~R   —   A Tautology

R	~R	(R ▼ ~R)
T	F	T
F	T	T

2.   ~G → ~G   A Tautology

~G	~G → ~G
T	T
F	T

3. *   R → (R ▼ S) A Tautology

R	S	(R ▼ S)	R → (R ▼ S)
T	T	T	T
T	F	T	T
F	T	T	T
F	F	F	T

4.   P → (M ▼ ~M)   A Tautology

P	M	(M ▼ ~M)	P → (M ▼ ~M)
T	T	T	T
T	F	T	T
F	T	T	T
F	F	T	T

5. *   (R & ~R) → (S ▼ ~S)   A Tautology

R	S	(R & ~R)	(S ▼ ~S)	[(R & ~R) → (S ▼ ~S)]
T	T	F	T	T
T	F	F	T	T
F	T	F	T	T
F	F	F	T	T

6.   I → (L & ~L)   A Contingent Statement

I	L	(L & ~L)	[I → (L & ~L)]
T	T	F	F
T	F	F	F
F	T	F	T
F	F	F	T

7. *   H → ~H   A Contingent Statement

H	~H	(H → ~H)
T	F	F
F	T	T

8.   (D ▼ ~D)   A Tautology

D	~D	(D ▼ ~D)
T	F	T
F	T	T

9. *   A Contingent Statement (which is true by definition)
10.   A Tautology (one is either married or not married)
11. *   A Contingent Statement
12.   A Contingent Statement
13. *   A Contingent Statement
14.   A Tautology (R → R)
15. *   A Contingent Statement
16.   A Contingent Statement
17. *   A Contingent Statement

18.   Can be argued in two ways:
       (A) It is a tautology because it says R ▼ ~R where wrong means the same thing as "not right," or
       (B) It is a contingent statement because it leaves out the possibility that it is neither right nor wrong but a matter of no moral significance; i.e., that it is amoral or non-moral.

TEST BANK

Multiple Choice Questions

1. Which of the following expresses two propositions that are contrary to each other?
    A. ~A & ~B
    B. ~A ▼ ~B
    C. ~A → ~B
    D. ~(A ▼ B)
    E. (A & B) ▼ (~A & ~B)

    ANSWER: B

2. What does it mean to say that two propositions are contrary to each other?
    A. They cannot both be false.
    B. They cannot both have the same truth value.
    C. Neither one of the two can be true.
    D. They cannot both be true at the same time.
    E. Knowing the truth value of one determines the truth value of the other.

    ANSWER: D

3. What is the difference between contradictory and contrary statements?
    A. There is no difference; they are the same thing.
    B. While both of them are false, contradictory statements are stronger than contrary statements.
    C. Contradictory statements have completely opposite truth values, while contrary statements may both be false.
    D. Contradictory statements are mean; contrary ones are ornery.
    E. None of the above.

    ANSWER: C

4. Which of the following statement forms are inconsistent?

           I.   contrary statements

           II.   contradictory statements

           III.   contingent statements

  A. I only

  B. II only

  C. III only

  D. I and II only

  E. I, II, and III

ANSWER: D

5. ~(A ▼ B) & (C ▼ D) represents which of the following kinds of statements?

  A. a contingent statement

  B. a contrary statement

  C. a contradictory statement

  D. a tautology

  E. a subcontrary statement

ANSWER: A

6. What is the difference between a contingent statement and a tautology?

  A. A contingent statement's truth value is determined by its content while a tautology's truth value is a matter of its form alone.

  B. A contingent statement's truth value depends on many different things while a tautology's truth value may be looked up in a dictionary.

  C. A contingent statement might end up being either true or false, but a tautology is always true, no matter what.

  D. A contingent statement could mean many different things in different contexts, but a tautology has no meaning at all.

  E. Both A and C above.

ANSWER: E

7. Which of the following does not express a contradiction?

  A. A & ~A

  B. (A & ~B) ▼ (~A & B)

  C. (A & B) & ~(A & B)

  D. (A ▼ ~B) & ~(A ▼ ~B)

  E. (A ▼ B) & ~(A ▼ B)

ANSWER: B

8. What is the difference between a contradiction and a tautology?
    A. A tautology is known by its form; a contradiction, by its content or meaning.
    B. A contradiction is known by its form; a tautology, by its content or meaning.
    C. Both are known by their content rather than their form; but, contradictions are always false while tautologies are always true.
    D. Both are known by their form and not by their content; but, contradictions are always false while tautologies are always true.
    E. None of the above.

ANSWER: D

9. The formal proposition ~(A ▼ B) expresses
    A. that A and B are contrary statements.
    B. a contradiction.
    C. a tautology.
    D. inconsistent statements.
    E. contingent statements.

ANSWER: E

10. The formal proposition ~(A & B) expresses
    A. That A and B are contrary statements.
    B. that A and B are contradictory statements.
    C. a tautology.
    D. that A and B are subcontrary statements.
    E. None of the above.

ANSWER: A

Short Answer Questions

State whether the following pairs of statements are inconsistent, contrary, contradictory, or logically compatible, and why:

11. (a) I believe in life after death.
    (b) I do not believe in immortality.

    ANSWER:
        This one can be handled several ways. First, if by "immortality" one means "life after death," then a contradiction results as if one were to say, "I believe in life after death, but I

don't believe in life after death." Second, one may want to maintain that there is a period after death in which there is some sense of survival or life, but that ultimately everything dies. In this case, there is no incompatibility. Third, there are other ways of reading this example, as long as one is able to justify that reading.

12. (a) All elephants are gray.
    (b) I did find one African elephant that was brown.

   ANSWER: Definitely a contradiction.

13. (a) Post Impressionists are my favorite painters.
    (b) Cubists are my favorite painters.

   ANSWER:
   The two statements are contrary and hence inconsistent, but they are not necessarily contradictory because both of them might be false.

14. (a) I love her.
    (b) I hate her.

   ANSWER:
   These two statements may not be contrary, contradictory, nor inconsistent in any way. We occasionally have conflicting feelings about one and the same person or object.

15. (a) The Soviet Union won World War II.
    (b) The United Kingdom won World War II.

   ANSWER:
   The two statements may both be true; therefore, they are not inconsistent, contrary, or contradictory.

State whether the following sentences are contradictions, tautologies, or contingent statements:

16. Either you passed the test or you did not pass it. (Assume you took it!)

   ANSWER: A tautology.

17. If you don't pass go, then you can't collect two hundred dollars.

   ANSWER: A contingent statement.

18. You cannot both go to the movies tonight and not go to the movies tonight.

ANSWER: This is the negation of a contradiction which makes it a tautology.

19. You are both left-handed and not left-handed.

ANSWER:
   On the face of it, this looks like a contradiction, but it is actually a contingent statement because a person can be ambidextrous.

20. The cake batter rose but it didn't rise.

ANSWER: Definitely a contradiction.

Use truth tables to test whether the following statements are contradictions, tautologies, or contingent statements.

21. (A & ~B) & ~(~A ▼ B)

ANSWER:

A	B	~A	~(~A ▼ B)	(A & B)	&	~(~A ▼ B)
T	T	F	T	T	F	F
T	F	F	F	F	F	T
F	T	T	T	F	F	F
F	F	T	T	F	F	F

This statement is a contradiction: all values for the conjunction are false.

22. (A ▼ B) ▼ ~(~A → B)

ANSWER:

A	B	(A ▼ B)	(~A → B)	~(~A → B)	(A ▼ B) ▼ ~(~A → B)
T	T	T	T	F	T
T	F	T	T	F	T
F	T	T	F	T	T
F	F	F	T	F	F

This is a contingent statement: the values for the entire disjunction are true in some instances (Lines 1 - 3) and false in others (Line 4).

23. (A → B) ▼ (A & ~B)

ANSWER:

A	B	(A → B)	(A & ~B)	(A → B) ▼ (A & ~B)
T	T	T	F	T
T	F	F	T	T
F	T	T	F	T
F	F	T	F	T

This is a tautology: the values for each line in the entire disjunction are always true.

24. (A & ~B) ▼ (~A & B)

ANSWER:

A	B	(A & ~B)	(~A & B)	(A & ~B) ▼ (~A & B)
T	T	F	F	F
T	F	T	F	T
F	T	F	T	T
F	F	F	F	F

This is a contingent statement: in two lines the disjunction is false and in two lines it is true.

Determine whether the following arguments contain or imply contradictions. First translate the statements into symbolic form, then try to derive a contradiction. Note, the conclusions are omitted, because the main function here is to search for inconsistent premises.

25. Either Al or Bob will attend the meeting. If Cindy does not go to the meeting, then neither will Al. It turns out that Cindy is attending the meeting. Bob will not attend the meeting.

ANSWER:
line 1	A ▼ B	given
line 2	~C → ~A	given
line 3	C	given
line 4	~B	given

| line 5 | A | lines 1, 4, Disjunctive Argument |

No contradiction: Al is going, Bob is not, Cindy is going.

26. You don't listen to Jazz and Rap music in the same afternoon. You are listening to Jazz right now. If you do not listen to Rap music, then you will have time to study. But you don't have time to study.

ANSWER:

    line 1   ~(J & R)   given
    line 2   J   given
    line 3   ~R $\rightarrow$ S   given
    line 4   ~S   given

---

    line 5   ~R   lines 1, 2 Conjunctive Argument
    line 6   R   lines 3, 4 Modus Tollens
    line 7   R & ~R   lines 5, 6 Conjunction
    This is a contradiction.

27. If a person pays lip service to the health hazards of smoking but continues to purchase cigarettes, then that person likes to smoke. On the other hand, if a person goes to great lengths to avoid designated smoking sections and spends a lot of time and money trying to stop smoking, then that person does not like to smoke. Now, John definitely pays lip service to the health hazards of smoking and goes to great lengths to avoid designated smoking sections. Moreover, he has spent a lot of time and money trying to stop smoking, although he continues to purchase cigarettes.

ANSWER:

    line 1   (L & P) $\rightarrow$ S   given
    line 2   (A & T) $\rightarrow$ ~S   given
    line 3   L & A   given
    line 4   T & P   given

---

    line 5   L   line 3 Simplification
    line 6   P   line 4 Simplification
    line 7   L & P   lines 5, 6 Conjunction
    line 8   S   lines 7, 1 Modus Ponens
    line 9   A   line 3 Simplification
    line 10 T   line 4 Simplification
    line 11 A & T   lines 9, 10 Conjunction
    line 12 ~S   lines 11, 2 Modus Ponens
    line 13 S & ~S   lines 8, 12 Conjunction
    This is a contradiction.

Essay Questions

28. How could you use a truth table to show that two statements were or were not contrary to each other?

ANSWER:

Construct a truth table such that all possible cases of truth values are considered. Then, look to see whether it is possible that both statements can have a value of "true" at the same time. If so, then the two statements are not contrary. However, if there are no lines in which both statements can be true at the same time, then the statements may be considered contraries.

29. Explain why a truth table can show two statements to be contradictory.

ANSWER:

A truth table can show that two statements are contradictory by showing that they cannot both be true at the same time, *and* they cannot both be false at the same time. In other words, when one of the statements is true, the truth value of the other statement must necessarily be false. Conversely, when the truth value of the first statement is false, the second must necessarily be true. Thus, the conjunction of these two statements in a truth table will yield a column with truth values that are always false.

30. What exactly is the "law of contradiction" in logic or critical thinking, and how would you assess its worth?

ANSWER:

The Law of Contradiction in logic holds that a statement cannot be both true and false at the same time. The Law of the Excluded Middle holds any statement must be either one or the other—true or false. The conjunction of any statement, simple or complex, and its negation will of necessity yield a contradiction.

Chapter 12

Inductive Reasoning

CHAPTER OUTLINE

12.1 Analogies and Metaphors
Exercises
12.2 Mill's Methods
Exercises
12.3 Hypotheses and Theories
Summary
Exercises
Case Study

KEY TERMS

Analogical Argument - An argument in which an analogy is used to support a conclusion.

Analogy - The comparison or contrast of two different objects, ideas, or situations.

Causal Explanation - An explanation based on the relationship between physical stimuli and their effects.

Combined Method - Using both the methods of agreement and difference, this method is helpful when the method

of difference should be used but the surrounding circumstances cannot be varied. Also called the *indirect method*.

Hypothesis - A prediction about a cause-and-effect relationship.

Illustrative or Explanatory Analogy - The clarification of a difficult or complex point by comparison with a simpler case or example.

Inductive Argument - An argument that does not guarantee the truth of the conclusion, even if the premises are known to be true.

Intentional Explanation - An argument explaining why an individual does some thing using as premises the *reasons* for their behavior.

Method of Agreement - The variation of the surrounding circumstances of a suspected cause.

Method of Concomitant Variation - The correlation of varying degrees of a cause with varying degrees of the effect.

Method of Difference - The technique of varying the suspected cause.

Method of Residues - Correlation of causes and effects with the resulting "residue" effects attributed to the "leftover" causes.

Mill's Methods - Techniques of inductive reasoning analyzed by the philosopher John Stuart Mill.

Speculative Analogy - The use of a comparison or contrast to guide behavior and actions.

Theory - A set of concepts that gives one a structure by which to make observations and to frame hypotheses.

OVERVIEW

In this chapter the technique is focussed upon the more prominent methods of inductive reasoning. Previously, we have learned to analyze and evaluate both the structure or form of reasoning in some of its deductive guises (in Chapters Six through Eleven), and we have looked at how to spot some of the more glaring types of content fallacies (in Chapter Five). Inductive reasoning, likewise, has both content and structural problems associated with it. Perhaps the primary difference between inductive and deductive reasoning is that the premises of the former do not and cannot guarantee the truth of the conclusion in the same way that deductive arguments do.

Metaphors and analogies are one of the most commonly found forms of inductive reasoning. They function by comparison; by pointing out similarities in things and events, other similarities are said to follow. While analogies tend to function on the denotative level, with explicitly drawn comparisons, metaphors have more of a symbolic function and tend to operate more on the connotative level. We use both of these inductive forms on several levels. First, they are probably most often used illustratively to make a more complex or opaque point a bit more understandable. Second, they are also used speculatively to suggest, influence, guide, or direct behavior to certain directions or away from others. Third, and most important for critical thinking, analogies are used argumentatively to establish conclusions.

Argumentative analogies are extraordinarily multi-purposed tools. They may be used by researchers to draw conclusions about how certain drugs and treatments will affect human beings based upon how they operate on other types of animals. Or, they may be used when we want to have the law applied to our case in the same way it was applied to a precedent that has been set and we must argue that our case is substantially the same as the previous one. Indeed, the list is limitless. All of these uses, however, may be assessed according to the degree to which the analogy has been established, the strength of the conclusion reached relative to the evidence given in support of it, the relevance of the main similarities and the absence of any crucial differences in the areas of comparison.

The nineteenth century philosopher and savant, John Stuart Mill, decided to codify some of the main ways that inductive reasoning is used, so that increased accuracy might be achieved. According to his "Methods," the technique of or method of agreement is used by holding the suspected cause constant while varying the surrounding circumstances. Although we can never be one hundred percent sure by this method, it is fairly reliable at ruling out potential or suspected causes. The method of difference, on the other hand, holds the surrounding circumstances constant while observing the effects first with, and then without, the suspected cause.

The combined method of agreement and difference (sometimes called the "indirect method") can be useful when one would like to employ the method of difference but it is impossible or implausible to hold the surrounding circumstances constant. The combined method, then, makes use of two groups with similar, but not identical, circumstances. In one group, the suspected cause is present; in the second, it is not. Often, when we utilize "control groups," we are using the indirect method. The method of residues is a technique whereby we correlate and assign known causes to or with known effects and there are some residual phenomena which need to be explained. We do so by associating the "leftover" effects with "leftover" causes. Finally, the method of concomitant variations is the mathematical assignment of correlations between suspected causes and effects attributed to them. Coefficients of correlation generally range from zero (meaning there is absolutely no correlation between the alleged cause and the supposed effect) to one (which would mean that there is a perfect one-to-one relationship between the two events).

Theories and hypotheses are explained in this chapter according to their use as aids in inductive reasoning. Theories, like those of relativity and evolution, give us a set of concepts and a conceptual framework to help us make sense of the world as we experience it. Hypotheses are the specific tools we use to make predictions about cause-and-effect relationships. Within this framework, we also distinguished between intentional and causal explanations of events. The intentional explanations relied more on personal motives and reasons for performing certain actions, while causal explanations tend to focus more on the physical, physio-chemical factors leading to the event in question.

Instead of looking for "validity," as we did in deductive forms of reasoning, we look more for "reliability" and "warranted assertibility" in terms of inductive reasoning, since these latter never purported to establish their conclusions with one hundred percent certainty.

Chapter 12

SOLUTIONS TO EXERCISE QUESTIONS

Answers to Exercises on Pages 281 and 282

Level A

1 *   *Inductive reasoning* is argumentation in which the conclusion goes beyond what is
      contained in the premises. Hence, the conclusion gives us new information. The premises
      may support this conclusion to a greater or lesser degree, but they can never guarantee it
      100%. It would not be a contradiction to say all the premises are true, relevant, and fair,
      but that the conclusion might still be false. In the case of *deductive reasoning*, the
      argument is put forward as if the premises definitely guaranteed the truth of the conclusion
      all by themselves. No new information is needed because the conclusion is already
      contained in the premises (allegedly). In *valid* deduction arguments, it would be an
      outright logical contradiction to maintain that the premises were true, but that the
      conclusion is false.

2. *   An *analogy* is a comparison of the similarities between two things, events, or ideas,
      usually for the purposes of illustration, speculation, or argumentation. Analogical
      reasoning is a form of logical inference based upon the assumption that if two things are
      alike in certain ways then they must be similar in other respects as well.

3. *   A *metaphor* is a figure of speech which may constitute a special class of analogies. Strictly
      speaking, they are probably non-argumentative, because they consist of the use of a word
      or phrase to describe or modify something to which they do not literally apply. Still they
      may be persuasive because of the connotative force they carry.

4. *   A *speculative analogy* is an explicit comparison of one situation with another in order to
      instigate or guide actions. While it does more than merely illustrate similarities between
      two things or ideas, it stops short of actually putting forward the reasons or premises
      necessary to constitute an argument.

5. *   An *illustrative analogy* is the clarification of a more difficult or complex point by
      comparing it with something simpler or more well known. A *speculative analogy* does not
      merely seek to enlighten or explain but to incite action or to direct behavioral tendencies
      and feelings.

6. *   True. (Ordinarily)

7. *   True

8. *   False. (Although they do not guarantee their conclusions, they are often the best form of
      reasoning available in the situation.)

9. *   Maybe True, but not necessarily (i.e., they do not have to be).

10. * True

Level B

1. *   Comparing the conduct of business with a football game is probably a *speculative*

analogy. That is, it is doing more than merely illustrating information about doing business, but it is not trying to prove or establish a conclusion about business on this basis. If it incites one's employees to work harder or to have a feeling of team spirit and camaraderie, perhaps it is effective for an employer. The problem here may be one of cultural bias: that is, people who do not grow up playing football or who do not like it may feel disenfranchised or slighted by this analogy as if business were not meant for them. Particularly women, Asians, physically challenged persons, to name a few may feel as if they were being intentionally excluded. It also slights or biases the connotation of business as essentially a competitive, not a cooperative, enterprise and also one which is insignificant or playful (like a game) and not of serious importance. Then, of course, we may have just performed overkill on an analogy that was not meant to be all that serious in the first place!

2. Again, this is probably meant to be a Speculative Analogy to the extent that it is designed to influence attitudes and behavior. Because there is absolutely no apparent need for a fish to have a bicycle, the comparison is meant to suggest (descriptively) that a woman does not have any apparent need for a male in her life. When this analogy was first formulated some two or three decades ago, it was vivid, illuminative, fresh, suggestive, and challenging to the prevailing norms that a woman would grow up, and, if she became educated at all, it was merely instrumental in her quest for a husband for whom she would bear children, keep house, and, if necessary, play nurse. Now, however, the analogy is slightly worn and dated, perhaps a bit less relevant that it was thirty years ago, but still there is some merit to the comparison.

3. * This one is a cute play on words but it does not explain or even illustrate very much. It is not an argument by analogy, nor is it speculative. If anything, its purpose may be to warn us about the dangers of using an argument by analogy when other forms are available.

4. This is probably a speculative analogy, designed to get people to see the connection between an endeavor that is normally regarded positively (playing the piano) and one which at first may be regarded as a nuisance. Then, it is meant to suggest that if we continue to practice using logical techniques, we will become more skilled, just as we might if we continued to practice playing the piano.

5. * The comparison is one of those which is so time worn that it has probably outlived any utility it may have. If there is a conclusion to this, it is unstated and would probably be that baseball teams cannot be meaningfully compared to basketball teams. If so, we have not been given any real evidence to support such a claim other than the disanalogy.

6. This one is probably illustrative and instructional and, for that reason, a bit speculative: if we are fair to the intended meaning, it seems to indicate that there are a number of similarities between having a "nonhuman animal companion" and raising a child and that we would do well to consider those points of comparison before doing either one. Some may be quick to point out that "pets" are not something to be "owned" any more and that "having a child" is ambiguous insofar as it could mean the actual carrying of a fetus to term and the consequent process of childbirth, or it could mean the nurturing of that child from birth to maturity (or both).

7. *   This one is actually a metaphor in which Marx has "poisoned the well" with the emotional appeal of the word "slave." It is calculated to have the effect of waking up salaried employees and wage earners into "realizing" that they are being exploited and enslaved. The fairness of such a metaphor would depend in part on how much actual evidence was given to support such a claim.

8.   Former President Bush's analogy is calculated to poison the well against Saddam Hussein by likening him to one of the more infamous characters in recent history. As such, it is not argumentative but probably speculative since it is designed to color attitudes and behavioral tendencies.

9. *   This is an illustrative analogy, not an argumentative or a speculative one. As such, it is helpful to a point, as long as we are mindful of some very key differences, such as family or personal interaction which centered around the fireplace but which is usually cut off by passive spectating around the television.

10.   This one is more of a metaphor and, although an older one, is meant to point out the horrible and lasting consequences of war.

11. * This is more of a literary metaphor. Perhaps it is illustrative, but it may also engender the Fallacy of Assuming Existence if it makes us uncritically believe in the existence of souls.

12.   This one is also a metaphor. It is not speculative nor is it argumentative. It is meant to illustrate that the Chief Executive is the person who, like our own head, is supposed to make decisions concerning what we are going to do and who is held responsible for implementing those decisions.

13. * Perhaps this is a speculative analogy if it is meant to advise someone to be ruthless in their business endeavors. The use of the term 'rat', which generally has negative connotations, may make this analogy unduly biased. If the analogy is meant to be illustrative, then it may also cause negative impressions about business.

14.   This one is a metaphor designed to poison people's attitudes about, as well as alert them to, the dangers of cigarette smoking. As such, it is speculative.

15. * This is an illustrative analogy, meant to explain the author's style. It is helpful to those who understand what a musical chord is.

Answers to Exercises on Pages 288 through 290

Level A

1. *   The method of agreement asks us to vary the surrounding circumstances, while keeping the suspected cause or effect the same.

2. *   The method of difference requires us to vary the suspected cause, while we keep the surrounding conditions constant or the same.

3. *   The method of concomitant variation is one in which we match variations in the suspected cause with variations that occur in the effect.

4. *   The method of residues is one in which we first correlate known causes with known effects and then conclude that the remaining effects must be the result of the remaining

causes.

5. * Hasty generalization is a fallacy in which one draws a conclusion about an entire population or a different portion of it from an insufficient number of cases within that population.

6. * In the fallacy of accident, one assumes that whatever quality is generally found to be true of a group must be present in each and every member of that group.

7. * True

8. * False

9. * True

10. * True. (It would also be a Fallacy of the Undistributed Middle Term if analyzed as a Categorical Syllogism.)

Level B

1. * Method of Agreement: Try the horn, the lights, the radio, the lighter.

2. Method of Difference: Keep all of the appliances plugged in and then turn them off one at a time (and then back on if they are not the culprit).

3. * Method of Concomitant Variation: Experiment with various temperatures.

4. Method of Concomitant Variation: Experiment with adding a bit more sugar to each successive batch that you make.

5. * Method of Concomitant Variation: Correlate speed with distance.

6. Combined Method: Use both the methods of Agreement and Difference in determining which particular food or combination of foods is causing the allergic reaction.

7. * Method of Concomitant Variation: Correlate crime rates with different phases of the moon.

8. Good Question: Probably the methods of Concomitant Variation and of Residues, although a case may also be made for using the Combined Method.

9. * Combined Method/Concomitant Variation: Establish "control groups," then vary the cholesterol intake.

10. Method of Difference.

Level C

1. This one could be the Combined Method, if we have two or more groups, one whose diet remains the same throughout the experiment; one, perhaps with a placebo; and one with the same diet but one extra quart of solids-fortified skim milk per week. Some may argue that the Method of Concomitant Variation is more appropriate, because surely there is a need to establish an upper limit for how much milk intake would be healthy.

2. Method of Concomitant Variation: As the concentration of CO_2 increases, the temperature of the earth increases.

3. Method of Concomitant Variation again: As the size of the brain relative to the body varies, so does the extent of the mental powers.

Chapter 12

4.   Method of Agreement.
5.   Method of Residues.

Answers to Exercises on Pages 296 and 297

Level A

1. *   Hypothesis
2. *   Hypothesis
3. *   A causal explanation is one based on the physical relationship between causes and their effects.
4. *   An intentional explanation is based on the reasons one cites for performing an action.
5. *   A direct cause is said to be a sufficient cause for producing an effect. A contributory cause relies on other causes to produce the effect.
6. *   A hypothesis is a prediction about a cause and effect relationship. A theory is a set of concepts which provide a structure for making observations and framing hypotheses.
7. *   True
8. *   True
9. *   False
10. *   False

Level B

1. *   Intentional
2.   Causal
3. *   Causal
4.   Intentional
5. *   Causal
6.   Causal/Intentional?
7. *   Causal
8.   Causal
9. *   Intentional
10.   Causal
11. *   Intentional
12.   Causal
13. *   Intentional
14.   Causal
15. *   Intentional
16.   Causal
17. *   Causal
18.   Causal/Intentional
19. *   Intentional

20.   Causal/Intentional

TEST BANK

Multiple Choice Questions

1. Arguments by analogy are always
    A. incorrect
    B. deductive
    C. inductive
    D. fallacious
    E. illustrative

    ANSWER: C

2. "When you're boiling mad, don't hold it in! If a tea kettle could not blow off steam, it would explode! Therefore, if you don't let the anger out when you're really mad, you'll blow up too." Which of the following BEST refutes this little gem of Pop Psychology reasoning?
    A. Explosions are O.K. as long as they don't get into someone else's personal space.
    B. People are not tea kettles and "boiling mad" is only a metaphor. There are too many relevant dissimilarities here, so this is a Faulty Analogy.
    C. Experiments are first needed to confirm that boiling tea kettles really will explode if the steam is not allowed to escape.
    D. This argument is actually inductive in nature and therefore only probably true.
    E. This is bound to be bad advice because it has gotten me into trouble more than once.

    ANSWER: B

3. The reason why analogical arguments cannot guarantee their conclusions with certainty is because
    A. there are no guarantees in logic or critical thinking.
    B. no one has ever proved conclusively that there are guarantees in logic.
    C. most people believe that arguments by analogy cannot have guaranteed conclusions.
    D. every argument by analogy assumes that the two things being compared are exactly alike, which is impossible.
    E. experts in the fields of sociology, anthropology, and related social scientists concurred that arguments by analogy cannot achieve certainty.

    ANSWER: D

4. All hypotheses

A. involve predictions.
B. are fallacious themselves or rely on fallacies.
C. are ultimately deductive in nature.
D. involve the hypothetico-inductive principle.
E. are metaphors.

ANSWER: A

5. Theories
A. are another word for hypotheses.
B. function as logical explanations.
C. are analogical generalizations.
D. must contain some intentionality.
E. All of the above.

ANSWER: B

6. A necessary cause
A. must occur every time an effect occurs.
B. can bring about an effect all by itself.
C. is discovered by the method of direct agreement.
D. is more important than a sufficient cause.
E. None of the above.

ANSWER: A

7. The method of analogy
A. compares two things by the use of a metaphor or poetic language.
B. must make use of a counterfactual conditional.
C. occurs when more of a cause results in more of an effect.
D. assumes one thing causes another if they are frequently found together.
E. assumes something possesses an unknown property if it closely resembles other things known to possess that property.

ANSWER: E

8. Mill's Method of Difference
A. works best in everyday, nonscientific situations.
B. works best in highly controlled, laboratory conditions.
C. works best when the cause and effect come in varying degrees or quantities.
D. is the one method that can absolutely guarantee its results.
E. is most effective when known causes have been assigned to known effects and there is

some leftover unexplained phenomena requiring an explanation.

ANSWER: B

9. A Fallacy of Hasty Generalization occurs when
   A. one uses cases which are not typical of the whole population being sampled.
   B. one assumes that an organic whole will possess the exact same properties that each of its parts possesses.
   C. one assumes something which is true as a general rule but which has not been substantially proven, and then misapplies that rule to a case to which it doesn't really apply.
   D. one jumps to a conclusion about a whole population or other unsampled parts of that population based upon an examination of an insufficient number of cases or examples.
   E. one has enough information, but is too hasty or quick in assembling that information in drawing a conclusion.

ANSWER: D

10. Mill's Method of Agreement
    A. keeps the surrounding circumstances constant while varying the suspected cause or effect.
    B. keeps the suspected cause constant while varying the surrounding circumstances.
    C. looks for differences in degree of change in the effect when differences in degree of change in the cause occur.
    D. looks for strong concurrence among the experts in the particular field in question.
    E. is useful when there are no available instances where the cause in question is absent.

ANSWER: B

Short Answer Questions

The following passages involve some kind of inductive reasoning. Identify the type; e.g., generalization, theory or hypothesis, analogy, causal argument (one of Mill's Methods), causal or intentional explanation. Also, rate the reliability you would give each, according to the following scale:

A	= extremely reliable	B	= for the most part reliable
C	= maybe, maybe not reliable	D	= poorly reliable (unreliable mainly)
E	= extremely unreliable		

11. The people of South Carolina are really boring. I know this because every time I travel through the state and stop for gas, the service station attendant never has anything interesting to say.

    ANSWER: A Generalization (probably the Fallacy of Hasty Generalization) either D,

253

mainly unreliable, or E, completely unreliable.

12. Mental disorders are, in general, the result of chemical imbalances in the brain.

ANSWER: This is an hypothesis about a causal relationship. It is probably testable using some form of the Method of Concomitant Variation or the Join Method of Agreement and Difference. Reliability, probably C or D. Perhaps, an example of Assuming the Cause Fallacy if the suspected cause turns out to be a symptom.

13. The war in Viet Nam, like the American Civil War, was fought to safeguard democracy.

ANSWER: This is an Explanation which is intentional rather than causal in nature. Reliability, anywhere from B to E.

14. For a long time law enforcement officers have noticed a connection between the phases of the moon and the amount of crime committed. In particular, every time the moon is full there is more petty crime. The fact that there is a full moon seems to be the only common element which accounts for this increase in crime.

ANSWER: This is a Causal Explanation based upon Mill's Methods, probably the Method of Agreement or the Combined Method. Reliability, anywhere from B to E.

15. The lights were out and the car was gone, so we concluded that nobody was home.

ANSWER: This one could be seen as an Analogical Argument or as a Generalization. If the former, then one is drawing a conclusion based upon the prior similar situations when the lights were out and the car was gone. Or, it may be a combination of both inductive forms. Reliability, perhaps B or C.

16. Since the Rockets have lost their last ten home games, there is no reason to believe that they won't lose the next one also.

ANSWER: A Generalization, perhaps hasty. Reliability B to D.

17. Yuck! This stuff must be the dog biscuits. It tastes just like the last set of dog biscuits we tried to eat two weeks ago.

ANSWER: An argument by analogy. Reliability, probably B.

18. Logic is like playing the piano because the more you practice, the more proficient you become.

ANSWER: A Speculative Analogy, probably designed to get you to study more and practice more. As such, reliability would not figure into this one.

19. No doubt, exercise and proper diet are important factors in good health. Still many people who eat right and exercise daily fall victim to such ailments as heart disease, cancer, etc. Surely, some other factor, such as heredity, must be responsible for such disorders.

ANSWER: A Causal Argument. Using Mill's Method, probably the Method of Residues.

20. Nearly everyone has seen sleeping pets whimper, twitch their whiskers, and seemingly move their legs as if in pursuit of some prey, or even growl. Evidently, these animals are dreaming.

ANSWER: An Argument by Analogy (perhaps an Hypothesis) based upon comparing animal behavior with human behavior and then correlating it with the intentions behind human behavior. Reliability, probably B to D.

For each of the problems below, determine which of Mill's Methods would be most appropriate for solving it. Propose a strategy for discovering the answer.

21. Determining whether the power is out in just your residence or in the whole neighborhood.

ANSWER: Either the Combined Method or the Method of Difference.

22. Figuring out whether the static and 'bad connections' are internal to your telephone or in the telephone line itself.

ANSWER: Again, the Combined Method or the Method of Difference.

23. Deciding whether eating ice cream causes increased cholesterol levels.

ANSWER: The Method of Concomitant Variations.

24. Seeing if there is a relationship between how much you exercise and how you feel.

ANSWER: The Method of Concomitant Variations.

25. Figuring out the weight of a chemical compound that has just been loaded into an empty railroad tank car.

ANSWER: The Method of Residues (Weigh the empty car and then weigh the car when it is fully loaded; then subtract the former from the latter.)

Essay Questions

26. What (if anything) can you tell about cause and effect in the following scenario? ("Y" means 'yes' the possible cause or effect was present.) Explain your answer as fully as possible.

Person	Possible Causes					Effect
	Chips	Beer	Wine	Dip	Pretzels	
Jake	Y	Y	Y	Y	Y	Y
Kym	Y	Y		Y		
Leo	Y	Y		Y		
Misha		Y			Y	Y
Niobe	Y			Y		

27. What (if anything) can you tell about the cause and effect relationship in the following case? (Again, assume "Y" means 'yes' the possible cause or effect was present.) Explain your answer fully.

Person	Possible Causes					Effect
	Chips	Beer	Wine	Dip	Pretzels	
Jake	Y		Y	Y	Y	Y
Kym	Y	Y	Y	Y		Y
Leo	Y		Y	Y		Y
Misha		Y		Y	Y	
Niobe	Y		Y	Y		Y

28. Explain the difference in logic or critical thinking between a theory and a hypothesis.

29. What is the difference between an intentional and a causal explanation in logic?

30. Explain why analogical arguments are always inductive in nature.

Chapter 13

Standardized Tests and Logical Puzzles

CHAPTER OUTLINE

13.1 Puzzles Involving Position Diagrams
Exercises
13.2 Problems Employing Matrices or Grids and The Liar's Paradox
Summary
Exercises
Case Study

KEY TERMS

Liar's Paradox Problems - Logical puzzles or riddles the solution to which hinges on discerning the truth value of particular statements within the puzzle. Usually self-referential paradoxes are involved.

Matrix Problems - Logical puzzles that involve the use of grids or matrices to determine what is true and what is false of the individual parts of the puzzle.

Position Problems - Logical puzzles that involve the spatial arrangement of the parts of the puzzle.

OVERVIEW

In this chapter, the study of Step Seven of the Technique continues: this time, logical puzzles and games are used to show how arguments may be diagrammatically represented so that conclusions may be drawn from them. Remembering part of the definition of deductive reasoning is that the conclusion is contained in the premises; this chapter displays some of the techniques for drawing unstated conclusions.

Three main types of problems or puzzles are the focus of the chapter, although there are many others to which these techniques may apply. Indeed, such puzzles and problems are often found on standardized tests and examinations. The first type of problem discussed is the position problem, a broad category that includes puzzles that involve the spatial arrangement of people or things and that generally become easier to solve through the use of some sort of visual representation. (An interesting question is to ask how your visually challenged students find it easiest to solve these types of problems.) In other words, by drawing diagrams to represent the possible positions and then filling in the positions with the people or things known to inhabit them, the remainder of the unknown factors in the puzzle are often brought to light. When all of the other possibilities have been determined, the answers to many of the heretofore unanswered questions become apparent.

Matrix problems may be considered a special brand of position diagram. These are puzzles that involve the use of grids or matrices to determine what is true and false of the individuals or things represented in the puzzle. In these problems, it is usually assumed that only one box in each row and each column may be true and that all the others must be false. Once that "true" box is found, it can be determined by a process of elimination that the remaining boxes in both the row and the column must contain values that are "false." Sometimes it is not necessary that every box in every row and column be completed. It may be helpful to look at the questions in advance to find out which information is going to be particularly relevant. Also, in both the position problems and the matrix problems, information is sometimes given that is either misleading or irrelevant or both. Knowing which information is not needed in advance would be very helpful, but is not always possible. Moreover, in both types of problems, questions are sometimes posed later that are hypothetical in nature. For example, "What if all of the X's are not Y's?" After the set of possible answers is given, it is assumed that the puzzle will revert to the initial set of given conditions. This is not always stated.

Liar's Paradox problems involve the supposition that each statement given must be either true or false (there is no middle ground) and that usually the persons or things making those statements always tell the truth or always lie. Frequently, problems of this nature specify the number of true or false statements that are involved so that further inferences may be drawn. The solution to these kinds of problems requires the comparison of statements with each other and the search for contradictions among the statements.

To be sure, there are a myriad of other kinds of puzzles and games. We included a manageable number of types, but often offer our classes a wider range, depending on their interests. In fact, one way I utilize this chapter is to begin each class period with one short puzzle or game, that I have given the students on a take-home basis, and work it in class, being careful to note the many different ways students find to solve these puzzles. Often they are able to give me or each other valuable suggestions that become part of their working habits for solving additional problems. Also, it can get their attention focused in on the material to be covered during the remainder of the class period. For students who are having problems working these types of puzzles, I refer them to Chapter Thirteen and use it as a resource chapter. Also, rather than quiz the student directly on the material in this chapter, on the tests, I offer a set of extra credit problems that make use of these kinds of problems. They are graded on the basis of how well they are able to explain how they arrived at the answers they did.

SOLUTIONS TO EXERCISE QUESTIONS

Answers to Exercises on Pages 315 through 325

Level A

1. *   One reason why a diagram might be helpful would be that it allows easy reference so that you may return to it again and again as needed when answering more than one question about a relationship or when answering long and protracted questions about the same relationship. On the other hand, if you are quick to visually imagine relationships or if they would require an inordinate amount of time to draw, you might be better off forgoing the diagram altogether.

2. *   Many standardized tests use analytical reasoning questions for several reasons:
     (a) they do have nice, neat, objective answers which can be justified;
     (b) they test different types of ability to conceptualize abstract relationships and to follow complex lines of reasoning;
     (c) they are not the kind of content questions which may be associated with a particular course of study or curriculum.

3. *   Usually, it is a good idea to diagram each set of relationships as they occur in the given part of the question, for each may in some way be dependent on the relationships that came before it. However, there are circumstances, for instance, when a given piece of evidence makes no sense by itself until it is combined with a later piece of evidence, when this rule of thumb would not apply. Another example would be in the case of syllogistic reasoning; the universal premises should be diagrammed before the particular ones simply in order to make less work and save time.

4. *   Not only would making assumptions be helpful; sometimes they are absolutely necessary to the solution of a problem or puzzle.

5. *   First look to the questions that are going to be asked and then utilize the information to sketch out what relationships you can. After all, one of the answers may be "cannot be determined from the information given above."

6. *   Binary relationships may be diagrammed each as they occur and later combined, or combined from the outset. Which of the two procedures to take will depend upon how much information is given. For example, if you are given that A weighs more than B and

259

that B weighs less than C, you cannot determine at this point whether A weighs more than C, less than C, or the same as C. You will have to await more information.

Level B

1. *   C
2. *   B
3. *   E   (D looks like a great answer, but you need more information before you can draw this conclusion.)
4. *   B
5. *   C
6. *   A

7. *   D   Do = Male   All are brothers and sisters. if we assume that the
8. *   E   Re = Female   relationships are transitive.
9. *   D   Mi = Male
10. * A   Fa = ?

11. * B
12. * B   A B C D   E F G H
13. * A   D ≠ H
14. * E   F + G
15. * C   East   West   1-3 / 3-1
16. * B

17. * C
18. * E
19. * C
20. * B   (!)
21. * E
22. * E

23. * A
24. * D
25. * B
26. * E
27. * D
28. * A

29. * D
30. * A
31. * B

32. *   C
33. *   E
34. *   C

35. *   D
36. *   C
37. *   C
38. *   A
39. *   B
40. *   A

41. *   A
42. *   C
43. *   E
44. *   B
45. *   C
46. *   A

Answers to Exercises on Pages 331 through 337

Level A

1. *   True
2. *   False
3. *   Generally False (but could be true on occasion)
4. *   True (or more)
5. *   True
6. *   True
7. *   True
8. *   False
9. *   True
10. * True

Level B

1. *   E
2. *   D
3. *   A
4. *   B
5. *   C
6. *   E

7. *   B
8. *   E
9. *   C
10. * A
11. * E
12. * D
13. * A
14. * B
15. * C

16. * C
17. * E
18. * D
19. * B
20. * B
21. * E
22. * A
23. * C
24. * C
25. * C

26. * B
27. * B
28. * B

29. * B
30. * B
31. * A

32. * A

Level C

1. *   Dr. Mitchell is in seat A
Professor Sachs is in seat B
General Glunn is in seat C
Astronaut Armstrong is in seat D
    Gen. Glunn is the murderer.
2. *   Peter is the murderer. Everything he says is true except C, his profession of innocence.
Quince is telling the truth about everything except A., about never having been in the
basement. Rota is telling the truth except in her statement D, where she accuses Quince.

And, Shelby is telling the truth in three cases A, B, and C; but, she is lying in her statement D where she denies that the candlestick is hers.

TEST BANK

Multiple Choice Questions

Questions 1 through 6:
ACME Properties owns a new strip shopping center that has six retail spaces in it. The stores are numbered from one to six in order from left to right. They are going to be leased to six retail shops: A, B, C, D, E, and F. Each one of the retail shops occupies one of the spaces, 1 through 6.
   Shops 2 and 3 are open to each other internally by arched doorways in the adjoining wall. None of the rest of the shops are linked to each other.
   A is a pizza parlor with hot ovens and C is an ice cream shop with a large refrigerator and freezer.
   A and C cannot be in spaces next to each other.
   D and E are businesses run by a husband and wife team who must always be next to each other.
   Two stores receive large packages and must be located in shops 1 and 6 at each end of the strip center.
   The only shop with a large refrigerator and freezer is shop 4.

1. If D receives large packages and E is located in one of the shops that is connected to the next door shop, then which one of the following must be false?
    A. E has to be in the second shop.
    B. D has to be in the first shop.
    C. A has to be in the sixth shop.
    D. F has to be in a shop next to C.
    E. B has to be in the third shop.

    ANSWER: E

2. Suppose A and B are the businesses that receive large packages and that F is next door to C. Which of the following has to be true?
    A. D has to be in the second shop.
    B. F has to be in the fifth shop.
    C. A has to be in the first shop.
    D. B has to be in the sixth shop.
    E. E has to be in the third shop.

    ANSWER: B

3. Suppose D is in the second shop and if B cannot be next door to D or F, which of the following must be true?

        I.   A can be in the first shop.

        II.   A can be in the fifth shop.

        III.   E has to be in the first or the third shop.

A. I only

B. II only

C. III only

D. II and III only

E. I and II only

ANSWER: C

4. If F has to occupy the first shop and B has to occupy one of the two connecting shops, which of the following has to be true?

        I.   A has to occupy the second shop.

        II.   E has to occupy the sixth shop.

        III.   B has to occupy the third shop.

A. I only

B. II only

C. III only

D. I and II only

E. I and III only

ANSWER: E

5. If F occupies one of the two end shops and if B occupies the third shop, then which of the following is true?

A. D can occupy the fifth shop.

B. E must occupy the sixth shop.

C. F can occupy the sixth shop.

D. A must occupy either shop one or shop six.

E. D can occupy the second shop.

ANSWER: A

6. Businesses D and E are a dry cleaners with an alteration shop with the husband running the latter and the wife running the former. The dry cleaners (D) is in shop two and the alteration shop (E) adjoins in shop three. Which of the following cannot possibly be true?

A. A is in the first shop and F is in the sixth shop.

B. F is in the fifth shop and B is in the sixth shop.

C. F is in the first shop and B is in the fifth shop.

264

D. B is in the first shop and F is in the sixth shop.
E. B is in the fifth shop and F is in the sixth shop.

ANSWER: D

Questions 7 through 12:
My grandmother gave me ten expensive ACMEware bowls. I am going to put each of them on one of three vertical shelves; a top shelf, a middle shelf, and a bottom shelf.

A, B, and C are dark blue.
D and E are light blue.
F, G, and H are red.
I and J are yellow.
I've decided not to put all of the bowls of the exact same color on the same shelf.
I always put D, G, and H on the top shelf.
I never put A and E on the same shelf.

7. What is the greatest number of bowls that can be displayed on any one shelf?
   A.   6
   B.   7
   C.   8
   D.   9
   E. 10

   ANSWER: A

8. What is the greatest number of bowls that can be displayed on the bottom shelf?
   A. 3
   B. 4
   C. 5
   D. 6
   E. 7

   ANSWER; C

9. If there are exactly six bowls on one shelf, among those bowls there must be at least one bowl having which of the following colors?
         I.   Dark blue
         II.   Light blue
         III.   Red
   A. II only
   B. III only
   C. I and III only

265

D. II and III only
E. I, II, and III

ANSWER: E

10. Which two bowls can never be displayed on the same shelf?
   A. E and F
   B. D and F
   C. B and F
   D. A and C
   E. A and D

   ANSWER: B

11. If A and C are displayed on the middle shelf, which of the following must be true?
   I.   F has to be on the middle shelf.
   II.   B has to be on the top shelf.
   III.   E has to be on the bottom shelf.
   A. I only
   B. II only
   C. III only
   D. I and II only
   E. I, II, and III

   ANSWER: C

12. If exactly three bowls are placed on the middle shelf and four bowls are on the bottom shelf, which of the following ACMEware bowls could be the three on the middle shelf?
   A. B, C, E
   B. B, F, I
   C. C, F, J
   D. A, F, I
   E. A, B, F

   ANSWER: D

Questions 13 through 24 pertain to the following puzzle:
A fusion restaurant combining the culinary skills of three international chefs employs nine persons. In addition to the Mexican, Japanese, and Italian chefs, there are three persons on the wait staff, a cashier/hostess, a busboy, and a dishwasher.
   1.   Antonelli and Yoshio each lost $50.00 playing poker with the waiters and waitresses.
   2.   The Japanese chef, the busboy, and Benito and Grvak were married; everyone else was

single.
3. Kramer and the cooks make up the company's four person bowling team.
4. The cashier/hostess (one person) is going to graduate from high school this year and her boyfriend is helping her write the valedictorian's speech; the busboy has his doctorate in philosophy from Emory University and is the only advanced degree in the company.
5. David was taller than the chefs and the waiters and waitresses, and twice as old as the cashier.
6. The employee named Rising Moon knew all of the chefs and the waiters and waitresses before going to work at the restaurant.
7. One of the employees, Dr. Eriksen-Amdahl, is married to the chef named Yoshio.
8. Sarjukamar has never been married, but is known for his signature dish, enchiladas con camarones y poblanos.

13. Who is the Mexican chef?
   A. Antonelli
   B. Benito
   C. Yoshio
   D. Kramer
   E. Sarjukamar

   ANSWER: E

14. Who is the Japanese cook?
   A. Antonio
   B. Benito
   C. Yoshio
   D. Sarjukamar
   E. Rising Moon

   ANSWER: C

15. Who is the Italian cook?
   A. Antonelli
   B. Benito
   C. Yoshio
   D. Sarjukamar
   E. None of the above.

   ANSWER: A

16. What job does Benito have?
   A. A cook

B. A waiter/waitress
C. The cashier/hostess
D. Busboy
E. Dishwasher

ANSWER: B

17. Grvak must be
    A. a cook.
    B. a waiter/waitress.
    C. the cashier/hostess.
    D. the busboy.
    E. the dishwasher.

ANSWER: B

18. The waiters and waitresses have to be
    I.   Kramer
    II.   Sarjukamar
    III.   Grvak
    A. I only
    B. II only
    C. III only
    D. I and III only
    E. I, II, and III

ANSWER: D

19. The cashier/hostess is
    A. Kramer
    B. Eriksen-Amdahl
    C. Davis
    D. Rising Moon
    E. Sarjukamar

ANSWER: D

20. The busboy is
    A. Kramer
    B. Eriksen-Amdahl
    C. Davis
    D. Rising Moon

   E. Sarjukamar

   ANSWER: B

21. The dishwasher is
   A. Grvak
   B. Benito
   C. Davis
   D. Rising Moon
   E. Kramer

   ANSWER: C

22. Which of the following are single?
   I.   One of the wait staff.
   II.   Two of the wait staff.
   III. All three of the wait staff.
   A. I only
   B. II only
   C. III only
   D. None of the above.
   E. Cannot be determined from the given information.

   ANSWER: A

23. Which of the following are married?
   A. Antonelli, Yoshio, and Benito
   B. Yoshio, Benito, and Grvak
   C. Benito, Kramer, and Eriksen-Amdahl
   D. Eriksen-Amdahl, Yoshio, and Kramer
   E. Eriksen-Amdahl, Grvak, and Davis

   ANSWER: B

24. Rising Moon must be
   A. a cook.
   B. a waiter or waitress.
   C. the dishwasher.
   D. married.
   E. single.

   ANSWER: E

Chapter 13

Questions 25 through 30 relate to the following scenario:
A nuclear explosion with an effective yield of 100 kilotons of dynamite was detonated by a terrorist who wanted revenge. Five suspects were nabbed as they tried to flee the country, one of whom was the actual culprit. When authorities forced them to talk, each suspect made four statements, three of which were true and one of which was false. Here is a record of what they said:

Abdul: (1) I didn't do it.
           (2) Dorito did it.
           (3) Cadiz and I are old pals.
           (4) Bono was with me when it happened.

Bono: (1) I didn't do it either.
           (2) El Khalli did it.
           (3) One of us is guilty.
           (4) I was with Abdul at the time.

Cadiz: (1) Well, I certainly didn't do it.
           (2) The bomb must have been a nuclear device.
           (3) I've known Abdul a long time.
           (4) El Khalli didn't do it either.

Dorito: (1) I definitely didn't do it.
           (2) I've never been to El Khalli's place.
           (3) I don't even know how to detonate a nuclear bomb.
           (4) Abdul lied when he accused me of detonating the bomb.

El Khalli: (1) I didn't do it either.
           (2) Dorito did it.
           (3) Dorito showed up at my place right after it happened.
           (4) One of these other guys knows how to detonate a nuclear fission bomb.

25. Which one of the five terrorists detonated the bomb?
    A. Abdul
    B. Bono
    C. Cadiz
    D. Dorito
    E. El Khalli

ANSWER: C

26. Which one of Abdul's statements is false?
    A. I didn't do it.

B. Dorito did it.
C. Cadiz and I are old pals.
D. Bono was with me when it happened.
E. None of the above.

ANSWER: B

27. Which one of Bono's statements is false?
    A. I didn't do it either.
    B. El Khalli did it.
    C. One of us is guilty.
    D. I was with Abdul at the time.
    E. None of the above.

ANSWER: B

28. Which one of Cadiz's statements is false?
    A. Well, I certainly didn't do it.
    B. The bomb must have been a nuclear device.
    C. I've known Abdul a long time.
    D. El Khalli didn't do it either.
    E. None of the above.

ANSWER: A

29. Which one of Dorito's statements is false?
    A. I definitely didn't do it.
    B. I've never been to El Khalli's place.
    C. I don't even know how to detonate a nuclear bomb.
    D. Abdul lied when he accused me of detonating the bomb.
    E. None of the above.

ANSWER: B

30. Which one of El Khalli's statements is false?
    A. I didn't do it either.
    B. Dorito did it.
    C. Dorito showed up at my place right after it happened.
    D. One of these other guys knows how to detonate a nuclear fission bomb.
    E. None of the above.

ANSWER: B

Chapter 14

Argumentative Writing

CHAPTER OUTLINE

14.1 The Argument's Format
Summary
Exercises
Case Study - Sample Student Essays

KEY TERMS

Analogical Argument - Reasoning based on a comparison between two things or states of affairs, one more familiar than the other, or one set as a precedent for the other.

Definitional Argument - Reasoning that attempts to establish the meaning of a word or phrase.

Moral Argument - A line of reasoning attempting to establish that something "ought" to be done or not done or that something is "right" or "wrong" or "good" or "bad."

Statistical Argument - Reasoning based on probability theory.

OVERVIEW

For this, the culminating chapter of the book, the different aspects of the Critical Technique are reassembled in the construction or reconstruction of arguments. It is helpful to establish the conclusion one wishes to make first (Step One), then determine which premises best support that

273

conclusion (Step Two). In developing these premises, be mindful of the logical assumptions and implications (Step Three) that accompany the lines of reasoning that are emerging. Be wary of unclear meanings, ambiguity, vagueness, and other problems in the area of meaning that may detract from the strength of the reasoning (Step Four).

As you begin to construct the argument, you will notice that it takes on a certain structure or form. You should be able to draw a picture of the structure of the argument schematically or diagrammatically. Once you have done this, you will be in a better position to assess the form of the reasoning (Step Six) and to identify any formal or informal fallacies that may have occurred (Step 5). Moreover, a determination of any other conclusions that may be drawn from your argument or premises can be assessed more readily (Step Seven). Finally, you should proceed to express your written argument clearly and understandably with an overview of how important rationality is in the particular case you have chosen (Step Eight).

By way of particulars, it is a good idea to begin to rank the premises in order of their importance for the purpose of determining which ones require further support and which ones need less. At this point it can be determined where and how much further research may be needed. It is also a good idea to anticipate possible objections to the arguments being constructed and to shore up the premises that might be attacked. Where necessary, make sure that the conclusions are not too strong for the support upon which they are based. Also, check to make sure that a fair picture has been given and that you are not open to attack for having unfairly biased or skewed the evidence in favor of your conclusion. Many more finer points of argument analysis would be useful to bring up in discussion at this point. To be sure, for those of us who believe that reasoning is a social process, it is often a good idea to get someone else to take a look at our reasoning to make sure that we have not overlooked something crucial.

Arguments can be constructed on the basis of several formats. Definitional arguments are the kind of reasoning that attempts to establish the meaning of a word or phrase. Frequently, these arguments require a preliminary argument against a currently accepted definition before proceeding to construct and justify a new definition. Analogical arguments attempt to justify their conclusions by comparing allegedly similar (or dissimilar) cases. To the extent that they are successful, the analogue should be much more familiar to the audience than the conclusion to which it is being compared. The comparison should be vivid, and there should be a number of relevant similarities between the two cases. Moreover, there should not be relevant dissimilarities that would detract from the comparison. And, the comparison should be fairly drawn, not a deliberate attempt to prejudice opinion.

Moral arguments assume many different forms, usually with the common thread that they are attempting to draw some normative or evaluative conclusion. Perhaps, they are trying to justify that something should be the case or that some particular course of action should (or should not) be taken. Maybe, a recommendation is being made or advice is being given. Almost assuredly, one of the logical assumptions of this kind of reasoning will be a normative or evaluative principle. For example, "Mr. So and So cheated on the test; therefore, he should be punished." In this moral argument, the author is assuming that "people who cheat should be punished."

Statistical arguments often purport to establish a conclusion on the basis of some type of probabilistic reasoning using quantitative premises. These arguments are subject to the strictures of Mill's Methods and should be wary of the fallacies of inductive reasoning.

SOLUTIONS TO EXERCISE QUESTIONS

Answers to Exercises on Pages 352 through 357

Level A

1. * The Conclusion or main point of the argument.
2. * To be able to state the conclusion as clearly, concisely, fairly, and adequately as possible in a single sentence.
3. * Look for unstated assumptions and implications, clarify meaning, be alert to spot fallacies.
4. * To get an overview of how the argument can be developed as well as to illuminate any structural flaws in the reasoning that may not be apparent otherwise.
5. * To determine which premises need stronger or more stringent defenses.
6. * This strengthens the reasoning by giving it more balance and by making it less susceptible to external attack.
7. * A line of reasoning supporting a definition that is not currently accepted or which is controversial.
8. * A line of reasoning comparing the point at issue with something better known or more simply understood in order to draw some conclusion about that point.
9. * To argue that something is right or wrong; to argue for adopting a course of action; to pass judgment on something; to make a recommendation....
10. * Arguments that use laws of probability to establish their conclusions. Remember the warnings regarding Mill's Methods when evaluating them.

Level B

1. * Moral Argument
2.   Moral Argument
3. * Definitional Argument
4.   Moral Argument
5. * Analogical Argument
6.   Moral Argument
7. * Statistical Argument
8.   Moral Argument (Might also use a Definitional Argument)

9. *   Moral Argument
10.   Moral Argument
11. *   D is most specific, followed by C, then B, and finally A
12.   C is probably the strongest reason. D and B are probably the next strongest pieces of evidence, followed by A and E.
13. *   A appears to be the strongest, followed by B and C, then D, and finally E.
14.   C
15. *   D
16.   A
17. *   B
18.   D

TEST BANK

Departing from the usual format of the earlier chapters, I will first list some additional writing topics in case you are pressed for some ideas. Generic topics might include questions of the moral justification or indefensibility of

-- Euthanasia
-- Abortion
-- Legalization of Drugs
-- Prohibition of Alcohol or Tobacco
-- Suicide
-- Hunting
-- Fishing
-- Military Defense
-- Pacifism
-- Conscientious Objection to War
-- Capital Punishment
-- Welfare
-- Prayer in School
-- Teaching of Creationism
-- Sex Between Consenting Teenagers
-- Sex Out of Wedlock
-- Gay Marriages

Second, we can be more specific in the kinds of questions we pose for writing topics. On the one hand, we can have the student respond in a critical essay to another essay he or she has read. I often give a couple of essays during the first half of a term in which the student is asked to employ something like the Critical Technique to one out of perhaps six passages that I give them. When grading the essays, I then use a chart such as the one below so that the student can understand exactly why they have earned the grade that they have.

ARGUMENT ANALYSIS

	N/A	Poor	Fair	Good	Very Good	Exc.	Outstanding
	____	____	____	____	____	____	_____

1. **Recognition of Main Point**
2. **Clarity of Main Point**
3. **Identify Premises and Conclusions**
4. **Portray Structure of Argument**
5. **Induction/Deduction Recognition**
6. **Explanation of Why Reasoning is Ind/Ded**
7. **Spotting Assumptions**
8. **Implications**
9. **Clarifying Meaning**
10. **Recognition of Fallacies**
11. **Evaluating the Argument**
12. **Overall Evaluation**

Comments:

Also possible are even more specific writing assignments. For instance, one, provided by Dr. Milton Snoeyenbos, is to write a critical assessment essay in response to the following article:

* * * * * * * * * *

THE HOMELESS

Most Americans can take their food, clothing, and shelter for granted. They think they will always have these necessities. But for many people in our great country this is not a reality. Many are on the streets at night, wondering where their next meal will come from. There have been many proposals to solve this problem, but they seem not to have had an effect. There are still people on the streets. In America we need homeless shelters that truly solve these problems. We should support homeless shelters that provide not only a place to stay but also job training

277

and communications skills.

Many Americans do not understand that most homeless people do not want to be homeless. Many of them merely had several problems at once and could not cope with the results. Some have lost their jobs and families at the same time and are left with no place to go. Others are desperately sick, have no insurance, and have lost hope and home. Some are alcoholics that want to change but have no support from friends or family. Once these men and women are homeless, they usually lack the skills needed to find jobs and lose all sense of hope.

Anyone can fall into homelessness. A person can suddenly develop a mental illness, not be able to keep a job, lose his home and family, and be on the streets. The rich may get cancer, lose their job, then lose their money and become homeless. If it happened to them, it can happen to you. That's reason enough why we should have homeless shelters.

Some people propose the alternative that we have no homeless shelters. This is based on the view that having shelters is the cause of the problem. This is ridiculous. Nobody gives up his home to go to a shelter. This ridiculous proposal wouldn't solve anything. We would still have these people on the streets. To say we don't need shelters is like saying we don't need social security and nobody believes that. Those people who say we don't need shelters are just the rich who think they will never be poor and homeless. Trini Rogers, of the U.S. Homeless Task Force, argued eloquently before the U.S. Senate that we need shelters, and that's proof enough.

Obviously, we need shelters, but today's shelters treat only the symptoms—they provide a meal and a bed. But people need to be self-sufficient. So shelters should provide job training. This would provide people with self-confidence. Giving them a shot at working will be a first step at becoming self-sufficient. Providing just a meal and a bed will not solve the problem. My solution will surely help solve it, though it is not the total answer. So, homeless shelters should provide job training in addition to just providing a meal and a bed for the homeless. Clearly, many homeless do not have the education to get a job. If they had the training they lack and which a homeless shelter could provide, they would be eligible for the job openings they apply for.

Another aspect in getting a job is being able to function in the job market. Teaching social skills, such as how to have a successful interview and how to interact with co-workers, can greatly improve their chances of rejoining the work force. Homeless shelters should also teach people these skills. It seems clear that a homeless shelter that taught social skills would be a better shelter than one that just provided the necessities. It would just be a better solution to the problem. Therefore, homeless shelters should teach social skills in addition to providing room and board.

While homeless shelters are good in their attempt to help people in need, they do far too little to help. They help the symptoms of homelessness, not having food and shelter, but they do not help the homeless people cure the problem. By implementing training for jobs and social skills, homeless shelters can better help those in need and provide them with the abilities needed to improve their lives. So, we should support such shelters by passing legislation at the federal level to support them.

* * * * * * * * * *

We create a grading sheet such as the following to help the students see exactly what is strong and what is weak in their critique. It also helps to simplify and speed up the process of grading.

QUALITY OF THE CRITIC'S DISCUSSION

	Not Disc.	Very Poor	Poor	Average	Good	Very Good
	___	___	___	___	___	___

THE HOMELESS

Ambiguity in <u>Writer's</u> thesis
T_1: We need homeless shelters that provide job training and com/soc skills
T_2: We need federal legislation to support homeless shelters and job training and communications skills

The <u>Critic's</u> thesis—adequately and clearly stated

Is the problem clearly defined in Paragraph's 2 and 3?

Paragraph 4: Argument for T_1
    Causal claim—Distortion
    Personal Attacks

Analogy—Underdeveloped/Asserted
Authority—Underdeveloped/Asserted
    SO: Argument in Para. 4 is very
    poor

Paragraph 5:
    No alternatives discussed to shelters
        providing job training
    Thus, no argument that this is best
        solution
    No evidence shelter-based job
        training would solve the problems
        mentioned in paragraphs 2 and 3.
    Poisoning the well—asserted certainty
        to start paragraph
    Possible Misuse of Hypothesis contrary
        to fact in last sentence

Paragraph 6:
    No alternatives to shelters providing
        communications skills
    So, no argument this is best solution
    No evidence this would solve problems
        mentioned in paragraphs 2 and 3

For T_2: No alternative solutions to
    federal funding (& assuming we
    need shelters)
    So, no argument this is best solution

Overall Presentation and Clarity of
    Critic's Essay

Other suggestions and ideas: For in-class essays I have sometimes utilized "Hot Sheets" where I pick out the best features or points in perhaps three to five of the in-class essays and put them on the board. Not only does it reinforce good technique, but also it has the advantage of getting the students to learn from each other and to accentuate the positive (rather than, say, picking out the five most egregious errors!). For take-home essays, I utilize longer formats. Occasionally, I will xerox entire articles, for example, Dr. Martin Luther King Jr.'s "Letter From the Birmingham Jail," or a letter to the editor about Dr. Jack Kevorkian and Euthanasia, or a short chapter from a book on the ideal of rationality and the social responsibility of corporations. Accompanying these pieces of writing (and usually I pick them depending upon the interests of students) will be a set of instructions that may be two to three pages in length and explaining what sorts of strategies, presentation, criteria, sometimes formats, are to be involved. On other occasions, I loosen up and let them pick their own topics and manner of critique or assessment. In any case, I find it helpful to offer a minimum of three to four written essays per term depending upon the size of the class.

TRANSPARENCY MASTERS

Transparency 1 A Technique for Thinking Critically A-1

Transparency 2 Disagreements and Arguments A-2

Transparency 3 Logical Assumptions, Implications, and Argument
Diagrams A-3

Transparency 4 Clarifying Meaning A-4

Transparency 5 Fallacies... A-5

Transparency 6 The Categorical Syllogism A-6

Transparency 7 The Syllogism Refined.. A-7

Transparency 8 Symbolizing Statements.. A-8

Transparency 9 Argument Forms A-9

Transparency 10 Truth Tables, Equivalence, and Validity A-10

Transparency 11 Statement Forms: Contraries, Contradictions, and
Tautology A-11

Transparency 12 Inductive Reasoning.. A-12

Transparency 13 Standardized Tests and Logical Puzzles A-13

Transparency 14 Argumentive Writing.. A-14

1

A TECHNIQUE FOR THINKING CRITICALLY

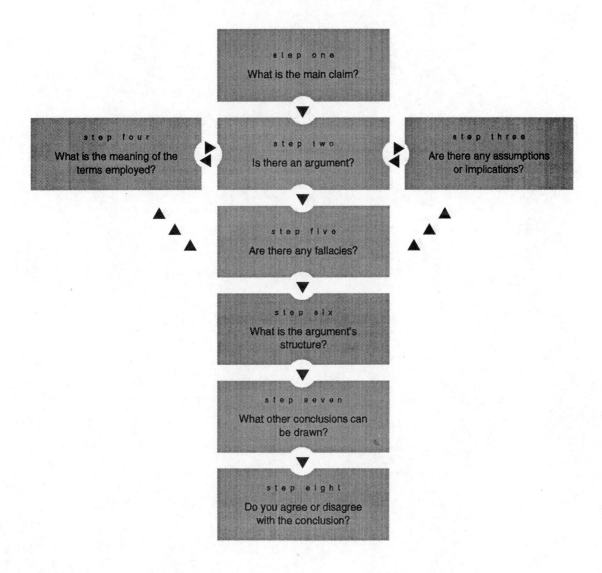

step one
What is the main claim?

step four
What is the meaning of the terms employed?

step two
Is there an argument?

step three
Are there any assumptions or implications?

step five
Are there any fallacies?

step six
What is the argument's structure?

step seven
What other conclusions can be drawn?

step eight
Do you agree or disagree with the conclusion?

2
DISAGREEMENTS AND ARGUMENTS

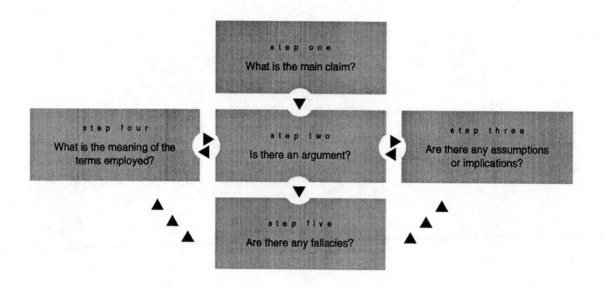

step one
What is the main claim?

step four
What is the meaning of the terms employed?

step two
Is there an argument?

step three
Are there any assumptions or implications?

step five
Are there any fallacies?

3

LOGICAL ASSUMPTIONS, IMPLICATIONS, AND ARGUMENT DIAGRAMS

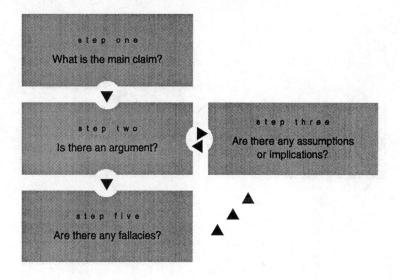

4
CLARIFYING MEANING

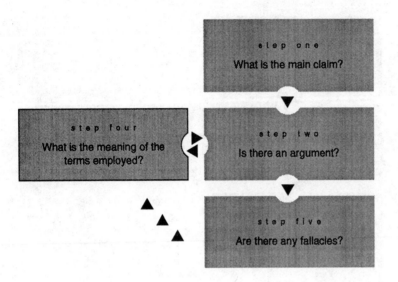

step one
What is the main claim?

step four
What is the meaning of the terms employed?

step two
Is there an argument?

step five
Are there any fallacies?

5
FALLACIES

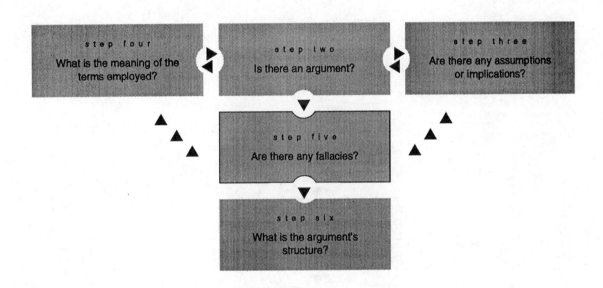

6

THE CATEGORICAL SYLLOGISM

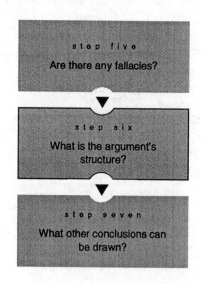

step five

Are there any fallacies?

▼

step six

What is the argument's
structure?

▼

step seven

What other conclusions can
be drawn?

7
THE SYLLOGISM REFINED

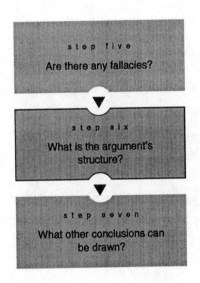

step five
Are there any fallacies?

step six
What is the argument's structure?

step seven
What other conclusions can be drawn?

8

SYMBOLIZING
STATEMENTS

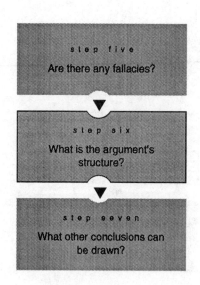

step five

Are there any fallacies?

▼

step six

What is the argument's
structure?

▼

step seven

What other conclusions can
be drawn?

9

ARGUMENT FORMS

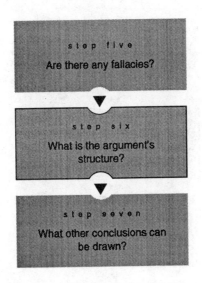

step five

Are there any fallacies?

step six

What is the argument's structure?

step seven

What other conclusions can be drawn?

10
TRUTH TABLES, EQUIVALENCE, AND VALIDITY

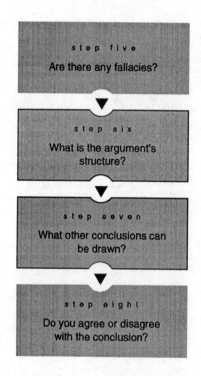

step five

Are there any fallacies?

▼

step six

What is the argument's structure?

▼

step seven

What other conclusions can be drawn?

▼

step eight

Do you agree or disagree with the conclusion?

11
STATEMENT FORMS: CONTRARIES, CONTRADICTIONS, AND TAUTOLOGIES

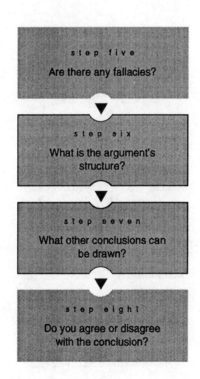

step five

Are there any fallacies?

step six

What is the argument's structure?

step seven

What other conclusions can be drawn?

step eight

Do you agree or disagree with the conclusion?

12

INDUCTIVE REASONING

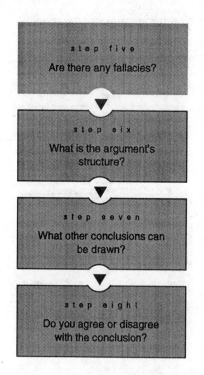

step five

Are there any fallacies?

▼

step six

What is the argument's structure?

▼

step seven

What other conclusions can be drawn?

▼

step eight

Do you agree or disagree with the conclusion?

13

STANDARDIZED TESTS
AND LOGICAL PUZZLES

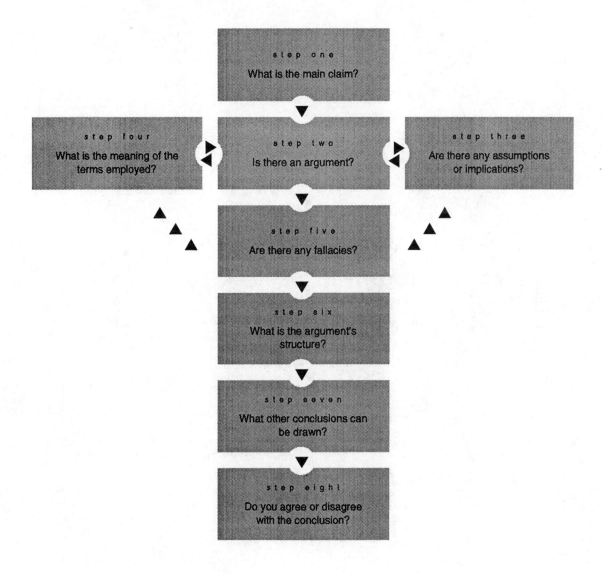

14
ARGUMENTATIVE WRITING

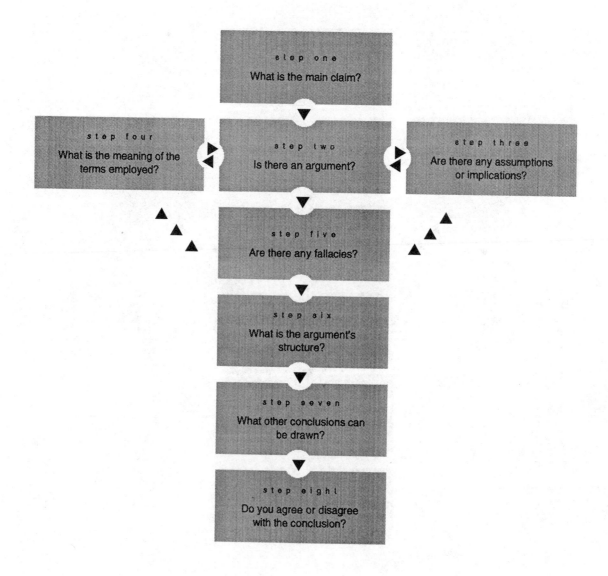

step one

What is the main claim?

step four

What is the meaning of the terms employed?

step two

Is there an argument?

step three

Are there any assumptions or implications?

step five

Are there any fallacies?

step six

What is the argument's structure?

step seven

What other conclusions can be drawn?

step eight

Do you agree or disagree with the conclusion?